Bloom's Modern Critical Interpretations

Bloom's Modern Critical Interpretations

Jack Kerouac's
ON THE ROAD

Edited and with an introduction by
Harold Bloom
Sterling Professor of the Humanities
Yale University

CHELSEA HOUSE
PUBLISHERS
A Haights Cross Communications Company

Philadelphia

Library of Congress Cataloging-in-Publication Data
On the Road / edited and with an introduction by Harold Bloom.
    p. cm. — (Bloom's modern critical interpretations) Includes
bibliographical references and index.
   ISBN 0-7910-7581-8
  1. Kerouac, Jack, 1922–1969. On the road. 2. Autobiographical
fiction, American—History and criticism. 3. Beat generation in
literature. I. Bloom, Harold. II. Series.
 PS3521.E735O536 2003
 813'.54—dc21

                                                    2003011504

Contributing editor: Jesse Zuba

Cover design by Terry Mallon

Cover: © Ken Kaminesky / CORBIS

Layout by EJB Publishing Services

Chelsea House Publishers
1974 Sproul Road, Suite 400
Broomall, PA 19008-0914

http://www.chelseahouse.com

Contents

Editor's Note

My Introduction amiably accepts *On the Road* as the Period Piece of Period Pieces, *The Rover Boys* for the counter-cultural Sixties.

Carole Gottlieb Vopat chronicles the flight from self-identity in Sal Paradise and his friends, after which George Dardess finds a complex structure in the book that conveys its sense of failed friendship.

For Tim Hunt, *On the Road* is an achievement worthy of such forerunners as *Moby-Dick*, *Huckleberry Finn*, and *The Great Gatsby*, but this is an assertion I do not believe any good reader will accept. Robert Holton, more cautiously, sees Kerouac's book *as* a crucial influence upon Thomas Pynchon, on Pynchon's own authority.

Jazz is viewed by Douglas Malcolm as more of an ideological than a structural element in *On the Road*, while Alex Albright attempts a parallel study of a superb poet, the late Archie Randolph Ammons, and of Kerouac on the basis of their employment of tape as manuscript.

James T. Jones emphasizes the barely repressed image of the mother in Kerouac's work, after which Omar Swartz regards *On the Road* as an instructive vision of American social alienation.

To Ben Giamo, transcendence is the keynote of *On the Road*, while to Mark Richardson, a nostalgia for childhood is the true tenor of the book.

HAROLD BLOOM

Introduction

I had not reread *On the Road* during the near half-century since its first publication, and I am not happy at encountering it again. The book has many admirers, including Thomas Pynchon, but I hardly understand what he, and others, discover in this rather drab narrative. And yet I remain fascinated by the phenomenon of Period Pieces, and by the sad truth that literary Period Pieces, unlike visual ones, in time become rubbish. Like the *Harry Potter* volumes, *On the Road* will be rubbed down and out. Since the once alienated counter-culture is now the prevalent vogue in our mediaversities, even the element of social protest in Kerouac has now faded away. Our society remains under the rule of corporate robber barons, and I have to startle myself sometimes in order not to believe that Benjamin Harrison or William McKinley or Warren Gamaliel Harding is still our president. Social reality has changed little in an America where the ruling party seems determined to so bankrupt the federal government that only the military will be funded by it.

Kerouac's vagrants are literate, self-pitying, afraid of women, and condescending towards Mexicans and African-Americans. No one will confuse them with Steinbeck's displaced Okies, and no grapes of wrath are trampled out by them. Nor are they doom-eager dreamers like Gatsby, or monomaniac questers like Ahab, or benign wanderers like Huckleberry Finn. Comparing *On the Road* to the masterpieces of Classic American fiction is most unkind to Kerouac.

I can locate no literary value whatsoever in *On the Road*, but I must admit the same blindness (if it is that) afflicts me when trying to reread the verse of Allen Ginsberg, a good acquaintance whom I miss personally. *Howl*, rather like *On the Road*, strikes me as an Oedipal lament, weeping in the wilderness for a mother's consolation. What both works lack sorely is the delicately nuanced artistry of our father, Walt Whitman, whose greatest poems may *look* easy, but actually are superbly difficult. *On the Road* and *Howl* look easy, and *are* easy, self-indulgent evasions of the American quest for identity.

CAROLE GOTTLIEB VOPAT

Jack Kerouac's On the Road: *A Re-evaluation*

Nothing has been published about Jack Kerouac for seven years. Most of what has been written is either hostile or condescending or both. While it may perhaps be true, as Melvin W. Askew suggests ("Quests, Cars and Kerouac," *University of Kansas City Review*, 28 [1962], 231–240), that to speak of Jack Kerouac in the same breath with Melville, Twain and Hawthorne is "to leave a smirch on the configuration of classic American literature" (p. 235), Kerouac has, as they have, provided an enduring portrait of the national psyche; like Fitzgerald, he has defined America and delineated American life for his generation. Certainly, Kerouac is not a great writer, but he is a good writer, and has more depth and control than his critics allow. *On the Road* is more than a "crazy wild frantic" embrace of beat life; implicit in Kerouac's portrayal of the beat generation is his criticism of it, a criticism that anticipates the charges of his most hostile critics. For example, Norman Podhoretz' assertion ("The Know-Nothing Bohemians," *Doings and Undoings* [New York: Noonday Press, 1964], 143–158) that "the Beat Generation's worship of primitivism and spontaneity ... arises from a pathetic poverty of feeling" (156), parallels Kerouac's own insights in *On the Road*.

In that novel Kerouac makes it clear that Sal Paradise goes on the road to escape from life rather than to find it, that he runs from the intimacy and responsibility of more demanding human relationships, and from a more

From *The Midwest Quarterly* 14, no. 4. © 1973 by *The Midwest Quarterly*, Kansas State College of Pittsburg.

demanding human relationship with himself. With all their emphasis on spontaneity and instinct, Sal and his friends are afraid of feeling on any other than the impassive and ultimately impersonal "wow" level. For Sal especially, emotion is reduced to sentimentality, roleplaying and gesture. His responses are most often the blanket, indiscriminate "wow!" or the second-hand raptures gleaned from books and movies; he thrills to San Francisco as "Jack London's town" and melodramatically describes leaving his Mexican mistress: "Emotionlessly she kissed me in the vineyard and walked off down the row. We turned at a dozen paces, for love is a duel, and looked at each other for the last time ..." (*On the Road* [New York: The Viking Press, 1957], 101). Sal is continually enjoying himself enjoying himself, raptly appreciating his performance in what seems more like an on-going soap-opera than an actual life: "She'd left me a cape to keep warm; I threw it over my shoulder and skulked through the moonlit vineyard.... A California home; I hid in the grapevines, digging it all. I felt like a million dollars; I was adventuring in the crazy American night" (100).

Sal's self-conscious posturing undercuts his insistence on the life of instinct and impulse, and indicates his fear of emotions simply felt, of life perceived undramatically and unadorned. He responds to experience in a language of exaggeration; everything is the saddest or greatest or wildest in the world. Although on page 21 he meets a "rawhide oldtime Nebraska farmer" who has "a great laugh, the greatest in the world," a few pages later he encounters Mr. Snow "whose laugh, I swear on the Bible, was positively and finally the one greatest laugh in all this world" (62). Reality is never good enough; it must be classified, embroidered and intensified; above all, the sheer reality of reality must be avoided. Sal's roleplaying shelters him from having to realize and respond to actual situations, and to the emotions and obligations, whether of others or of himself, inherent in those situations. He is protected from having to face and feel his own emotions as well as from having to deal with the needs and demands of other people. What Sal enthuses over as "a California home" Kerouac reveals as a place of poverty, frustration, anger and despair, but Sal's raptures cushion him from recognizing the grimness of the existence to which he is carelessly consigning his mistress and her small son, a child he had called "my boy" and played at fathering. By absorbing himself in the melodramatics of a renunciation scene, Sal is protected from the realities of Terry's feelings or her future, nor must he cope with his own emotions at parting with her. When the melodrama fails and the scene threatens him with its potentiality for suffering and loss, Sal is able to escape from feeling by escaping from the scene:

'See you in New York, Terry,' I said.... But we both knew she wouldn't make.... She just walked on back to the shack, carrying my breakfast plate in one hand. I bowed my head and watched her. Well, lackadaddy, I was on the road again (101).

Sal is far more comfortable in the role of wayward child than as friend or brother, much less father and husband. His early trips end in a return home to be babied by his aunt: "Poor little Salvatore ..., you're thin, you're thin. Where have you been all this time?" (107). Sal is a failure as a friend, unable to sustain even the least demanding friendships. His idyll with Remi and Lee Ann breaks down partially because of his own irresponsibility. Although he knows Remi wants desperately to impress his doctor stepfather, Sal appears at their rendezvous drunk and outrageous, knowing he is ruining their friendship but unable to control himself: "I gave up, I got drunk.... Everything was falling apart" (77). Kerouac's characters take to the road not to find life but to leave it all behind: emotion, maturity, change, decision, purpose, and, especially, in the best American tradition, responsibility; wives, children, mistresses, all end up strewn along the highway like broken glass. Sal refuses responsibility not only for the lives of others but for his own life as well. He does not want to own his life or direct his destiny, but prefers to live passively; to be driven in cars, to entertain sensations rather than emotions. A follower, Sal is terrified of leading his own life; he is, as Kerouac points out, "fearful of the wheel" and "hated to drive;" he does not have a driver's license. He and Dean abdicate self-control in a litany of irresponsibility: "It's not my fault, it's not my fault ..., nothing in this lousy world is my fault" (213). Both of them flee from relevance and significance, telling long, mindless stories and taking equally pointless trips. They avoid anything—self-analysis, self-awareness, thinking—which would threaten or challenge them, for with revelation comes responsibility for change and, above all, they do not want change. They demand lives as thin and narrow as the white lines along the road which so comfort and mesmerize them, and are content with surfaces, asking for no more. Thus they idolize Negroes as romantic and carefree children, seeing in the ghetto not the reality of poverty and oppression, but freedom from responsibility and, hence, joy.

Sal and his friends are not seeking or celebrating self, but are rather fleeing from identity. For all their solipsism, they are almost egoless. They do not dwell on the self, avoid thinking or feeling. They run from self-definition, for to admit the complex existence of the self is to admit its contingencies: the claims of others, commitments to society, to oneself. Solipsism rather than an enhancement of self is for them a loss of self, for the self is projected until it loses all boundaries and limits and, hence, all definition. Sal in the Mexican jungle completely loses his identity; inside and outside merge, he becomes the atmosphere, and as a result knows neither the jungle nor himself. For Sal and Dean, transcendentalism, like drugs, sex, liquor, and even jazz, leads not to enlightenment but to self-obliteration. Erasing both ego and world, nothing remains save motion and sensation, passive, self-effacing and mechanical. Only the sheer impetus of their frantic, speeding cars holds their scattered selves together.

Their selves have no definition and their lives no continuity. Nothing is related, neither self nor time; there is no cause and effect, life is not an ongoing process. Rather, there is only the Eternal Now, the jazz moment, which demands absolutely nothing. Their ideals are spontaneity and impulse because both are independent of relation to what has gone before and what may come after. Spontaneity and impulse are the ethic of disjunction, recognizing neither limit, liability or obligation. Their emphasis on spontaneity is a measure of their fear of life. In their cars they are suspended from life and living, as if in a capsule hurtling coast-to-coast above the earth. They seek out not truth nor values but this encapsulated almost fetal existence as an end in itself, an end that is much like death.

For even their much touted ideal of Freedom is in reality a freedom from life itself, especially from rational, adult life with its welter of consequences and obligations. Dean is utterly free because he is completely mad. He has defied maturity and logic, defied time with its demands that he grow up to responsibility. Like Nietzsche's superman, he is beyond good and evil, blame and expectation, nor must he justify his existence through work and duty, a state Sal sorely admires: "Bitterness, recriminations, advice, morality, sadness—everything was behind him, and ahead of him was the ragged and ecstatic joy of pure being" (195). Sal's own longing for freedom is embodied in a mysterious Shrouded Traveler, a figure who unites the road and death. In many avatars, he pursues Sal in his headlong flight down the highway, offering, through solitary travel, the "lost bliss" which is the death of the self: "The one thing that we yearn for in all our living days, that makes us sigh and groan and undergo sweet nauseas of all kinds, is the remembrance of some lost bliss that we probably experienced in the womb and can only be reproduced (though we hate to admit it) in death" (124).

"Free love" is rather freedom from love and another route down that same dark deathwish. For Sal the love-bed is "the deathbed," where he goes to obliterate himself and to find the safe "lost bliss" of the womb, "blindly seeking to return the way he came" (132). But Sal is only able to find this particular version of "lost bliss" when he has reduced his partner to the non-threatening role of fellow child. He has trouble succeeding with adult women; he fills Rita with nothing but talk and is convinced Theresa is a whore until he discovers with relief that she is only a baby, as fragile and vulnerable as he: "I saw her poor belly where there was a Caesarian scar; her hips were so narrow she couldn't bear a child without getting gashed open. Her legs were like little sticks. She was only four foot ten. I made love to her in the sweetness of the weary morning. Then, two tired angels of some kind, hung-up forlornly in an LA shelf, having found the closest and most delicious thing in life together, we fell asleep ..." (84). Sex here is not a wild explosion but the desperate, gentle solace two babes in the woods haltingly offer each other. Sex, like love, is passive and accepting; it is child-love: one only stands there and is showered in undemanding, protective affection. Sal says he ought to be seeking out a wife, but his true search is, as is Dean's, not for lover but for father, for someone to shelter him from life and responsibility. He turns to Terry not for ecstasy or even sensation, but as a respite from his search, an escape from the demands of life: "I finally decided to hide from the world one more night with her and morning be damned" (89).

In short, for all their exuberance, Kerouac's characters are half in love with easeful death. And this Sal Paradise and his creator well know. Neither is deceived about the nature of beat existence. Kerouac is able to step back from his characters to point out their follies; to show, for example, Dean's pathetic justification of life on the road and Sal's equally pathetic hunger, despite his friend's unmistakable deterioration, to believe him: "'What's your road man?—holy boy road, mad man road, rainbow road, guppy road, any road. It's an anywhere road for anybody anyhow. Where body how?' We nodded in the rain" (251). Sal himself is able to articulate his own fear of feeling and responsibility and his resultant, overwhelming emptiness: "Well, you know me. You know I don't have close relationships with anybody anymore. I don't know what to do with these things. I hold things in my hand like pieces of crap and don't know where to put it down.... It's not my fault! It's not my fault! ... Nothing in this lousy world is my fault, don't you see that? I don't want it to be and it can't be and it won't be" (213). He realizes that he has "nothing to offer anybody except my own confusion," and marks the deaths of his various illusions with the refrain, "Everything is collapsing."

Kerouac further points out that the shortcomings of his characters parallel the shortcomings of the country to which they are so intimately connected. Kerouac's response to America is typically disillusioned. America is a land of corruption and hypocrisy, promising everything and delivering nothing, living off the innocence and opportunity, the excitement and adventure of the past. In particular Kerouac indicts America for failing to provide his searching characters with any public meaning or communal values to counteract the emptiness of their private lives. Sal looks to America much as he looks to Dean, to provide him with direction, purpose and meaning, to offer him a straight line, an ordered progression to a golden destination, an "IT" of stability and salvation. But IT never materializes, and the straight line itself becomes an end; the going, the road, is all. Dean's response to continual disillusionment is to forsake the destination for the journey: "Move!" Sal follows his leader but eventually becomes disgusted with the purposeless, uncomfortable jockeying from coast to coast, just as he becomes disgusted with Dean. Unlike Dean, Sal is able to recognize and identify his despair and, ultimately, to act on the causes of it; where for Dean change is merely deterioration, Sal undergoes true development.

In addition to Sal's growing insight, Kerouac equips his narrator with a double vision, enabling Sal to comment on the people and events of the novel as he saw them when they happened, and as he views them now that they are over, a sadder-but-wiser hindsight which acts as a check upon his naive, undiscriminating exuberances and provides a disillusioned alternative view of the beatifics of the beat generation.

While the younger Sal idolized Dean upon first meeting him, the older Sal reminds the reader that "this is all far back, when Dean was not the way he is today ..." (4), and notes that "the whole mad swirl of everything that was to come began then; it would mix up all my friends and all I had left of my family in a big dust cloud over the American night" (8). He observes the sad effect of Time upon his old friends who once "rushed down the street together, digging everything in the early way they had, which later becomes so much sadder and perceptive and blank" (8). He corrects himself when his earlier view of Dean intrudes upon the more precise voice of his older self: "Dean ... had finished his first fling in New York. I say fling, but he only worked like a dog in parking lots" (9). Sal continually checks and repudiates his youthful self, and deflates his naive view of Dean and life on the road: "I could hear a new call and see a new horizon, and believe it at my young age; and a little bit of trouble or even Dean's eventual rejection of me as a buddy, putting me down, as he would later, on starving sidewalks and sick-beds— what did it matter? I was a young writer and I wanted to take off" (11). He is even able to poke fun at his melodramatic posturings: "I hid in my corner with my head between my knees. Gad, what was I doing three thousand miles from home? Why had I come here? Where was my slow boat to China?" (75).

Sal's double vision does more than correct his impulses. It projects the reader forward in time and provides the sense of continuity the disjunctive characters, including the younger Sal, lack. This older voice offers relations and connections, causes and effects, connects past with present and projects into the future. It firmly anchors reader and narrator to the familiar world of change and conjunction. It knows the discrepancy between appearance and reality and realizes sadly that Time eventually captures even frantically speeding children. It is the view of a man who has, in Dean Moriarty's words, come to "know Time," it prepares the reader for Sal's eventual disillusionment with beat life and "the sordid hipsters of America."

Sal's double vision is proof of his eventual recapitulation to time and change, a recapitulation which he battles for most of the novel. It is this battling, perhaps, so constant and monotonous, which has infuriated readers used to traditional novels of development and, makes them wonder, indeed, whether anything happens to anyone in the novel at all. Sal alone of the characters continually perceives the futility and insanity of his journeys, yet continually makes them, always with the same childlike innocence and expectation, always to follow the same pattern of hopefulness ending in disillusionment as he learns and relearns the same weary lessons about America and Dean Moriarty. Nonetheless, Sal does finally accept the obligations of his insights and revelations, decides to bear the heavy weight of change and responsibility, and grows up to understand, evaluate and finally repudiate Dean Moriarty, the American Dream, and life on the road.

Kerouac makes it clear from the first sentence of the novel that Sal's relationship with Dean is a less demanding, less intimate substitute for a relationship with a wife, a relationship which the newly-divorced Sal has proven himself unable to handle. His liaison with Dean is intimately connected with his fears of emotions, of himself, and of life. He is able to work through with Dean some of the fears, inadequacies and reservations that have prevented him from forming meaningful or lasting alliances, and have prompted him to search for meaning in cars or countries rather than in himself and with a woman.

When the novel opens, Sal is drifting. His marital and college careers have broken down and, as he says of his friend Remi, he has "fallen on the beat and evil days that come to young guys in their middle twenties;" he is "hanging around waiting for a ship" (61). Unable to provide himself with direction or purpose, haunted by the "feeling that everything was dead," Sal seizes on an impetus from without, a strong force which promises to order his life. His ship comes in, navigated by that "crazy Ahab," Dean Moriarty, who, for all his madness, is able, as was Ahab, to provide his crew with direction and purpose. With his constant schedules and plans, his frantic attempts to order, use and outrun Time, his paring down of life to the essentials of motion and survival, Dean is a figure of order and authority for Sal. As long as he is in Dean's car, Sal has a direction and a destination: California, Mexico or New York, in as straight a line as possible. Even more, he has a purpose. Sal and Dean manage, at least at first, to endow their trip with great spiritual significance. They are not tourists, as Sal often points out with contempt, but pilgrims in search of all the "IT" America has to offer, seekers after paradise and salvation, as Sal's name suggests. Denver and San Francisco are not mere cities but, respectively, "the Promised Land" and "the greater vision." Their trip is to be a straight and holy march across the continent, a quest endowed, as all quests ought to be, with monastic purity, rigid order, and singleness of purpose, goals Sal is unable to carry out but nonetheless upholds: "I rued the way I had broken up the purity of my entire trip, not saving every dime, and dawdling and not really making time, fooling around with this sullen girl and spending all my money" (35).

Dean offers Sal more than direction and meaning; he simultaneously provides both a quest and an escape, a hiatus from adult life and adult feelings, a moratorium on maturity. Sal associates Dean with his own childhood: "... he reminded me of some long-lost brother ..., made me remember my boyhood.... And in his excited way of speaking I heard again the voices of old companions and brothers under the bridge ..." (10). Indeed, although Sal is older than Dean, he regards Dean at first not so much as "long lost brother" but as Father whom he passively follows, trusting to be protected, loved and directed. Sal is disenchanted with Dean at the end of Part Two not because Dean has proven himself a poor friend, but because he has turned out to be yet another bad father: "Where is Dean and why isn't he concerned about our welfare?" (171).

Sal's disillusionment with Dean in California is paralleled by his disenchantment with Los Angeles and the perversion and despair he finds there. Fed up with his adoptive fathers, with Dean and America, Sal falls in with the Chicanos whom he regards as a nation of beautiful children, leading lives free from ambition, success, pressure and responsibility: "Nothing had been accomplished. What was thereto accomplish? Manana ... Manana, man" (92). Sal attempts to find an antidote to Dean's frenzy, California's emptiness, and all the adult voices haranguing him to make a choice in the slow, primitive case of Chicano life. He finds Theresa, another child, and plays house with her. But this too collapses; the chill of winter is in the air and he tires of playing at husband and father. He can romanticize the life of the migrant workers, but their suffering is real: "Nothing was going to happen except starvation for Terry and me" (95).

Once again he takes to the road, heading back to his old life, having managed to ignore all the disillusionment along the way. But the stern prophet figure which has haunted him on his journey West appears in real form, not as father but as fool, a warning to Sal that his journey has been foolish and in the wrong direction, that he is heading nowhere and towards nothing, that he must take hold of and change his life.

The Ghost of the Susquehanna arrives like the prophet Sal had been expecting; "he walked very fast, commanding me to follow, and said there was a bridge up ahead we could cross" (103). But "as far as I could see he was just a semi-respectable walking hobo of some kind" (104). Instead of father and son, they are only "bums together." The old man's message is not a revelation but a recital of free meals cadged from the Red Cross. Lost and confused, he is unable to conduct Sal into paradise; "we never found that bridge." But although he does not live up to Sal's romantic expectations, he does function as a genuine prophet, offering through his example a warning and a prophecy: he and Sal are traveling on the same road. The "poor little madman," stubbornly headed out in the wrong direction "on the wrong road," is an aging reflection of Sal himself, who, empty, lost, starving, mired in the past, is as well a "poor forlorn man, poor lost sometimeboy, now broken ghost of the penniless wilds" (104).

That Sal understands the connection between the Ghost and himself is immediately evident. Shaken by this new view of his life, he wakes to a morning with "a whiteness like the whiteness of the tomb," a "day of the Laodiceans, when you know you are wretched and miserable and poor and blind and naked, and with the visage of a gruesome grieving ghost you go shuddering through nightmare life." He understands that he is no longer "a sweet child believing in everything under your father's roof" (105); the lonely road along which he stumbles is "terrifying" now and "mournful," lit by hellish fires. Nor will the road and its denizens shelter him: "I was starving to death." Yet the alternative to innocence, childhood, dreams and the road is even more "terrifying" and "mournful." To be an adult, to settle down, is to be one of the "millions and millions hustling forever for a buck among themselves, the mad dream-grabbing, taking, giving, sighing, dying, just so they could be buried in those awful cemetery cities beyond Long Island" (106). Sal's temporary compromise is to forsake the road and return home, where he can have both roots and irresponsibility, safe with his aunt and her laden refrigerator, in his room with the rug "woven of all the clothes in my family for years" (107).

Yet, after he has been home awhile, his family begins to wear on him. Adult life is reduced to "talking in low whining voices ... about the weather, the crops, and the general weary recapitulation of who had a baby, who got a house, and so on ..." (109). The prospect of settling down "to marry a girl ... so I can rest my soul with her till we both grow old" (116) is enough to send Sal straight into Dean's battered Hudson for another sail around the road; as always Dean appears to "save" his friend from having to grow up. However, rather than a holy quest, Sal introduces this second journey as nothing less than a species of madness. They have no particular destination; Sal is going merely because "the bug was on me again." Although Dean's madness endows everything with frenetic significance, Sal knows that "It made no sense.... It was a completely meaningless set of circumstances that made Dean come, and similarly I went off with him for no reason" (116). Now only pot can make him believe that IT, the moment of decision and revelation, is at hand; "that everything was about to arrive—the moment when you know all and everything is decided forever" (129).

Dean's madness has "bloomed into a weird flower" (113), and it becomes more and more difficult for Sal to enthuse away his friend's "compulsive psychosis dashed with a jigger of psychopathic irresponsibility and violence" (147). Sal grows colder, hungrier, more frustrated and miserable, haunted by "that feeling when you're driving away from people and they recede on the plain till you see their specks dispersing" (156). He yearns after the "comfortable little homes with chimneys smoking," wants to "go in for buttermilk and beans in front of the fireplace" (161). Dean retreats further and further until "we didn't know what he was talking about anymore," and Sal comes to view their furious rushing with disgust and rue: "It was sad to see [Hingham's] tall figure receding in the dark as we drove away, just like the other figures in New York and New Orleans.... Where go? What do? What for? ... But this foolish gang was bending onward" (167). Onward is only once more to California, as "broken-down," "withered" and "disenchanted" as before. Demanding more of his travels than mere distance ("What I accomplished by coming to Frisco I don't know"), abandoned again by Dean ("Dean didn't care one way or the other"), Sal ends his second journey with a catalogue of madness, perversion, and despair, and decides to strike off on his own ("We were all thinking we'd never see one another again and we didn't care" [178]).

He moves to Denver, gets a job, and thinks of "settling down there" to be a "patriarch" and live alone in the adult world. Once again, his cautious foray into adult life is followed by a frenzied retreat. Unable to bear the "loneliness" and emptiness of his new life style ("In God's name and under the stars, what for?"), he longs to be a Black or a Chicano or "even a poor overworked Jap," anything but a "disillusioned 'white man'" caught up in respectability and dreariness (p. 180). While he cannot be a Black or a Chicano or a "Jap," and share what he deems their "boyish human joy," he can rejoin Dean Moriarty who, by virtue of his madness, is one with the "happy true-hearted ecstatic Negro," beyond respectability, responsibility and the grim white workaday world. Suppressing his earlier disenchantment,

Sal vows to keep "faith" in Dean, for his alternatives are either the white wasteland of adult life, the depression of living completely without meaning, or the awesome responsibility of having to provide order and direction for himself, beyond what either Dean or modern America can offer.

Yet when Sal "runs immediately to Dean ... burning to know ... what would happen now," he finds his friend sunk into pitiable madness, and realizes with shock and pity that "it was up to me. Poor, poor Dean—the devil himself had never fallen farther; in idiocy, with infected thumb, surrounded by the battered suitcases of his motherless, feverish life across America and back numberless times, an undone bird" (189). Sal accepts the responsibility for his "undone bird" and commits himself "resolutely and firmly" to Dean and his "burdensome existence." Their roles reverse; now Sal provides the direction and purpose ("Come to New York with me; I've got the money"), decides, plans and answers all questions. He becomes, in short, Dean's father, his adult, feeling "sudden concern for a man who was years younger than I...." This change in Sal is nothing short of momentous. In effect, he enters into a marriage with Dean "whose fate was wound with mine ...," a pact as solemn as any with a woman. He asks for Dean's hand like a nervous fiancé, looking into his eyes and blushing, "for I'd never committed myself before with regard to his burdensome existence," and waits for Dean's answer, "my eyes ... watering with embarrassment and tears" (189). But "something clicked in both of us;" standing "on top of a hill on a beautiful sunny day," Dean accepts him; "he became extremely joyful and said everything was settled." The two plight their troth ("we would stick together and be buddies till we died"), witness an actual wedding party (p. 190), then go off on their honeymoon ("'Well,' said Dean in a very shy and sweet voice, 'shall we go?'"), forsaking all others ("we paid absolutely no attention to Roy and sat in the back and yakked"). Although both are afraid of this rather formal intimacy and involvement, and feel "perplexed and uncertain," true to his vows Sal takes care of Dean, defending him against his enemies, responding to him with love and protecting him from worry. Although not yet ready to settle down with a woman, Sal can travel intimately with his dependent friend to whom he shyly but resolutely offers sympathy, commitment and responsibility.

Sal's emotional maturation is evident in his first "lover's quarrel" with Dean. Enraged by Dean's casual reference to his growing old ("You're getting a little older now"), Sal turns on him, reducing him to tears, but immediately afterwards realizes that his anger is directed at aging rather than at Dean: "I had flipped momentarily and turned it down on Dean" (212). He takes responsibility for hurting Dean, and apologizes to him, humbly and lovingly: "Remember that I believe in you. I'm infinitely sorry for the foolish

grievance I held against you ..." (217). He sees that his present anger springs
from sources buried in his youth ("Everything I had ever secretly held
against my brother was coming out ..."). This insight into himself helps him
to understand Dean, who is, like him, mired in a past whose anger and frenzy
he is compelled to act out, but, unlike Sal, without benefit of apology or
insight: "All the bitterness and madness of his entire Denver life was blasting
out of his system like daggers. His face was red and sweaty and mean" (221).
Regarding his friend without desperate idealism, Sal sees that Dean's frantic
moving and going is not a romantic quest for adventure or truth but is
instead a sad, lost circling for the past, for the home and the father he never
had. He sees that both he and Dean are as frightened and lost as "the Prince
of Dharma," going in circles in the dark lost places between the stars,
searching for that "lost ancestral grove" (222). The road on which they run
is "all that old road of the past unreeling dizzily as if the cup of life had been
overturned and everything gone mad. My eyes ached in nightmare day"
(234). True to his vow, he takes Dean back to New York with him, yet knows
that for them a "permanent home" is impossible. Their marriage breaks
down; Dean returns to his crazy welter of wives and children, Sal to his, aunt
and his disillusionment.

Reminders that he is aging and must decide what to do with his life
become inescapable. Dean's gloomy forecast of their futures as desperate
bums ("someday you and me'll be coming down an alley together at sundown
and looking in the cans to see" [251]) is frightening rather than romantic.
Playing basketball with a group of "younger boys," he is forced to admit that
he is no longer legitimately young, and cannot compete with the "boys" who
"bounced all around us and beat us with ease" while "we huffed and puffed."
Nor does he miss their condemnation of his frantic pursuit: "They thought
we were crazy" (253). As usual, his response to pressure is flight; he tries to
deny the facts of age and decision by running off with Dean in search of
ecstasy in timelessness. In leaving America behind, Sal hopes to leave behind
all he has realized there ("behind us lay ... everything Dean and I had
previously known, about life and life on the road" [276]), as well as his
identity as a "disillusioned white man" confronted with the American way of
life. But this final foray with Dean only brings to a head all the forces of Time
and Change that have borne down upon him in the course of his journeys.

In Mexico Sal hopes to escape from the self, civilization, and their
discontents. At the bottom of his primitivism is a desire to confront the
primal sources of pure being, to discover life as it was—shapeless, formless,
dark—before being molded into self or society; in short, to find once and for
all the womb he has been seeking all his life. If nothing else, he hopes to

search out his final, true and ultimate parents among the Indians who are the source of mankind and the fathers of it."

But the "strange Arabian paradise we had finally found at the end of the hard, hard road" is only "a wild old whore house" (290) after all. The Indians are coming down from the mountains drawn to wristwatches and cities. They and the Mexicans welcome Sal and Dean not as brothers or fellow children, but as American tourists to be exploited. The brothel where they converge for their ultimate mind- and time-blowing fling is a sad, frantic, desperate place, full of eighteen-year-old drunks and child whores, "sinking and lost," "writhing and suffering." The children cry south of the border too: "The baby ... began a grimace which led to bitter tears and some unknown sorrow that we had no means to soothe because it reached too far back into innumerable mysteries and time" (286). Their great primitive playground is no more than "a sad kiddy park with swings and a broken-down merry-go-round ... in the fading red sun ..." (292). And in that "sad kiddy park" Sal leaves behind his faith in the possibility of an infantile paradise and, with it, his faith in Dean.

Dean first induced Sal to accompany him over the border with the happy announcement that "... the years have rolled severally behind us and yet you see none of us have really changed ..." (262). In Mexico Sal finds this denial of time not a reprieve but a condemnation. Dean cannot change and he cannot rest, not even in "the great and final wild uninhibited Fellahin childlike" Mexico City. Wedded forever to his terrible, changeless compulsions, not the love of his friend nor the possibility of paradise can stay him from his rounds.

He leaves the "delirious and unconscious" Sal to return to "all that again," for, as he himself announces, "the road drives *me*." Sal understands and pities him ("I realized what a rat he was, but ... I had to understand the impossible complexity of his life, how he had to leave me there, sick, to get on with his wives and woes" [302]), realizing his friend is the least free of anyone. Dean leads not a primitive life of spontaneity and instinct but instead a sorry, driven existence of joyless "sweats" and anxieties. Sal has a "vision" of Dean not as sweet, holy goof but as the Angel of Death, burning and laying waste whatever he touches:

> Suddenly I had a vision of Dean, a burning shuddering frightful
> Angel, palpitating toward me across the road, approaching like a
> cloud, with enormous speed, pursuing me like the Shrouded
> Traveler on the plain, bearing down on me. I saw his huge face
> over the plains with the mad, bony purpose and the gleaming

eyes; I saw his wings; I saw his old jalopy chariot with thousands
of sparking flames shooting out from it; I saw the path it burned
over the road; it even made its own road and went over the corn,
through cities, destroying bridges, drying rivers. It came like
wrath to the West.... Behind him charred ruins smoked. (259).

On the Road ends with a rejection of beat life. Sal turns his back on
Dean and the life of "bursting ecstasies" and frantic traveling, for he knows
now that it, too, is meaningless, "making logics where there was nothing but
inestimable sorrowful sweats" (305), that it is, ultimately, the way of Death.
Sal himself must opt for life, and for growth.

Returning to America, Sal meets up once more with the Shrouded
Traveler, a symbol of the fatal lure of the road and the restless, nomadic beat
life. Sal wonders if this "tall old man with flowing white hair ... with a pack
on his back" is a sign "that I should at last go on my pilgrimage on foot on
the dark roads around America" (306). He wonders, in short, if he ought to
become the Ghost of the Susquehanna, to enter the darkness from which the
old man appeared and into which he vanished. He responds to the romance
of this suggestion, but is haunted by its loneliness. Later, in New York, he
calls out his name in the darkness and is answered by Laura, "the girl with
the pure and innocent dear eyes that I had always searched for and for so
long" (306). Settling his dreams of paradise and salvation in her, he gives up
the road.

Sal's emphasis has shifted from moving to staying, from road to home.
His relationship with Laura is described simply; they can communicate with
and respond to one another without the sentimental, self-important
posturings that have marked Sal's previous interludes. He and Laura have
long-range plans; they will take a trip, but it will be a migration rather than
a flight, not impulsive but carefully planned out, a moving from one home to
another, bringing with them furniture, a future, and roots: "We planned to
migrate to San Francisco, bringing all our beat furniture and broken
belongings with us in a jalopy truck" (306). Sal is now able in himself to
consummate straight lines, to carry through on his plans with Laura and his
decision to make it up with Remi; he is able to fulfill his promises. But to
make it up with Remi and continue his orderly relationship with Laura, to
remain in the world of intimacy and responsibility he has newly entered, he
must reject Dean.

In a sense, Sal's growth as an adult can be measured through his
responses to Dean and in the changing aspects of their relationship. Sal
moves from idolatry to pity, from a breathless, childlike worship of Dean as

alternately Saint and Father, to a realization of Dean's own tortured humanity, marked by Sal's attempt to be brother, then Father, to his friend, sensitive to Dean's needs without melodrama, facing responsibility and decision, allowing himself to feel blame and love, yet, eventually, for the sake of his own soul, rejecting, deliberately and sadly, his lost, perpetually circling friend.

When Dean arrives to rescue him once more from the world of age and obligation, Sal refuses to go. He discards Dean's plan to leave for San Francisco before he himself is absolutely ready ("But why did you come so soon, Dean?"), and, deciding that he "wasn't going to start all over again ruining [Remi's] planned evenings as I had done ... in 1947" (309), he pulls, away from Dean and leaves him behind.

Sal's final view is of his friend as the Shrouded Traveler. Looking back he sees Dean, ragged, freezing, shrouded in "a motheaten overcoat," alone, and on the move: "Dean, ragged in a motheaten overcoat ... walked off alone, and the last I saw of him he rounded the corner of Seventh Avenue, eyes on the street ahead, and bent to it again" (309), to a lower-case "it" of frustration, futility and despair.

In the course of his scattered journeys Sal has learned, perhaps to his regret, what rather tentatively might indeed finally matter, and to this tenuous value he cautiously decides to commit himself, giving up the ghost of the Shrouded Traveler, of Dean Moriarty and Old Dean Moriarty and dead America, and accepting in their place feeling, responsibility, and roots—not in a place but in another person, Laura. Sal's relationship with Dean has served as an apprenticeship during which he has learned how to accommodate to intimacy, as his disillusionment with America has prepared him to look beyond the road for salvation and paradise. Neither America nor Dean can successfully order his life, provide him with direction or meaning. Neither can father him; ultimately, he must father himself, must look inward for purpose and belief. For America has lost her innocence and her sense of purpose just as Dean has and, like Dean, is continually making bogus attempts to pretend it still has all the potential and grace of its youth ("Hell's bells! It's Wild West Week.... Big crowds of businessmen, fat businessmen in boots and ten-gallon hats, with their hefty wives in cowgirl attire, bustled and whooped on the wooden sidewalks of old Cheyenne.... I was seeing to what absurd devices [the West] had fallen to keep its proud tradition" [33]).

On the Road ends with an elegy for a lost America, for the country which once might have been the father of us all, but now is only "the land where they let children cry." Dean Moriarty is himself America, or rather the dream of America, once innocent, young, full of promise and holiness, bursting with potential and vitality, now driven mad, crippled, impotent ("We're all losing our fingers"), ragged, dirty, lost, searching for a past of security and love that never existed, trailing frenzy and broken promises, unable to speak to anybody anymore.

GEORGE DARDESS

The Delicate Dynamics of Friendship:
A Reconsideration of Kerouac's On the Road

W hen Norman Mailer asserted, in *Advertisements for Myself*,[1] that Jack Kerouac "lacks discipline, intelligence, honesty and a sense of the novel," he was giving voice to an opinion so generally accepted that no critic to this day has attempted to refute or even qualify it. Yet Kerouac's books continue to be read, and even his unpublished manuscripts are receiving attention. (*Visions of Cody*, a work written in 1951–1952, was published in January 1973 by McGraw-Hill.) In addition, a full scale biography has recently appeared (Ann Charters, *Kerouac*, Straight Arrow Press, 1973), and another is in progress. Nevertheless, critical reassessment lags. Readers admire hesitatingly, even helplessly, as if they were unsure how to describe a writer for whom few terms, except pejorative ones, have been invented. What is needed to counteract the negative influence of unproved opinions like Mailer's is not, however, a vocabulary of praise but one of careful critical judgment like that recently accorded Mailer himself.[2] Kerouac's work deserves understanding. If, after treating the work fairly, we find condemnation justified, we can pass with good conscience to worthier objects.

A close look at Kerouac's work suggests that his "sense of the novel," though not identical to Mailer's, is carefully and rigorously developed; and his "discipline, intelligence, honesty" are indeed evident, perhaps most clearly so in the novel for which he is best known, *On The Road*. For though

From *American Literature* 46, no. 2. © 1974 by Duke University Press.

many readers of *On The Road* have thought it a modern version of the picaresque,[3] its structure is formidably complex. Here is no loose scribbling of notes whose only organization is geographical and chronological, but a delicately constructed account of the relation between the narrator, Sal Paradise, and his friend, Dean Moriarty—an account built according to a classic dramatic design. *On The Road* is a love story, not a travelog (and certainly not a call to Revolution). It is told with all the "art"—the conscious and unconscious shaping of verbal materials—one expects from the best writing. Kerouac may legitimately be, even on the basis of *On The Road* alone, a great American author—an author the equal of Mailer himself.

A comparison between the opening and closing paragraphs of *On The Road* gives a preliminary idea of the book's structural complexity. Where the book begins cautiously, with careful distinctions made between the narrator's present, his Moriarty past, and his pre-Moriarty past, it ends with a complicated paragraph in which temporal and spatial boundaries are obliterated. A similar change occurs in the emotional associations attributed to each paragraph's treatment of time. Where the book opens with a gleam of happiness ("the part of my life you could call my life on the road"[4]) preceded by darkness (by "the miserably weary split-up" between the narrator and his wife), it ends with a mix of hope and discouragement, of expansiveness and resignation. (In the last paragraph, for instance, the discouraged wisdom of the phrase "nobody, nobody knows what's going to happen to anybody besides the forlorn rags of growing old" is contained within a panoramic gesture embracing the entire American continent.) The book begins with the narrator's construction of distinctions and boundaries; it ends with his discarding them—a discarding which indicates his desire to suspend opposites in a perhaps continuous state of flux. The book moves from hierarchy to openness, from the limitation of possibilities to their expansion.

Such a movement might seem to suggest that *On The Road* becomes incoherent: a book in which the ending does not resolve complexities might seem careless or meaningless. Alan Friedman, in *The Turn of the Novel*,[5] assures us, however, that absence of resolution need not deny fictional closure. It can substitute closure of a different kind, one appropriate to the narrated experience. As for *On The Road*, its narrated experience is such that an open ending is appropriate. The experience consists in the narrator's desire, as shown in the first paragraph of the book, to render events of a happier "part" of his life without, as much as possible, contaminating his feelings about that "part" with his feelings about other parts of his life, including his feelings about the present. The narrated experience also consists, however, in the narrator's final assimilation of the events he is dramatizing with the moment of dramatization itself. In the book's last paragraph the narrator speaks from a present tense ("So in America when the sun goes down and I sit on the old broken-down river pier ...") in which all parts of his life, together with the part from which he is now speaking, are included.

Yet the assimilation of times just referred to does not disturb the book's classic dramatic shape. One of Kerouac's accomplishments in *On The Road* is in fact to unify the open ending (in which all points of view in the novel are combined without being resolved) with a time-honored novelistic and dramaturgic structure. The structure is evident in a narration divided into five Parts, the third of which contains what can be called the climax of Sal's and Dean's friendship. Parts One and Two record Sal's gradual development of excited interest in Dean, while Part Four records Sal's development of an apocalyptic fear of him. Accompanying the growing complexity of Sal's relation to Dean is an outfanning geographical movement. Each Part records a circuit of the United States with New York, Denver, and San Francisco serving as the main geographical and cultural axes. In Parts Two and Three, important detours are made from more or less straight lines of progress connecting one axis with another, the first detour by way of New Orleans, the second by way of Chicago. In Part Four, the friends spin off the board altogether towards Mexico City and the "end of the road." In Part Five, Sal and, Dean go their separate ways, each friend towards opposite shores of the American continent.

The men's relations are intimately connected to the direction and scope of their geographical movements. As their geographical range increases, so does the range and complexity of their relation. In Part One, for instance, Dean is mostly on the periphery of Sal's experience. Consequently, this is the innocent section of *On The Road*, the one most unqualifiedly romantic. Sal is making his first road trip, alone, across the country, and his feelings are those of boyish delight. Though there are perceptions of *lacrimae rerum* (the "tears of things"), the perceptions do not achieve dramatic coherence. They do not achieve coherence even when Dean enters the center of Sal's life in Part Two, since Sal's attitude towards Dean is at this point too wide-eyed, too bedazzled by admiration. The negative aspects of Dean's conduct are hinted at but never in this Part confronted systematically. Beginning with Part Three, however, Sal begins to confront the consequences of Dean's vulnerability to "IT," to ecstasy, to the promise of being able to reduce time and space to smaller and smaller increments until they disappear altogether as measurements of activity. Where in Parts One and Two "IT" functions as an ultimate mystery to which Dean's relation is priest-like (and Sal's is that of the neophyte), in Part Three Sal takes custodianship not only of Dean but of the "IT" which Dean embodies more consistently and dramatically than anyone else Sal knows. And by taking custody of Dean and "IT," Sal changes from being little more than an admirer caught up in Dean's wake to becoming Dean's father-defender. The change occurs just after Sal arrives at Dean's house and finds that Dean and his wife Camille are at war:

"Why did Camille throw you out? What are you going to do?"

"Eh?" he said, "Eh? Eh?" We racked our brains for where to go and what to do. I realized it was up to me. Poor, poor Dean— the devil himself had never fallen farther; in idiocy, with infected thumb, surrounded by the battered suitcases of his motherless feverish life across America and back numberless times, an undone bird. "Let's walk to New York," he said, "and as we do so let's take stock of everything along the way—yass." I took out my money and counted it; I showed it to him.

"I have here," I said, "the sum of eighty-three dollars and change, and if you come with me let's go to New York." ... "Why yass," said Dean, and then realized I was serious and looked at me out of the corner of his eye for the first time, for I'd never committed myself before with regard to his burdensome existence, and that look was the look of a man weighing his chances at the last moment before the bet. There were triumph and insolence in those eyes, a devilish look, and he never took his eyes off mine for a long time. I looked back at him and blushed.

I said, "What's the matter?" I felt wretched when I asked it. He made no answer but continued looking at me with the same wary insolent side-eye.

I tried to remember everything he'd done in his life and if there wasn't something back there to make him suspicious of something now. Resolutely and firmly I repeated what I said— "Come to New York with me; I've got the money." I looked at him; my eyes were watering with embarrassment and tears. Still he stared at me. Now his eyes were blank and looking through me. It was probably the pivotal point of our friendship when he realized I had actually spent some hours thinking about him and his troubles, and he was trying to place that in his tremendously involved and tormented mental categories. (pp. 188–189)

This passage marks the "pivotal point" not only of the friendship but of the book as well. Sal's assuming responsibility for what he now calls Dean's "burdensome existence"—that is, seen as "burdensome" in the act of taking responsibility for it—brings out unexpected responses both in himself and his friend. What's more, those responses begin to affect almost immediately the way both of them see the world. The remainder of *On The Road* is concerned with working out the consequences of the new responses dramatically. Later, in Part Three, Sal himself receives possession of "IT" during the friends' journey east; and before they leave San Francisco Sal stands up in defense of Dean before a "jury" composed of Dean's former friends. These would seem, however, more or less predictable consequences of Sal's behavior in the "pivotal" scene. Far trickier psychologically and metaphysically are the consequences of Dean's "devilish look" and Sal's blush.

When Sal says, at the beginning of the passage quoted, that "the devil himself has never fallen farther," we may either dismiss the analogy as hyperbolic or say that the analogy connects Dean not with the devil but with the devil's falling. According to the latter view, Sal would be trying to indicate only the suddenness of Dean's loss of self-control; where "IT" had sustained Dean in Part Two above the world of hurt and family obligation, "IT" abandons him in Part Three. But when Sal assumes the sustaining function of "IT" here, he sees Dean in a new and terrible light. Dean's "weighing his chances at the last moment before the bet" has about it the calculating coldness of the devil himself. Or is Sal the devil? When one adult assumes absolute responsibility for the existence—"burdensome" or not—of another adult, he does so at what seems a great risk, since both parties sacrifice to each other their independence. Everything one does has direct, immediate, and perhaps mortal effects on the other; there is no escaping the implications of each other's conduct. Later in Part Three, for instance, Sal begins to see Dean in terms of titanic evil: "the Angel of Terror" (p. 233), a "mad Ahab" (p. 234), and finally, at the beginning of Part Four, as "a burning, frightful Angel, palpitating toward me across the road, approaching like a cloud, with enormous speed, pursuing me like the Shrouded Traveler on the plain" (p. 259)—the same "Shrouded Traveler" whom Sal had earlier, in Part Two, identified with Death (p. 124).

These apocalyptic forebodings acquire their greatest significance in Part Four, when Dean, Sal, and another friend make their trip to Mexico City and to what they call the "end of the road" (p. 276). After leaving the United States, the three men suppose that they are entering the land of "basic, primitive, wailing humanity" (p. 280). And in this land they feel close to the source of all understanding. But they feel also—and particularly the narrator, Sal, feels this—a strain between apocalyptic truths and the sensory evidence that ought to support them unequivocally. Mexico City's status as "end of the road" has to be put beside the fact that while there Sal contracts dysentery. And Dean's status as leader has to be put beside his abandoning Sal at the "end of the road." (He does so in order to return to New York with a Mexican divorce from his second wife, Camille, in order then to commit himself to yet a third.) Sal's comment on Dean's shabby act shows a further dimension of the responsibility he took for Dean in Part Three: "When I got better I realized what a rat he was, but then I had to understand the impossible complexity of his life, how he had to leave me there, sick, to get on with his wives and woes. 'Okay, old Dean, I'll say nothing'" (p. 303).

To have responsibility for your friend means not only providing him with companionship or with money, not only defending him before a jury of his peers; it means also—and painfully—maintaining a sense of how your friend sees himself apart from the way you see him. But, perhaps more painfully, it means maintaining a sense of how the friend sees you apart from the way you see yourself. Maintaining such difficult senses is an act of generosity few people care to perform unless they are in love. And if they are in love, they are people—like Sal Paradise—susceptible to the wild contradictory splendors of human behavior. There certainly is justice in Sal's calling Dean a "rat," though earlier in Part Four Sal claimed, during a particularly strong marijuana "rush," that Dean "looked like God." The one view doesn't cancel out the other; they exist side by side, the sides being defined by the division established throughout the book between those human possibilities which lead to "IT" and those which lead to failure and exhaustion.

But the division is established only to be held in suspension. By choosing one side or the other, by declaring once and for all that Dean is a "rat" and nothing else or by declaring that he is "God" and nothing else, Sal could rest on the security of an unambiguous position. Yet what price security? Taking the first option, Sal commits himself to a resigned cynicism; taking the second, to a mindless hero-worship. The third option—to make no choice at all—is described by a writer whom Kerouac strongly resembles, F. Scott Fitzgerald, in *The Crack-Up*: "... the test of a first-rate intelligence is the ability to hold two opposed ideas in the mind at the same time and still retain the ability to function. One should, for example, be able to see that things are hopeless and yet be determined to make them otherwise."[6]

If under the term "function" we can assume that Fitzgerald would include writing (and it is hard to see how we cannot), then *On The Road* is an example of such a test's being taken—and passed, though passing would have to be subjected to the same conditions as those which obtain in the test situation. That "first-rate intelligence" has to see that even a "first-rate intelligence" is, from one point of view, "hopeless." Writing a book about friendship does not allow for tidy endings or unmixed feelings. What takes their place is a fragile, impossible, contradictory structure sustained by the energy of intelligence alone. But such energy is not supplied without cost, and perhaps much of the despair Kerouac (speaking through other narrators) displays in his subsequent writing[7] can be attributed to his awareness of how exorbitant that cost was, though it was a cost he never ceased to pay.

NOTES

1. See *Advertisements for Myself* (New York: Berkeley Medallion Ed., 1966), p. 428.

2. Particularly by Richard Poirier in *Mailer*, in The Modern Masters Series, ed. F. Kermode (New York, 1972).

3. Even someone so close to Kerouac as Allen Ginsberg thinks the book's structure picaresque. See Ginsberg's interview in *Writers at Work, The Paris Review Interviews*, Third Series, ed. George Plimpton (New York, 1967), p. 288.

4. *On The Road* (New York, 1957), p. 3. The book was written in 1951, six years before it was finally published. All subsequent page references to *On The Road* will refer to this edition and will be found in the text directly after the quoted passages.

5. Alan Friedman, *The Turn of the Novel* (New York, 1966), esp. pp. 179–188.

6. F. S. Fitzgerald, *The Crack-Up* (New York, 1956), p. 69.

7. Especially in *Desolation Angels* (written in 1956 and 1961) and *Big Sur* (written in 1961).

TIM HUNT

An American Education

Part one of *On the Road* is an extended confrontation between the "sadder-but-wiser" hindsight of the narrator Sal and his earlier "exuberances." In this first section, Sal as a character is most naive and open to ridicule. Throughout his trip west, Sal's fantasies about himself, Dean, and the road bring him into conflict with a world unconcerned with his fantasies, and Sal looks back on his trip of rude awakenings with a mixture of tolerance and embarrassment. Sal's reasons for crossing the country underscore his optimistic shallowness. After his initial encounter with Dean, Sal decides to explore the West and the road for himself in order to become what he imagines Dean to be, a "sideburned hero of the snowy West." Sal certainly hopes to escape the weary oversophistication of his New York circle and his own depression over recent illness and a failed marriage. Sal's springtime pilgrimage, it should be noted, begins not with adolescent enthusiasm but with adult despair. Sal is not encountering adult realities for the first time. His naiveté as a character stems from the faith that Dean awakens in the redemptiveness of America. Like the hero of the second version of *On the Road*, Sal decides that he has failed to realize his "inheritance" and that the West is the appropriate place to search for it.

In part one, Sal is the college boy on a lark. He plays at being Dean in much the same way that Tom Sawyer plays at being Huck Finn. Sal, like

From *Kerouac's Crooked Road: Development of a Fiction.* © 1981 by Tim Hunt.

Tom, can always count on his aunt to bail him out. Like Huck, Dean relies on himself. He has no aunt, and his alcoholic father is probably dead. Kerouac seems aware of this parallel between the family situations of Sal and Dean and of Tom and Huck. In fictionalizing his own situation, Kerouac changes his mother into an aunt, and in part two as Sal and Dean travel west together, they pick up a series of hitchhikers who each earn their rides by claiming they have an aunt at their destination who will contribute gas money. The aunts all turn out to be fictitious, and Dean finally complains, "Everybody has an aunt!" Everybody has one, that is, except Dean, who must rely on his own resources, primarily his cunning, to keep the gas tank full and everyone in motion. Sal, as it turns out, is not the only "Tom Sawyer" in the book who substitutes an aunt for a mother.[6]

Setting off, Sal is convinced that the world will serve him if he only shows up and gives it the chance. "Somewhere along the line I knew there'd be girls, visions, everything; somewhere along the line the pearl would be handed to me" (OR, 11). "Filled with dreams" and confidence, Sal chooses to hitchhike Route 6 to Denver because it makes such a straight red line on the map. When Route 6 turns out to be a minor highway with little traffic and he is drenched in a thunderstorm, Sal must retrace the little distance he has covered "in a bus with a delegation of school teachers" (OR, 13). As Sal in his role of narrator says,

> It was my dream that screwed up, the stupid hearth-side idea that
> is would be wonderful to follow one great red line across America
> instead of trying various roads and routes. (OR, 13)

Dean's world and the reality of the road is not governed by the aesthetics of maps, and America will not turn out to be a single reality but a series of conflicting realities.

In spite of the fiascoes, much in the trip is positive to Sal. He is a great tourist, and the Mississippi River, his first truck driver, his first cowboy, and the vistas of the range all trigger descriptive epiphanies.

> And here for the first time in my life I saw my beloved Mississippi
> River, dry in the summer haze, low water, with its big rank smell
> that smells like the raw body of America itself because it washes
> it up. (OR, 15)

But even the tourist sights are not always up to his l expectations.

> We arrived at Council Bluffs at dawn; I looked out. All winter I'd
> been reading of the great wagon parties that held council there

before hitting the Oregon and Sante Fe trails; and of course now
it was only cute suburban cottages of one damn kind and another,
all laid out in the dismal gray dawn. (OR, 19)

And in Cheyenne, instead of the old West of his imagination, he finds the old
West as imagined by the chamber of commerce of the new West, the West
of "Wild West Week" where

> fat businessmen in boots and ten-gallon hats, with their hefty
> wives in cowgirl attire, bustled and whooped on the wooden
> sidewalks.... I was amazed, and at the same time I felt it was
> ridiculous: in my first shot at the West I was seeing to what
> absurd devices it had fallen to keep its proud tradition. (OR, 33)

Initially as he travels, Sal alone is inconvenienced by his mistakes and
illusions. Impatient with hitchhiking, he wastes money on bus rides. At the
Wild West Week, he throws away his money buying drinks for a hitchhiking
buddy and trying to seduce a farm girl only to wind up the next morning in
the bus station alone, hung over, and broke. But as Sal moves westward, his
mistakes increasingly have serious consequences for people he is with. In
California, Sal moves into a shack with his bohemian, merchant seaman
buddy Remi Boncoeur and Boncoeur's shrewish girl friend. Sal becomes
embroiled in their domestic quarrels and their schemes for getting rich.
Boncoeur puts Sal to work writing a film script to make his girl a star and the
three of them rich. When that fails, the triangle begins to disintegrate, and
at a dinner party Sal insults Boncoeur's stepfather even though he knows it is
important to Boncoeur to impress the gentleman. Sal humiliates Boncoeur
needlessly and must move on.

In the fiasco with Boncoeur's stepfather, Sal is only partly at fault. In his
affair with the Mexican girl Terry that follows, though, he is wholly to blame.
The guilt for meddling in someone else's world is his alone, and he is forced
to recognize that his actions affect others. When Sal spots Terry on the
evening bus to LA, he is "so lonely, so sad, so quivering, so broken, so beat"
that he manages to get up "the courage necessary to approach a strange girl"
(OR, 81). What follows is a pastiche of Sal's fantasies of Dean and of half-
remembered movie images. Sal's language becomes an imitation of Dean's so
that "it was mutely and beautifully and purely decided that when I got my
hotel room in LA she would be beside me" (OR, 82). Sal makes their arrival
in LA real to himself by equating it with a Hollywood fantasy. "The bus
arrived in Hollywood. In the dirty dawn, like the dawn when Joel McCrea
met Veronica Lake in a diner in the picture *Sullivan's Travels*, she slept in my
lap" (OR, 82). The reference to *Sullivan's Travels*, though seemingly random,

is actually quite suggestive. The hero of the movie is a director of cartoons who flees Hollywood and takes to the road to find out what life is *really* like, only to find it more violent and dangerous than his romanticized image. By a twist of plot and amnesia, the director becomes first a hobo and then a prison inmate before his chance rescue. Back in Hollywood, he decides to return to making cartoons and lighten the load of the poor by entertaining them. The character Sal is interested only in the meeting between two cinema lovers, but it seems likely that Kerouac, and probably the narrator Sal as well, are aware of the more suggestive parallel between the film director's dangerous fantasies about life on the road and Sal's fantasies.

The references to *Sullivan's Travels* comments ironically on Sal's affair with Terry. Throughout the encounter, the narrator juxtaposes his earlier fantasies with the details that undercut them and reveal their reality. When Sal and Terry hit Los Angeles, Sal worries that she may be a "tramp" setting him up for a mugging. Confused by his nervousness, Terry in turn assumes that Sal must be a pimp rather that the "nice college boy" she originally took him to be. The affair is consummated, but sorrowfully at best. When the two get to Terry's home town in the San Joaquin Valley, Sal-the-college-boy approaches the episode as a pastoral interlude of sex in William Saroyan's sun-warmed valley. After Terry collects her little boy from her family, Sal sets to work picking cotton only to find that without the help of Terry and her little boy, he is incapable of picking enough to support them. Gradually Sal is forced to recognize that while he wants simply "experience," Terry wants and deserves a father for her son. Finally Sal has no choice but to wire his aunt for bus fare and leave, and the guilt he feels shows that even the optimistic Sal cannot completely ignore the demystifying force of Dean's world with its painful underside of poverty and rootlessness.

Episodes like the affair with Terry reveal the somber undercurrent beneath the often comic surface of *On the Road*. By the time Sal is ready to return to New York in the fall ("everybody goes home in October" just as "everybody" takes a trip in the spring), the spring dreams that had led him west have given way to the sense of isolation and mortality that turns the trip into a nightmare. In Los Angeles, Sal first claims the rejected movie script he had written for Boncoeur. He then has four hours before his bus to Pittsburgh.

> First I bought a loaf of bread and salami and made myself ten sandwiches to cross the country on. I had a dollar left. I sat on the low cement wall in back of a Hollywood parking lot and made the sandwiches. As I labored at this absurd task, great Kleig lights of a Hollywood premiere stabbed the sky, that humming West

Coast sky. All around me were the noises of the crazy gold-coast
city. And this was my last night in Hollywood, and I was
spreading mustard on my lap in the back of a parking lot john.
(OR, 102)

Through the passage, the word *Hollywood* is repeated almost as a dirge, and
the description is organized as a series of movie shots. The figure in the
foreground is juxtaposed against the panoramic night, kleig lights, and
excitement of the premiere. Then the camera pans in to emphasize the
mustard-stained Sal, his rejected script an emblem of his collapsed fantasies.

When Sal reaches Pittsburgh, he is "wearier than [he has] been for
years," and has a dime in his pocket and 365 miles left to hitchhike to his
aunt's house in New Jersey. Outside Harrisburg he meets "the Ghost of the
Susquehanna ... a shriveled little old man with a paper satchel who claimed
he was headed for 'Canady' (OR, 103). Sal first sees him as a "semi-
respectable walking hobo" and follows when the Ghost claims he can lead Sal
to a bridge that will shorten the trip. As the Ghost maintains a hypnotic
stream of disconnected details of past handouts, Sal gradually realizes the
little man's insanity, abandons him, and flags down a ride only to find he has
been travelling west not east, back to the world of the road and not toward
home. For Sal, the encounter with the Ghost becomes an experience of
terror, a vision of hell faintly reminiscent of "The Try-Works" in *Moby-Dick*
in its colors and sense of inversion.

We were bums together. We walked seven miles along the
mournful Susquehanna. It is a terrifying river. It has bushy cliffs
on both sides that lean like hairy ghosts over the unknown waters.
Inky night covers all. Sometimes from the railyards across the
river rises a great red locomotive flare that illuminates the horrid
cliffs. (OR, 104)

The perpetual disappointment of missed rides, aimless wanderings, and
isolation is not an escape across the bridge into a land of free meals and free
lodging but a shortcut to insanity and death.

I thought all of the wilderness of America was in the West till the
Ghost of the Susquehanna showed me different. No there is a
wilderness in the East. (OR, 105)

There is also wilderness in the self, society, and history, and the discovery
drives Sal to despair.

That night in Harrisburg I had to sleep in the railroad station on a bench; at dawn the station masters threw me out. Isn't it true that you start your life a sweet child believing in everything under your father's roof? Then comes the day of the Laodiceans, when you know you are wretched and miserable and poor and blind and naked with the visage of a gruesome grieving ghost you go, shuddering through nightmare life. I stumbled haggardly out of the station; I had no more control. All I could see of the morning was a whiteness like the whiteness of the tombs. (OR, 105)

Sal's vision of "whiteness" echoes the famous passage in *Moby-Dick* and epitomizes his new awareness of death and loss. He can no longer play Tom Sawyer but must, when he reaches home, "lay [his] head down and figure the losses and figure the gain that ... was in there somewhere too" (OR, 106–7).

The encounter with the Ghost is an indictment of Sal's reasons for travelling west. In imitating Dean, Sal in effect parodies what is perhaps the archetypal American tale: he flees the constrictions of the East hoping to find freedom and regeneration in the West. But Sal's vision of the West is childish and superficial. He refuses to recognize the possibility that his actions may involve cost to himself or others much as, in the final section of *Huck Finn*, Tom Sawyer refuses to recognize the dangers and immorality of playing at freeing the already freed slave Jim. Tom's belief in the inviolability of the child's world is so strong that he can refuse to recognize the wound from an adult bullet. As Sal travels west, he is convinced he can make it on his own and that the world will shape itself to his "dream." By the time he encounters the Ghost on his return, Sal has begun to see the consequences of this attitude. Sal, like Tom Sawyer presumably an orphan, discovers his need for direction only to find that there is no one to provide it. When Sal turns to the Ghost as a surrogate father, the Ghost can offer him only loss, isolation, and death. The Ghost awakens Sal to his need for the father that he, in his childish confidence, has not even seemed to miss, but the Ghost is as unable to be a father to Sal as Sal was to Terry's little boy. The Ghost reveals to Sal that the father is as lost as the son and that each son must confront his own inadequacy and mortality, must become his own father.

Understanding the Ghost, we can see the importance of chapter 4 of part one, where Sal hitches "the greatest ride in my life." Although this scene is one of the novel's most comic, it prefigures Sal's grim return in the fall. Sal's ride is with "two young farmers from Minnesota" who haul farm machinery on their flat bed truck from Los Angeles to the Midwest and then pick up whoever they pass on their return. On the truck Sal finds, in addition to the two drivers, "two young farmer boys," "two young city boys,"

"Mississippi Gene and his charge" (a "tall blond kid ... running away from something"), and "a tall slim fellow who had a sneaky look" called Montana Slim. With the exception of Slim and Sal, everyone on the truck is paired. Three pairs are innocuous; they suggest the pattern but contribute little else. Mississippi Gene, his charge, and Montana Slim, though, are of interest, and Sal's failure to understand the contrast between Gene's responses to being on the road is the crux of the episode.

Gene is patient and soft-spoken. He accepts his way and makes the best of it. When Sal asks about his charge, Gene explains,

> "He got into some kind of trouble back in Mississippi, so I offered to help him out. Boy's never been out on his own. I take care of him best as I can, he's only a child." Although Gene was white there was something of the wise and tired old Negro in him.... (OR, 28)

There is perhaps as well something of Twain's Jim in Mississippi Gene. Gene has not sought his comrade but accepts him and offers what support he can. Slim, on the other hand, is "all insinuation," a loner who feels no compunction about using people. Slim boasts that he always knows where to get money, and when Sal asks him to explain, Slim replies,
" 'Anywhere. You can always folly a man down an alley, can't you?' " (OR, 26).

Kerouac carefully contrasts Gene and Slim.

> Gene was taking care of [his charge], of his moods and his fears. I wondered where the hell they would go and what they would do. They had no cigarettes. I squandered my pack on them, I loved them so. They were grateful and gracious. They never asked, I kept offering. Montana Slim had his own but never passed the pack. (OR, 30)

In spite of the contrast between Gene and Slim, Sal declines Gene's invitation to go to Ogden with him and aligns himself with Slim, who drinks up Sal's money and leaves him flat in the Cheyenne bus station. Sal is not yet ready to accept Gene's example. He intuitively recognizes that Gene's ease and gentleness are a result of how little he demands from the world, but Sal is too optimistic and too sure of his own self-reliance to accept Gene as a guide or to accept Gene's gentle fatalism. Sal is still convinced that "the pearl" will be "handed" to him, and cannot deal with Gene's well-intentioned question about where he is going. When Gene sings what Sal takes to be "'the prettiest song,'" Sal offers, " 'I hope you get where you're going, and be happy when you do.'"

Sal does not understand that Gene is always wherever he is going and, because he is without goals, able to respond calmly to whatever comes his way. Gene's reply, "'I always make out and move along one way or another'" (OR, 32), is finally too stark and simple for Sal, and so he hops off the truck to follow the more exciting but destructive Slim, a comrade who requires no allegiance and offers none in return. Sal's search for excitement and fear of responsibility make him unable to share in the relationship of comrades. He is neither Jim nor Huck, Gene nor his charge; he is the orphan Tom not yet recognizing his own poverty and illusions. Unable to share in Gene's world, Sal makes inevitable the collapse at the end of his trip in October. Sal does not understand Gene or Slim anymore than he later understands the Ghost, but these three figures reveal that the Indian Territory is no longer, if it ever was, an option. One can give up like Gene, turn sly and predatory like Slim, or, like the Ghost, escape into insanity. Sal rejects all three options, but all are relevant to his fantasy of America and the West.

Throughout part one, Sal is essentially alone, and the experiences of his trip teach him the implications of his solitariness and the inadequacy of his fantasies. Early in part one, Sal finds himself halfway West. Ahead is the "Promised Land" of Denver and "the greater vision of San Francisco." Behind is the college world of his past, of which Sal is reminded when he hitches a ride with two University of Iowa students who "talk of exams." The students drop Sal in Des Moines, where he takes a room in "a gloomy old Plains inn of a hotel by the locomotive roundhouse." There,

> I woke up as the sun was reddening; and that was the one distinct time in my life, the strangest moment of all, when I didn't know who I was—I was far away from home, haunted and tired with travel, in a cheap hotel room I'd never seen, hearing the hiss of steam outside, and the creak of the old wood of the hotel, and footsteps upstairs, and all the sad sounds, and I looked at the cracked high ceiling and really didn't know who I was for about fifteen strange seconds. I wasn't scared; I was just somebody else, some stranger, and my whole life was a haunted life, the life of a ghost. I was halfway across America, at the dividing line between the East of my youth and the West of my future, and maybe that's why it happened right there and then, that strange red afternoon. (OR, 17)

Sal, here, recognizes his need to go forward and establish a new identity but does not recognize the cost that will be involved. In America, the future is always in the West and a source of hope. In its attainment, the future, in becoming present, ceases to be West, ceases to be a matter of place, and necessarily involves admitting failure.

The themes established in part one—the search for identity, the relationship between comrades, the problem of the father, and the belief in the West—intersect for Sal in the figure of Dean and the three trips Dean and Sal take in parts two, three, and four. Unlike Gene, Slim, and the Ghost, Dean is a Huck Finn not yet defeated, an active figure willing to attempt to create his freedom, and from the beginning of their trips together, Sal looks to Dean as a brother. Unlike the "intellectuals" of Sal's crowd, Dean

> reminded me of some long-lost brother; the sight of his suffering bony face with the long sideburns, and his straining muscular sweating neck made me remember my boyhood in those dye-dumps and swim-holes and riversides of Paterson and the Passaic. (OR, 10)

And Dean is consistently searching for his hobo father, a search that Sal makes in part his own in aligning himself with Dean.

> At dusk I walked. I felt like a speck on the surface of the sad red earth. I passed the Windsor Hotel, where Dean Moriarity had lived with his father in the depression thirties and as of yore I looked everywhere for the sad and fabled tinsmith of my mind. Either you find someone who looks like your father in places like Montana or you look for a friend's father where he is no more. (OR, 180)

But most basically, Sal responds to Dean's amazing energy, his seemingly limitless vitality which contrasts sharply with Sal's own lethargy at the beginning of the book. Sal admires Dean's freedom from social constraint, his success with women, and his ability to ignore social patterns. Dean is a "natural" and Sal sees in that a traditional American ethos more fundamental than any Protestant work ethic. Dean is Whitman's (and R. W. B. Lewis's) "American Adam." His "dirty workclothes" have that fit earned "from the Natural Tailor of Natural Joy" (OR, 10). Dean is a "cowboy" and evokes in

Sal a nostalgia for the frontier and escape from adult responsibilities. And, finally, Dean projects an aura of "knowing time" that Sal comes to feel might offer a way beyond the despair of his encounter with the Ghost of the Susquehanna.

Even though the plot action from part two on makes *On the Road* seem more Dean's than Sal's story, it is Sal's stake in the action that structures the book and gives it coherence. If this is forgotten, the trips do blur together. But each one is a distinct stage in Sal's understanding of the images associated with Dean. Viewed from Sal's perspective, each trip shows a common pattern. Sal begins by breaking out of an established routine or order in search of kicks and the knowledge of time. He then proceeds through a series of road experiences that end in vision, exhaustion, and a return to the established order. Sal flees the order of his aunt's home, enters the disorder of the road, and returns at the end of each trip to figure his losses and gains. As early as 1949 in the second version, Kerouac thought of *On the Road* as a quest or pilgrimage, and Sal, not Dean, is the one who reaches the moment of vision on each trip. Dean, at times the guide, at times the goal, at times the obstacle, gives Sal a focus for his search and gives the book much of its energy, but Dean does not grow in the way Sal does. His trips end in a defeat quite different from Sal's partial defeat of losses and gains. Dean leaves his wives and children for the disorder of the road only to settle with a new woman and new children, creating an increasingly oppressive "order" of domestic and economic obligations.

In one way, part two, Sal's initial trip with Dean, resembles part one. The optimistic Paradise is still being disabused of his illusions. No longer confident in his self-sufficiency, he is still infatuated with a romanticized image of Dean and must learn firsthand the cost of Dean's ecstasy. Sal must also experience for himself the callous way Dean often uses the people close to him. Sal admits near the end of the section, "I lost faith in [Dean] that year" (OR, 177). But there is also a new dimension to Sal in part two. For the first time he thinks of his travelling explicitly and consciously as a "quest."

> I only went along for the ride, and to see what else Dean was going to do, and finally, also, knowing Dean would go back to Camille in Frisco, I wanted to have an affair with Marylou. (OR, 129)

Kerouac here points out that Sal's notion of questing is inadequate and that his motives in travelling are still mixed, but Sal is not longer the college boy on a lark. He is Dean's disciple, and Dean is "a monk peering into the manuscripts of the snow." When Sal resorts to religious language in part one, it reveals his shallowness and lack of self-control. He talks of the Hudson's "mysterious source," the "Promised Land" of Denver, and laments at one point having compromised "the purity of his trip," but Sal's experience of the Hudson is being stranded in a thunderstorm, Denver is a series of missed connections, and the trip's purity was compromised from the beginning. When Sal goes to the Central City opera in part one, it is no accident that he sees *Fidelio* and that the tenor is named "D'Annunzio or some such thing." But Sal, for all of his excitement at the opera, is basically unaffected. He is primarily interested in playing out drunken Hemingway fantasies with his friend Roland Major. At one point, Sal pauses to say,

> The night was getting more and more frantic. I wished Dean and Carlo were there—then I realized they'd be out of place and unhappy. They were like the man with the dungeon stone and the gloom, rising from the underground, the sordid hipsters of America, a new beat generation that I was slowly joining. (OR, 54)

The "dungeon stone" image refers to a scene from the opera, and the reference is ironic. As Sal finds out later, Dean and Carlo have been in Central City that night, and Sal has been, figuratively, blind to the fact. Sal may, in retrospect, realize that his wandering education is already leading him to be a subterranean seeker, but at the time of the trip to Central City, Sal is frightened by the intense, though erratic, self-exploration of Dean and Carlo. Just before the Central City episode, Sal watches them through one all-night manic session and wants no part of it. Sal may sing "Ah me, what gloom!" in imitation of D'Annunzio, but he is playing a role and knows it:

> I wondered what the Spirit of the Mountain was thinking, and looked up and saw jackpines in the moon, and saw ghosts of old miners, and wondered about it. In the whole eastern dark wall of the Divide this night there was silence and the whisper of the wind, except in the ravine where we roared; and on the other side of the Divide was the great Western Slope, and the big plateau that went to Steamboat Springs, and dropped, and led you to the western Colorado desert and the Utah desert; all in darkness now as we fumed and screamed in our mountain nook, mad drunken Americans in the mighty land. We were on the roof of America and all we could do was yell, I guess—across the night, eastward over the Plains, where somewhere an old man with white hair was probably walking toward us with the Word, and would arrive any minute and make us silent. (OR, 55)

Sal's shallow and childish version of the American past traps him into aligning himself with the facileness of the new West's "Old West Week" in order not to confront the problematic heritage of the actual old West. Sal aligns himself with the spirit of boosterism and shuts out the spirit of a Whitman, avoiding in the process the demands of a visionary past and avoiding, as well, having to recognize society's and history's betrayal of that past. The Ghost of the Susquehanna is neither Whitman nor the "old man ... with the Word," but Sal's intense response to the Ghost reveals, in any case, the gloom and silence (that is, lack of language to "figure the losses and the gain") that comes from confronting the reality and extent of the American "wilderness."

The different character of part two is suggested early in the trip by the encounter with the Jewish bum Hyman Solomon. Dean and Sal find Solomon in "the Virginia wilderness" and carry him with them to the town of Testament. The conjunction of "Solomon," "wilderness," and "Testament" is not accidental. Solomon is

> a ragged, bespectacled mad type, walking along reading a paperback muddy book he'd found in a culvert by the road ... We asked him what he was reading. He didn't know. He didn't bother to look at the title page. He was only looking at the words, as though he had found the real Torah where it belonged, in the wilderness. (OR, 137)

For Solomon to find the "real Torah" in the wilderness is, appropriately, both American and biblical. However, in Testament, Solomon promises to "'hustle up a few dollars'" and continue with Sal and Dean, but he simply disappears.

> Solomon never showed up so we roared out of Testament. "Now you see, Sal, God does exist, because we keep getting hung-up with this town, no matter what we try to do, and you'll notice the strange Biblical name of it, and that strange Biblical character who made us stop here once more, and all things tied together all over like rain connecting everybody the world over by chain touch ..." Dean rattled on like this; he was overjoyed and exuberant. He and I suddenly saw the whole country like an oyster for us to open; and the pearl was there, the pearl was there. (OR, 137–38)

Dean's and, through Dean, Sal's response to Solomon mixes religious fervor and American opportunism. Sal is no longer convinced that "the pearl [will] be handed to [him]" (OR, 10). But he and Dean are still convinced that "the pearl" exists. They see the world as their "oyster." In spite of this juxtaposition, Sal, both at the time of the action and retrospectively, is convinced of the legitimacy of Dean's "Mysticism." Early in the trip, Sal notes that Dean is "out of his mind with real belief," and Dean rambles on about "God," "time," and his ability to transcend the troubles of his life. Sal concludes,

> There was nothing clear about the things he said, but what he meant to say was somehow made pure and clear. He used the word "pure" a great deal; I had never dreamed Dean would become a mystic. These were the first days of his mysticism, which would lead to the strange, ragged W.C. Fields saintliness of his later days. (OR, 121)

Although Dean communicates his faith in the "rain connecting everybody" through the force of his enthusiasm, his religious impulse has no shape or definition and, as a result, even though Sal and Dean *are* following "the white line in the holy road," they are wandering and lack a map. The naive American, Dean is out to make it on his own, sure that "God does exist," untroubled by the fact that the "real Torah" is unread or that God's prophet is a fool who wanders off and abandons them.

Solomon is an avatar of the Ghost of the Susquehanna, revealing Sal's and Dean's lack of any testament other than perhaps that all-American book, the landscape which Sal reads with descriptive fervor:

> we leaned and looked at the great brown father of waters rolling down from mid-America like the torrent of broken souls— bearing Montana logs and Dakota muds and Iowa vales and things that had drowned in Three Forks, where the secret began in ice. (OR, 141)

Sal and Dean are not playing at being "on the road," as Sal was in part one. They are serious about "leaving confusions and nonsense behind and performing [their] one and noble function of the time," which is to "*move*" (OR, 133). Yet, however real the faith and energy, Sal and Dean are not so much searching for vision as they are attempting to avoid certain realities of their lives, and this escapist energy at the center of their travels dooms the trip.

The escapist nature of the trip is apparent to Sal's and Dean's friends. Early in part two, Sal's girlfriend Lucille notices Sal's behavior when he is with Dean.

> When Lucille saw me with Dean and Marylou her face darkened—she sensed the madness they put in me. "I don't like you when you're with them."
>
> "Ah, it's all right, it's just kicks. We only live once. We're having a good time."
>
> "No, it's sad and I don't like it." (OR, 125)

And Carlo Marx, now settled in New York after "a terrible period" of visions and introspection, confronts Sal and Dean several times in a reversal of the Denver situation in part one.

> Carlo watched this silly madness with slitted eyes. Finally he slapped his knee and said, "I have an announcement to make."
>
> "Yes? Yes?"
>
> "What is the meaning of this voyage to New York? What kind of sordid business are you on now? I mean, man, whither goest thou, America, in thy shiny car in the night?"
>
> "Whither goest thou?" echoed Dean with his mouth open. We sat and didn't know what to say; there was nothing to talk about any more. The only thing to do was go. (OR, 119)

Even Bull Lee, "a teacher" from whom they've all learned, is "curious to know the reason for this trip." He gets no more answer than Carlo. Carlo and Bull can only warn that the maniacal energy sustaining Dean must eventually run out. Carlo pronounces,

> "The days of wrath are yet to come. The balloon won't sustain you much longer. And not only that, but it's an abstract balloon. You'll all go flying to the West Coast and come staggering back in search of your stone."
>
> In those days Carlo had developed a tone of voice which he hoped sounded like what he called The Voice of the Rock; the whole idea was to stun people into the realization of the rock. (OR, 130)

"The rock" Dean and Sal try to avoid dealing with is at least in part the mystery of evil and death. Leaving New Orleans after the visit with Bull Lee, Sal and Dean lose their way in a swamp.

> We were surrounded by a great forest of viny trees in which we could almost hear the slither of a million copperheads. The only thing we could see was the red ampere button on the Hudson dashboard. Marylou squealed with fright. We began laughing maniac laughs to scare her. We were scared too. We wanted to get out of this mansion of the snake, this mireful drooping dark, and zoom on back to familiar American ground and cowtowns. There was a smell of oil and dead water in the air. This was a manuscript of the night we couldn't read. (OR, 158)

The one landscape "manuscript" that Sal and Dean cannot read is the one that would force them to deal with the reality of darkness. They can attempt to trivialize evil by imitating a Hollywood thriller, but they cannot confront it without admitting its reality which would, in effect, burst "the balloon" and reveal the emptiness of the encounter in Testament. Sal and Dean are running from the superficial banalities of modern America but are equipped only with a superficial idealism and the complete faith in self that perhaps has led to what they would escape. Sal and Dean insist that "the golden land's ahead" (OR, 135), and that faith is based on their ability to ignore or forget the "smell of oil and dead water."

Sal's sense of death is tied to his dream of the "Shrouded Traveler."[7]

> Just about that time a strange thing began to haunt me. It was this: I had forgotten something. There was a decision that I was about to make before Dean showed up, and now it was driven clear out of my mind but still hung on the tip of my mind's tongue ... It had to do somewhat with the Shrouded Traveler. Carlo Marx and I once sat down together ... and I told him a dream I had about a strange Arabian figure that was pursuing me across the desert; that I tried to avoid; that finally overtook me before I reached the Protective City ... I proposed it was myself, wearing a shroud. That wasn't it. Something, someone, some spirit was pursuing all of us across the desert of life and was bound to catch us before we reached heaven. Naturally, now that I look back on it, this is only death: death will overtake us before heaven. The one thing that we yearn for in our living days, that

makes us sigh and groan and undergo sweet nauseas of all kinds, is the remembrance of some lost bliss that was probably experienced in the womb and can only be reproduced (though we hate to admit it) in death. But who wants to die? In the rush of events I keep thinking about this in the back of my mind. I told it to Dean and he instantly recognized it as the mere simple longing for pure death; and because we're all of us never in life again, he, rightly, would have nothing to do with it, and I agreed with him then. (OR, 124)

Sal interprets his dream correctly, but his response is problematic. Dean's arrival prevents Sal from coming to terms with his own death, and this leaves Sal haunted and pursued. The fact is, Sal and Dean do want to die just as they want to live and Sal's interpretation avoids recognizing this conflict. Dean's strategy is to ignore and avoid the recognition of death if at all possible, and this is his advice to Sal. The concluding phrase shows that Sal agreed with Dean at the time but leaves open the possibility that Sal is less sure about the matter retrospectively.

Neither Sal nor Dean is able to be as blasé about their own death as their companion Ed Dunkel, who tells Sal,

"Last night I walked clear down to Times Square and just as I arrived I suddenly realized I was a ghost—it was my ghost walking on the sidewalk." He said these things to me without comment, nodding his head emphatically. Ten hours later, in the midst of someone else's conversation, Ed said, "Yep, it was my ghost walking on the sidewalk." (OR, 130)

By refusing to see their "ghost," Sal and Dean become their own pursuers. At two points, Sal, Dean, and those in the car are described as a "band of Arabs," and at times Dean himself is described as an "Angel of terror" (OR, 237), "a burning shuddering frightful angel ... pursuing me like the shrouded traveler" (OR, 259). The doubleness of Dean's motivation is suggested by his response to women:

I could hear Dean, blissful and blabbering and frantically rocking. Only a guy who's spent five years in jail can go to such maniacal helpless extremes; beseeching at the portals of the soft source, mad with a completely physical realization of the origins of life-bliss; blindly seeking to return the way he came. This is the result of years looking at sexy pictures behind bars; looking at the legs and breasts of women in popular magazines; evaluating the hardness of the steel halls and the softness of the woman who is not there. Prison is where you promise yourself the right to live. Dean had never seen his mother's face. Every new girl, every new wife, every new child was an addition to his bleak impoverishment ... Dean had every right to die the sweet deaths of complete love of his Marylou. (OR, 132)

In his passion, Dean both affirms and denies. His involvement with Marylou demonstrates his intense experiences of the world but also his lack of perspective. Blind to everything but the moment, Dean experiences the world, even in the confused demands he makes on it, with visionary intensity, but his blindness also sets in motion the social forces, the increasingly complicated series of marriages, divorces, and children that constrict his ability to experience the moment. In New York, Sal and Dean spend an evening with Rollo Greb whose "excitement," like Dean's, "blew out of his eyes in stabs of fiendish light" (OR, 127). Dean tells Sal,

"That Rollo Greb is the greatest, most wonderful of all. That's what I was trying to tell you—that's what I want to be. I want to be like him. He's never hung-up ... he knows time ... You see, if you go like him all the time you'll finally get it."
"Get what?"
"IT! IT! I'll tell you—now no time, we have no time now."
(OR, 127)

Dean seems to be too busy to notice the irony, as Sal does retrospectively, of having "no time" in the middle of "knowing time."

Almost inevitably, the intense self-absorption of Dean leads to his own exhaustion and the exhaustion of those with him. As Sal notes at the end of the visit to Bull Lee, "Con-man Dean was antagonizing people away from him by degrees" (OR, 155), and even Sal is antagonized when Dean abandons him in San Francisco. Dean is so intensely into his own world, as Sal discovers, that no one else's world exists. And in San Francisco, not only is Sal abandoned by Dean but his affair with Marylou turns into a fiasco. Rather than manipulating the jealousies of Marylou and Dean for his ends, Sal becomes the pawn of Dean and Marylou in their conflict. Instead of the masterful and adult lover, Sal is reduced to the level of miscreant child, doubly abandoned and "out of" his "mind with hunger and bitterness." As in part one, exhaustion and failure lead to a vision of death. In his despair, Sal imagines a woman to be his "strange Dickensian mother." She begs him to "go" on his "knees and pray for deliverance" for his "sins and scoundrel's acts," and her plea leads Sal to remember an earlier vision of his father. These two visions of parentage give way immediately to "the point of ecstasy":

> I walked around, picking butts from the street. I passed a fish-'n-chips joint on Market Street, and suddenly the woman in there gave me a terrified look as I passed; she was the proprietess, she apparently thought I was coming in there with a gun to hold up the joint. I walked on a few feet. It suddenly occurred to me this was my mother of about two hundred years ago in England, and that I was her footpad son, returning from gaol to haunt her honest labors in the hashery. I stopped, frozen with ecstasy on the sidewalk. I looked down Market Street. I didn't know whether it was that or Canal Street in New Orleans: it led to water, ambiguous, universal water, just as 42nd Street, New York, leads to water, and you never know where you are. I thought of Ed Dunkel's ghost on times square. I was delirious. I wanted to go back and leer at my strange Dickensian mother in the joint. I tingled all over from head to foot. It seemed I had a whole host of memories leading back to 1750 in England and that I was in San Francisco now only in another life and in another body ... for just a moment I had reached the point of ecstasy that I always wanted to reach, which was the complete step across chronological time into timeless shadows, and wonderment in the bleakness of the mortal realm, and the sensation of death kicking at my heels to move on, with a phantom dogging its own heels, and myself hurrying to a plank where all the angels dove off and flew into the holy void of untreated emptiness, the potent and inconceivable radiancies shining in bright Mind Essence, innumerable lotus-lands falling open in the magic mothswarm of heaven ... I realized that I had died and been reborn numberless times but just didn't remember especially because the transitions from life to death and back to life are so ghostly easy, a magical action ... I realized it was only because of the stability of the intrinsic Mind that these ripples of birth and death took place, like the action of wind on a sheet of pure, serene, mirror-like water. I felt sweet, swinging bliss ... I thought I was going to die ... But I didn't die.... (OR, 172–73)

Death no longer evokes so deep a terror for Sal it did in part one; he sees it in a larger context of birth and rebirth. He describes literally an experience of "ecstasy," of moving beyond physical limits, and the effect is strangely calming and reassuring. By moving outside of himself, Sal is able to feel less threatened by his own eventual death and also for the first time to feel a degree of empathy for others. Sal may be wrong about the details behind the "terrified look" of the proprietess, but he is intensely aware of her response nonetheless and is willing to try to imagine her situation.

The gain in perspective evident in Sal's vision at the end of part two controls part three. More at ease with his own mortality, more aware of the emotional life of others, and more able to admit his own isolation, Sal begins to act purposefully, instead of drifting as in part one or taking his direction from someone else as in part two. Instead of simply responding to Dean's invitation to travel, as in part two, Sal now sets out for Denver where he is "thinking of settling down." Sal sees himself becoming "a patriarch" in "Middle America." He sees himself, that is, halfway between the isolation of the West and the stultification of the East, but in Denver Sal has no idea of how to become "a patriarch." He finds that his friends have all left Denver, and ends up a day laborer.

> At lilac evening I walked with every muscle aching among the lights of 27th and Welton in the Denver colored section, wishing I were a Negro, feeling that the best the white world had offered was not enough ecstasy for me, not enough life, joy, kicks, darkness, music, not enough night. I stopped at a little shack where a man sold hot red chili in paper containers; I bought some and ate it, strolling in the dark mysterious streets. I wished I were a Denver Mexican, or even a poor overworked Jap, anything but what I was so drearily, a "white man" disillusioned. All my life I'd had white ambitions; that was why I'd abandoned a good woman like Terry in the San Joaquin Valley.... (OR, 180)

Some have attacked Sal's condescension, but Sal, though "disillusioned," has yet to find anything to replace his original values. He mistrusts his original middle-class, success-oriented perspective, but it still shapes his view of the world. Sal's nostalgia reflects his sense of his own problems and not necessarily Kerouac's solution to these problems.

Coming on a neighborhood softball game, Sal laments,

> Never in my life as an athlete had I ever permitted myself to
> perform like this in front of families and girl friends and kids of
> the neighborhood, at night, under lights; always it had been
> college, big-time, sober-faced; no boyish, human joy like this.
> Now it was too late. Near me sat an old Negro who apparently
> watched the games every night. Next to him was an old white
> bum; then a Mexican family, then some girls, some boys—all
> humanity, the lot. Oh, the sadness of the lights that night! The
> young pitcher looked just like Dean. A pretty blonde in the seats
> looked just like Marylou. It was the Denver Night; all I did was
> die. (OR, 181)

The one entry that Sal has into this world is Dean, and Sal is so lonely that
he flees west to him in San Francisco. At first glance, this suggests the
escapism of parts one and two, but the trip that follows is of a different sort
altogether. For one thing, Sal and Dean now travel east instead of west. Not
only do they travel in the direction associated in the book with family,
society, and history, but their ultimate destination, though never reached, is
Italy, the Old World. More importantly, Sal's sense of his relationship to
Dean is radically different. Dean is no longer a fantasy figure or a rival to be
studied and bested. Dean is now a comrade. When Sal finds Dean near
"idiocy" and his wife throws them out, Sal responds unexpectedly by
assuming responsibility for Dean. Sal becomes, in a sense, Mississippi Gene
and Dean "his charge," and part three explores Sal's and Dean's attempt to
make a go of this relationship which, for the first time, involves Sal as the
active partner.

     The relationship between Sal and Dean is metaphorically a marriage.
Unlike the situation with Mississippi Gene and his "charge," Sal and Dean
choose to enter into an alliance. Sal proposes and Dean accepts:

> —"Come to New York with me; I've got the money." I looked at
> him; my eyes were watering with embarrassment and tears ... It
> was probably the pivotal point in our friendship.... Something
> clicked in both of us. He became extremely joyful and said
> everything was settled. (OR, 189–90)

The description that follows this "pivotal point" suggests how much is at
stake for Sal and Dean. As they stand on the sidewalk after settling their
affairs, a Greek wedding party files out of the tenement next door:

We gaped at these ancient people who were having a wedding
party for one of their daughters, probably the thousandth in an
unbroken dark generation of smiling in the sun.... Dean and I
might have been in Cyprus....

"Well," said Dean in a very shy and sweet voice, "shall we go?"
(OR, 190)

The description of the wedding party echoes Sal's description of the Denver
world he has just left. It also reflects Sal's notion of marriage in which being
absorbed into the context of the extended nuclear family takes precedence
over the actual relationship between husband and wife. At the beginning of
part two, Sal tells Dean and Marylou,

"I want to marry a girl ... so I can rest my soul with her til we both
get old. This can't go on all the time—all this franticness and
jumping around. We've got to go someplace, find something."

"Ah now, man," said Dean, "I've been digging you for years
about the *home* and marriage and all those fine wonderful things
about your soul." (OR, 116)

And at the end of part one, Sal describes how Dean

spent afternoons talking to my aunt as she worked on a great rag
rug woven of all the clothes in my family for years, which was
now finished and spread on my bedroom floor, as complex and as
rich as the passage of time itself... (OR, 107)

These passages link with Sal's desire at the beginning of part three to be a
"patriarch." Sal's sense of marriage is a response to isolation and his dread of
death. By becoming a "patriarch," by submerging himself into the cyclical
pattern of generation succeeding generation, Sal seems to see his own
individual death subsumed into and overcome by the ongoing process of the
family.

It is worth noting that these images of "generation" are primarily
associated with the "old world." Lucille and Sal's aunt are both Italian, and
Sal presents them as stereotypical first generation immigrants. Similarly, the
Greek wedding party makes Sal feel as if he and Dean are in Cypress. These
images suggest that Sal's nostalgia for an Old World peasant order may
actually be the impulse behind his romanticized version of Denver slum life,

but Sal's actual choice of a partner, Dean, represents the New World at its most a anarchistic and individualistic. For this reason, if no other, Dean's "marriage" to Sal is fated to end in divorce, as are all his other marriages. The disintegration of the relationship, though, defines for Sal a basic dichotomy. He can respond to his vision of death by accepting "marriage," by believing in the purposefulness of death in the cyclical, Old World pattern; or he can respond by becoming an "American" like Dean, by taking his isolation, his individuality, as an opportunity to ignore death by ignoring time and social pattern. He can try to overcome death by living as if outside time and society, cultivating the moment and torturing the senses to attain the "timeless" through temporary vision and ecstasy. The problem with the first response is that it is likely to result in the shallowness and social constriction that Sal flees in the book's beginning. The problem with the second, as Dean knows and as Sal discovers in part three, is that it leads to exhaustion and quite probably an early death.

In part three by assuming responsibility for Dean, Sal comes to understand the cost of Dean's attempt to "know time." Before leaving San Francisco for the East, Sal must watch the friends of Dean's wife confront him with the social consequences of his freedom and irresponsibility. Galatea, Dunkel's wife, reminds Dean of his children and his obligations. Not surprisingly, she "looks like the daughter of the Greeks with the sunny camera" (OR, 192). Dean's response is silence. He stands as if "tremendous revelations were pouring into him.... He was BEAT—the root, the soul of Beatific" (OR, 195). When Dean leaves the apartment to wait for the others to make up their minds "about time," Sal sees him

> alone in the doorway, digging the street. Bitterness, recriminations, advice, morality, sadness—everything was behind him, and ahead of him was the ragged and ecstatic joy of pure being. (OR, 195)

Sal is beginning to realize that Dean is the victim or scapegoat as much as the "con man" or manipulator.

Sal is also realizing that Dean is at least partly aware of the cost of his attempt to have "IT," to "know time." That last night in Frisco, Dean, Sal, Galatea and the rest of the crew find a sax player who has "IT," and the next day Dean tries to explain to Sal.

> "Now, man, that alto man last night had IT—he held it once he found it; I've never seen a guy who could hold so long." I wanted to know what "IT" meant. "Ah well"—Dean laughed—"now

you're asking me impon-de-rables—ahem! Here's a guy and everybody's there, right? Up to him to put down what's on everybody's mind. He starts the first chorus, then lines up his ideas, people, yeah, yeah, but get it, and then he rises to his fate and has to blow equal to it. All of a sudden somewhere in the middle of a chorus he *gets it*—everybody looks up and knows; they listen; he picks it up and carries. Time stops. He's filling empty space with the substance of our lives, confessions of his bellybottom strain, remembrance of ideas, rehashes of old blowing. He has to blow across bridges and come back and do it with such infinite feeling soul—exploratory for the tune of the moment that everybody knows it's not the tune that counts but IT—" Dean could go no further; he was sweating telling about it. (OR, 206)

Logically, the alto man's performance is a series of contradictions. He releases his audience from their oppression by celebrating it. He escapes time by being preternaturally aware of it. He crosses the bridge of the tune as if it were the Ghost of the Susquehanna's bridge beyond death by willing himself to recognize the temporary and doomed quality of his gesture. The alto man wills himself to create in the face of his despair at recognizing his own inevitable decline and inability to create. He escapes by accepting momentarily that there is no escape.

Dean's sense of the alto's relationship to his audience is also important. The alto suffers not only to attain his own fleeting moments of ecstasy but in order to renew his audience by creating a momentary experience of community among them based, paradoxically, on each one's recognition of his own isolation. And this sense of community has nothing to do with the Old World community of hierarchy where one inevitably has a role and place. This community is a Whitmanesque community of undifferentiated equals. Each member is isolated but still free to attain on his own the highest pitch of vision, and thereby recognize his similarity to the other isolates and experience a belonging beyond space, time, or social role. It is the community of "Crossing Brooklyn Ferry" which Whitman imagines among those who have crossed, are crossing, and will cross, a community more complete than any offered by the Old World and yet a community that exists at best momentarily, and then primarily in the imagination.

As Sal comes to realize in part three, Dean serves the same function for their circle as the alto player for his. Sal sees Dean as a scapegoat figure, "the Saint of the lot" (OR, 193), "the HOLY GOOF" (OR, 194), and as they ride east in a travel bureau car swapping the megalomaniacal fantasies of childhood, both Sal and Dean get "IT."

At one point the driver said, "For God's sakes, you're rocking the boat back there." Actually we were; the car was swaying as Dean and I both swayed to the rhythm and the IT of our final excited joy in talking and living to the blank tranced end of all innumerable riotous angelic particulars that had been lurking in our souls all our lives.

"Oh, man! man! man!" moaned Dean. "And it's not even the beginning of it—and now here we are at last going together, we've never gone east together, Sal, think of it, we'll dig Denver together and see what everybody's doing although that matters little to us, the point being that we know what IT is and we know TIME and we know that everything is really FINE." Then he whispered, clutching my sleeve, sweating, "Now you just dig them in front. They have worries, they're thinking about where to sleep tonight, how much money for gas, the weather, how they'll get there—and all the time they'll get there anyway, you see. But they need to worry and betray time with urgencies false and otherwise, purely anxious and whiny, their souls really won't be at peace unless they can latch on to an established and proven worry...." (OR, 208)

But as it turns out, Sal and Dean are also apt to "betray time." Even that least constraining of all possible "marriages," the idealized marriage of male comrades, inevitably involves a confrontation with aging and the ultimate constraint of death.

In Denver, Dean advises Sal to take care of himself physically "'because you're getting a little older now'" and eventually there will be the "'years of misery in your old age ... when you sit in parks'" (OR, 212). Although Dean means well, Sal lashes out, and Dean retreats in tears. When Dean returns, Sal tells him bitterly, "'You don't die enough to cry.'" Dean, too, confronted with the Denver scenes and memories of his barren childhood, turns bitter. His search for kicks loses its joyous quality. "All the bitterness and madness of his entire Denver life was blasting out of his system like daggers. His face was red and sweaty and mean" (OR, 221).

Once Sal and Dean get back on the road, though, Dean recovers his equilibrium.

It was remarkable how Dean could go mad and then suddenly continue with his soul—which I think is wrapped up in a fast car, a coast to reach, and a woman at the end of the road—calmly and sanely as though nothing had happened. "I get like that every

time in Denver now—I can't make that town any more. Gookly,
gooky, Dean's a spooky. Zoom!" (OR, 230)

The ecstasy and community of "IT" are at best temporary states and thrive
perhaps only at moments of transition or outside the normal social order.
Like Huck and Jim on the raft or Whitman on the ferry, Sal and Dean in the
car pass through the world but are not forced (at least temporarily) to be of
it. They are free to respond to the landscape as it "unreels, with dreamlike
rapidity," just as Huck and Jim muse on the stars and Whitman on the
"fluttering pennants" along the shore. But the inevitable result of being on
the road is exhaustion. As Huck and Jim know always in the backs of their
minds, the river ends. Even the car cannot escape, finally, the presence of the
outside world. As Dean drives on after Denver, he again goes mad and
becomes for Sal an "Angel of Terror." By the time the two comrades reach
New York, they are so consumed by their travels that they

> walk all over Long Island, but there was no more land, just the
> Atlantic Ocean, and we could only go so far. We clasped hands
> and agreed to be friends forever. (OR, 246)

Five days later when Sal introduces Dean to a woman at a party, she is so
infatuated with the image of Dean as a "cowboy" that she becomes his wife
and eventually the mother of Dean's fourth child.

> With one illegitimate child in the West somewhere, Dean then
> had four little ones and not a cent, and was all troubles and
> ecstasy and speed as ever. So we didn't go to Italy. (OR, 247)

Dean the "cowboy" can no more go to Europe than he can bring order to his
domestic affairs.

Dean's liaison with a third wife is in effect a double betrayal, a double
failure. It is a betrayal of his comradely marriage with Sal, and a betrayal of
the freedom of action and movement that goes with "IT." Sal's response to
this and the failure to make it to Italy is surprisingly mild and understated.
Perhaps this is in part because Sal has come to recognize the inherent
mismatch between his nostalgia for an Old World order of pastoral stability
and his desire to participate in Dean's anarchistic, New World search for
moments of individual ecstasy. But the experience of travelling with Dean as
his "brother" and participating fully in the life of the road has also led Sal to
question the desirability of "IT." This is in part because of the chaos,
isolation, and exhaustion necessary to attain "IT," but it is also because of the
nature of "IT" itself.

The ambiguity of "IT" shows up as Sal and Dean make their way from Denver to Chicago. At first, the car functions much as Huck's and Jim's raft. The comrades regain their equilibrium after the chaos of Denver. Like Huck and Jim, Sal and Dean muse on the landscape and reminisce, but then a glimpse of some bums by a fire reminds Dean of his missing wino father. He turns first morose and then demonic. For Sal, and perhaps Dean as well, "all that old road of the past" is soon "unreeling dizzily as if the cup of life had been overturned and everything gone mad. My eyes ached in nightmare day." (OR, 234). The openness and hypersensitivity that leads to the joy of "IT" also leaves one vulnerable and open to a sense of horror. As Dean's driving becomes increasingly wild, Sal crawls into the back seat.

> I got down on the floor and closed my eyes and tried to go to sleep. As a seaman I used to think of the waves rushing beneath the shell of the ship and the bottomless deeps thereunder—now I could feel the road some twenty inches beneath me, unfurling and flying and hissing at incredible speeds across the groaning continent with that mad Ahab at the wheel. When I closed my eyes all I could see was the road unwinding into me. When I opened them I saw flashing shadows of trees vibrating on the floor of the car. There was no escaping it. I resigned myself to all. (OR, 234)

Sal, like Ishmael, has signed on for the cruise and must see it through whether or not a mad captain holds the wheel. The reference to Dean as Ahab is more than a mere tag. In chapter 60 of *Moby-Dick*, "The Line," Melville describes the unfurling whale line in the same terms that Sal uses to describe the flying and hissing road. For Melville, the hissing "halter" that surrounds whalers as they work is a conceit for the way people live surrounded by, yet usually oblivious to, death. It is hardly necessary to catch this echo of Melville to catch Sal's sense of fear, but this and other parallels to *Huck Finn* and *Moby-Dick* (consider such things as the marriage of Dean and Sal, Ishmael and Queequeg, and the comradeship of Mississippi Gene and his charge, Huck and Jim) underscore that it is finally a question for the narrator and reader whether Dean is Huck or Ahab, whether the car is the raft or the *Pequod*. Is Dean the "Holy Goof," a saint who knows time, or is he a destructive and revenging "angel" who pursues Sal to destroy him? Is it monomania to step out of society or is it an experience of grace in nature? Is the American past with its emphasis on vision, individuality, freedom, and movement, a life-giving or life-denying heritage? Is the road salvation or damnation? These questions are not easily answered, as regards either Dean or the American tradition. Certainly Melville understood the potential for inverting Emerson's optimistic transcendentalism, understood how easily the emphasis on an idealistic universe and individualism could open one to both the beatific view from the masthead and the damning look into the try works. And Twain also had some sense of the lonesome deathlike sounds a boy is apt to hear when alone, or the arrogant but compelling power of a Colonel Sherburn that went hand in hand with the beauty of the river and the exhilaration of lighting out. In his recent book *Mystery Train*, Greil Marcus is writing about rock and roll politics, but his comments help explain the doubleness of Dean's example and the doubleness of "IT":

> one of America's secrets is that the dreams of Huck and Ahab are not always very far apart. Both of them embody an impulse to freedom, an escape from restraints and authority that sometimes seems like the only really American story there is. That one figure is passive and benign, the other aggressive and in the end malignant; the one full of humor and regret, and the other cold and determined never to look back; the one as unsure of his own authority as he is of anyone else's, the other felling authority only to replace it with his own—all this hides the common bond between the two characters, and suggests how strong would be a figure who could put the two together. For all that is different about Ahab and Huck Finn, they are two American heroes who say, yes, they will go to hell if they have to: they will go as far as anyone can.[8]

Like the two previous sections, part three ends with a vision of death that summarizes the lessons Sal learns from the road and Dean, and the vision that closes the third trip shows how clearly Sal is aware of the duality of "IT." By the time Sal and Dean reach Detroit, they are as "ragged and dirty as if [they] had lived off locust" (OR, 243), and must wait a day before pushing on to New York. The decide to spend the night in a skid row movie house.

> If you sifted all Detroit in a wire basket the beater solid core of dregs couldn't be better gathered. The picture was Singing Cowboy Eddie Dean and his gallant white horse Bloop, that was number one; number two double-feature film was George Raft, Sidney Greenstreet, and Peter Lorre in a picture about Istanbul. We saw both of these things six times each during the night. We saw them waking, we heard them sleeping, we sensed them dreaming, we were permeated completely with the strange Gray

Myth of the West and the weird dark Myth of the East when morning came. All my actions since than have been dictated automatically to my subconscious by this horrible osmotic experience. I heard big Greenstreet sneer a hundred times; I heard Peter Lorre make his sinister come-on; I was with George Raft in his paranoiac fears; I rode and sang with Eddie Dean and shot up the rustlers innumerable times. People slugged out of bottles and turned around and looked everywhere in the dark theatre for something to do, somebody to talk to. In the head everybody was guiltily quiet, nobody talked. In the gray dawn that puffed ghostlike about the windows of the theatre and hugged its eaves I was sleeping with my head on the wooden arm of a seat as six attendants of the theatre converged with their night's total of swept-up rubbish and created a huge dusty pile that reached to my nose as I snored head down—till they almost swept me away too. This was reported to me by Dean, who was watching from ten seats behind. All the cigarette butts, the bottles, the matchbooks, the come and the gone were swept up in this pile. Had they taken me with it, Dean would never have seen me again. He would have had to roam the entire coast to coast before he found me embryonically convoluted among the rubbishes of my life, and the life of everybody concerned and not concerned. What would I have said to him from my rubbish womb? "Don't bother me, man, I'm happy where I am." (OR, 244–45)

Most simply this passage suggests that Sal has given up. He is buried in "the rubbishes" of his life. Metaphorically, his past is dead. He is perhaps haunted, but there is no indication that he has the volition to act to change his situation. He is no longer "disillusioned"; he is simply illusionless, neither happy nor unhappy, simply exhausted and apathetic. Sal is also buried among "the rubbishes" of his culture which have been so much a part of his experiments with the road. The scene in the movie house suggests the extent to which the economy functions by discarding at least some people. Sal, here, is far removed from the fantasies of success that barred him from Terry. And the movies themselves amount to a kind of cultural rubbish: the lowest example of a popular medium that has picked up, simplified, and debased imaginative patterns critical to the culture's awareness of itself. As such, the two movies that are etched into Sal's "subconscious" parody the double experience of "IT," the double experience of the car as the raft and the Pequod.

In a letter to John Holmes of 24 June 1949, Kerouac writes about the people of the Colorado foothills who belong to no social class. These people do not read newspapers but make a social and imaginative reality out of Tex Ritter and Gene Autry movies. They allude to the movie figures in the same way Eastern intellectuals allude to literary ones.[9] Here, almost two years before *On the Road* and the trip portrayed in part three, the "Gray Myth of the West" is unambiguously positive. It represents a democratic classless ideal and evokes a time when goals were clear and morality as simple as white hats and black hats. By the time of *On the Road*, though, Kerouac has come to see the "Gray Myth" as facile and superficial in spite of its appeal. This indictment has obvious implications for an understanding of Sal's and Kerouac's attitude toward Dean at this point, since several factors connect Dean to the "Gray Myth of the West." Sal introduces Dean to the woman who becomes his third wife as a "cowboy," and Sal first thought of Dean as a "young Gene Autry ... a sideburned hero of the snowy West" (OR, 5). There is also the partial overlap between "Eddie Dean" and "Dean Moriarity." Even without these indicators, it is obvious that Dean initiates Sal's interest in the "West" and to some degree symbolizes it for him, but the sarcasm Sal directs at the western movie reveals the extent to which he has come to realize that Dean's absolute faith in the self-sufficiency of the individual is more complicated and volatile than anything admitted to in the adolescent and optimistic fantasies that typically pass for America.

The connection of "the weird dark Myth of the East" to the "Gray Myth of the West" may at first seem unclear, but the inevitable counterpart of a myth of absolute goodness and life is a myth of absolute evil and death. If Emerson's transcendentalism is one side of the coin, Poe's nightmare of the Arabesque is the other. If one side of the Hollywood imagination is the western, Busby Berkely musicals, and the romantic comedy, the other side is the film noir, the horror film, and the uncompromising aggression of a gangster film like *Little Caesar*. As the example of Poe and stories like "Ligeia" suggest, there is an American tradition of evoking fantasies of evil with Arabian and Middle Eastern imagery. Even in *Moby-Dick*, Ahab's monomania is fueled and given its particular tinge by the figure of the fire worshipping Parsee "devil" Fedallah. Certainly, Sal experiences the "Myth of the East" as a counterpoint to the "Myth of the West," and this myth is also linked to Dean through the dream of the Shrouded Traveler and the book's earlier Arabian imagery. In effect, the two films link with and reinforce even as they burlesque motifs that have run through the entire book. In addition, they show Sal for the first time aware of how each of these myths or ways of looking at the world are simultaneously part of his "subconscious," and this amounts to a recognition, though perhaps not articulated by the character

Sal, that Dean can be both "Saint" and "Angel of Terror," that Sal himself may be both searching for life and running toward death to escape life, that one's cultural heritage is perhaps based on a kind of simultaneous schizophrenia and amnesia. This implicit recognition of his own dualistic nature and the dualistic nature of experience is what gives Sal the sense of being buried in the "rubbishes of [his] life," but Sal's seeming acceptance of his discovery is what prepares him to move on toward some further confrontation with, some final attempt to understand, the mystery of death. And it is this acceptance that justifies the image of rebirth suggested by the words "womb" and "embryonically."

Sal's discovery of the dualistic nature of things is itself a dualistic matter. On the one hand, the character Sal is discovering the way good and evil, positive and negative, life and death, east and west interpenetrate and make his experience of the world inherently ambiguous. But at the same time that the character Sal is recognizing this, the narrator Sal, as he reflects on and expresses his own experiences, is coming to recognize a second duality between the world as it exists for others—that is, the world as it is by agreed social convention or verifiable measurement—and the world as it exists in the imagination. This double perspective helps explain the tone of Sal's description of the Detroit movie house. For the character experiencing the movies in his exhaustion following his epic ride and disorienting brush with the positive and negative facets of "IT," the movies are indeed a sinister and even mythic experience of the interpenetration of good and evil. Sal, though, looking back and trying to interpret and give form to his experiences, is aware of both the intensity of the experience and the shallow, ephemeral nature of the actual stimulus. The movies are Hollywood pap, but they are experienced with an intensity that suggests something much more profound because of the imagination's power to transform what it encounters. Sal may, looking back, satirize the movies themselves, but he recognizes the validity of his imaginative reception of the "Myth of the West" and the "Myth of the East." The imaginative reality of the individual does not deny the social reality of the group, nor does the reality, the realism, of the group deny the imagination's ability to perceive and create. Rather, they interact just as the competing myths interact. The point, as Sal is coming to recognize, is not to subjugate one to the other, not to deny the romantic experience of the self for the naturalistic experience of the group or vice versa, but to understand the way these different modes interrelate.

Sal's attempt retrospectively to order the competing realities of imagination and social world explains in part the pervasiveness of references to earlier American texts. Ahab and Huck offer Sal a yardstick for measuring his own experiences against earlier cultural models. It is as if Sal is able to give significance to his experiences only as he is able to relate them to the cultural patterns evoked in these earlier texts. The question of the car as raft or *Pequod* is not for Sal as narrator or Kerouac a matter of literary play but a matter of substance, a question of the first order. The typically American patterns of *On the Road* have, of course, long been recognized.[10] Dean embodies the conflict between the autonomous, visionary isolation of the adolescent and the constricting but sustaining social world of the adult. Dean is Huck Finn a few years older and refusing to give in to the fact that there is no more "Indian Territory." He is Gatsby living as if he can control time. And *On the Road* is typically American in the way it opposes fluidity and form, ecstasy and reason, individual and society, East and West, frontier past and urban present. But this Americanness has not usually been taken as a point in the book's favor. When Leslie Fiedler complains that Kerouac's "transparent, not-quite-fictional representations of himself and his friends emulate Huck Finn when they, at best capture the spirit of Tom Sawyer and, at worst, Becky Thatcher,"[11] he seems not to notice that Kerouac is aware of this.

Kerouac's sense of earlier American texts is more complex and serious than Fiedler recognizes. Kerouac uses the allusions and parallels to classic American texts along with such obviously iconographic images as cowboys and hobos to define the substance of Sal's education. For Sal, understanding Dean is also a matter of confronting the culture and the images that have shaped Dean since these underlie Sal's fascination with him. Sal is not fascinated with cowboys, the West, and travelling because of Dean; he is fascinated with Dean because Dean crystalizes Sal's recognition of these images. Dean reminds Sal of his romantic American heritage and does so at precisely the moment when Sal's allegiance to that other stereotypical American pattern, the middle-class faith in education, marriage, and success has left him "feeling that everything was dead" (OR, 3). Dean motivates Sal to explore his heritage, and this means grappling not only with the real world of Cheyenne's Wild West Week but with the symbolic landscape of East, West, and Mississippi, and the imaginative past of Huck, Ahab, and frontier; and this enables Kerouac to use these images and patterns to measure the progress of Sal's education.

Each trip and section of *On the Road* is characterized by a distinct attitude on Sal's part toward his cultural heritage. In part one, Sal's sense of America, Dean, and the West is a nostalgic fantasy of adolescent adventure that assumes life can be reduced to a matter of fences to be whitewashed, and that someone else will always be there to ply the brush. It may be a bit strong to equate this fantasy with Becky Thatcher as Fiedler does, but the limitations of Sal's view are obvious, first to the reader and, finally, eve to Sal.

Fantasies about red lines on maps and the great ride or greatest laugh reinvigorate Sal from his initial despair at the opening of the book, but they finally obscure reality. They provide escape but offer no growth. They offer Sal an approach to the solitary world of hitchhiking but offer no guidance for the more complex and social situations that he encounters in the later stages of the trip.

In part one, Sal's shallow use of cultural myths obscures reality and leads ultimately to the insanity of the Ghost of the Susquehanna. In part two, Sal attempts to do without cultural models altogether. In effect, he blames the failure of the first trip on his use of cultural models rather than his shallow understanding of them. In part two Sal and Dean have no map; their "testament" is an unread paperback found by the side of the road. Ironically, Sal, in trying to ignore his cultural heritage, fulfills it even more slavishly in his second trip than his first. Nothing is more American than Sal's programmatic dismissal of precedent and his faith that immediate experience indulged in for its own sake will yield meaning.

If parts one and two show Sal discovering the liabilities of individualism, part three shows him searching for an alternative to it. Figuratively, the comradely marriage of Sal and Dean echoes such pairings as Natty and Chingachgook, Ishmael and Queequeg, and Huck and Jim. Like their precursers, Sal and Dean search for a compromise between the isolation of the individual and the entrapment of society and family. Their failure to create a timeless society of two comes as no surprise. Their own characters are perhaps too erratic for a lengthy relationship and, even were this not the case, rivers end, ships sink, and the westward creep of civilization, Christianity, and old age separate even the most mythic of pairs. It is unclear whether Sal realizes at the time of the trip the Americanness of his pact with Dean or the questions it implies, but he certainly recognizes these matters retrospectively. As he narrates the trip, Sal actually discovers and defines its ambiguous nature through his recognition of such analogues for Dean and the car as Huck and the raft and Ahab and the *Pequod*. These analogues cannot solve Sal's experiences for him, but they allow him to define what is at stake and are Sal's means for grappling with the ambiguities of his American journey. While Sal assumed in part one that the ambiguities were not there and in part two that the heritage was not there, in part three he is aware of both the compelling nature of cultural heritage and the conflicts within such a heritage. He is aware of his compulsion to discover an individuality and freedom, yet aware also that this attempt opens him to the conflict between the shallow innocence of the "Gray Myth of the West" and the corruption of the "weird dark Myth of the East." Sal may still, as Fiedler suggests, be more of a Tom Sawyer than a Huck Finn, but if so, he is Tom

Sawyer in the process of becoming Nick Carraway. Like Nick, Sal must mediate between East and West and between the sanctity of the imagination and the corruption of history.

Like Nick, Sal must distinguish between the symbolic truth of the hero as he exists for the imagination, and the much more indeterminate reality of the hero as he exists in the actual world. In part three, Sal begins to recognize that the imagination is a fundamental tool for interpreting experience. It allows a coherence and depth not possible in the real world. For Sal, the car is raft, *Pequod*, and simply a car being driven into a wreck. Sal's recognition of the car's symbolic possibilities is not an attempt to escape the experience but to interpret it through images that suggest a truth the situation itself can only partly contain. In this sense, the failure of the comradely alliance of Sal and Dean comes not from choosing inappropriate roles, but from their inability to distinguish between the imaginative truth of the timeless partnership of comrades and the time-bound relationship of actual friends. As Sal becomes increasingly clear in part four about the relationship between the life one lives imaginatively and the life one lives in society, he attains, finally, the seemingly contradictory but liberating recognition that Dean is both "God" and a "rat," both the mythic avatar of the free and independent American and the victim of his society and his own personal excesses. He begins to understand that his recognition of the myths of East and West is a discovery of the necessity of the imagination, as well as a discovery of the competing principles of good and evil.

Initially in part four, Sal is simply marking time, waiting for something to indicate the direction he should take. As with the earlier sections, his lethargy is disrupted by spring and the urge to travel. Also as before, Sal's decision to travel is in part an attempt to avoid issues and in part an attempt to respond to them. When he goes to say good-bye to Dean before heading for Denver, Sal is reminded of Dean's essential westernness. Dean "the cowboy" is out of place in crowded parties and looks "more like himself huddling in the cold ... rain on empty Madison Avenue" (OR, 251). Space and isolation are integral to the "Myth of the West." As Dean later tells Sal, the inscriptions on the toilet walls in the East and West are

> entirely different; in the East they make cracks and corny jokes and obvious references, scatological bits of data and drawings; in the West they just write their names, Red O'Hara, Blufftown Montana, came by here, date, real solemn, like, say, Ed Dunkel, the reason being the enormous loneliness that differs just a shade and cu[n]t hair as you move across the Mississippi." (OR, 267)

To travel west means Sal must confront again his loneliness and lack of identity. Yet to stay amounts to giving up. The image of Dean on Madison Avenue also evokes the way urban life has encroached on the heritage of open space. Social relationships and urban sprawl leave Dean no "Indian Territory," and Sal realizes that Dean's recognition of this or something like it has left him at least temporarily defeated. As Dean admits,

> "I've decided to leave everything out of my hands. *You've* seen me try and break my ass to make it and *you* know that it doesn't matter and we know time—how to slow it up and walk and dig and just old-fashioned spade kicks, what other kicks are there? We know." (OR, 251–52)

Dean's abdication from decision reminds Sal that his own refusal to "decide" is in effect a decision. Sal claims to agree when Dean looks to their future and says,

> "You see, man, you get older and troubles pile up. Someday you and me'll be coming down an alley together at sundown and looking in the cans to see."
>
> "You mean we'll end up old bums?"
>
> "Why not, man? Of course we will if we want to, and all that. There's no harm in ending that way. You spend a whole life of non-interference with the wishes of others.... (OR, 251)

But Dean's fatalism is of a piece with Mississippi Gene's and is something Sal cannot yet accept. When he sees Dean "the following Sunday," Sal admits, "'All I hope, Dean, is someday we'll be able to live on the same street with our families and get to be a couple of oldtimers together'" (OR, 254). And Dean responds by showing Sal a snapshot of his ex-wife in San Francisco and their new child.

> He took out a snapshot of Camille in Frisco with the new baby girl. The shadow of a man crossed the child on the sunny pavement, two long trouser legs in the sadness. "Who's that?"
>
> "That's only Ed Dunkel. He came back to Galatea, they're gone to Denver now. They spent a day taking pictures." (OR, 254)

Sal notes Dunkel's "compassion," but at least in part it is Sal's remembrance of Dunkel's "ghost" and other ghosts that shapes his next comments:

I realized these were all the snapshots which our children would look at someday with wonder, thinking their parents had lived smooth, well-ordered, stabilized-within-the-photo lives and got up in the morning to walk proudly on the sidewalks of life, never dreaming the raggedy madness and riot of our actual lives, our actual night, the hell of it, the senseless nightmare road. All or it inside endless and beginningless emptiness.... Dean walked off in the long red dusk. Locomotives smoked and reeled above him. His shadow followed him, it aped his walk and thoughts and very being.... All the time he came closer to the concrete corner of the railroad overpass. He made one last signal. I waved back. Suddenly he bent to his life and walked quickly out of sight. I gaped into the bleakness of my own days. I had an awful long way to go too. (OR, 254)

Sal as yet can accept neither the compromises that might lead to the security of being an "oldtimer" nor the cost that comes with the freedom of remaining alone. When Sal sets out the "following midnight," he sings, "Home in Missoula / Home in Truckee, / Home in Opelousas, / Ain't no home for me. / Home in old Medora, / Home in Wounded Knee, / Home in Ogallala, / Home I'll never be" (OR, 255). Even though the West still lures Sal, it offers him no home, and yet, since the East itself is no home either, Sal prefers to travel rather than sit tight.

Like the earlier trips, the fourth one begins with Sal, unable to deal with his obsessions, wandering off to escape for a time the pressures that build up when he stays in one place. But this time, Sal is free of the illusion that the trip will resolve anything. He does not assume that he will find "the pearl" nor does he intend to found a patriarchy. He's travelling because he "can't stand the suggestions of the land that come blowing over the river." In Denver, Sal has a "wonderful time." He finds that "the whole world" opens for him because he has "no dreams." Because he has no dreams, Sal is able and willing to see clearly what he encounters. Things are no longer the greatest or most fantastic. He is willing to enjoy what comes his way without justifying himself through hyperbole.

Sal's realistic acceptance is typified by his dealings with Henry Glass, whom Sal meets on the bus to Denver. Glass, a "curly-haired kid of twenty," has just gotten out of jail, and Sal agrees to chaperone him as far as his brother's in Denver.

His ticket was bought by the feds, his destination the parole. Here was a young kid like Dean had been; his blood boiled too

much for him to bear; his nose opened up; but no native strange
saintliness to save him from the iron fate. (OR, 257)

Sal in no way romanticizes Glass even though superficially he is of a type
with Dean. Glass is ultimately pathetic and vicious, and Sal perceives the
difference between Glass and Dean even though Sal's buddies in Denver
from his college days do not. "They loved Henry and bought him beers"
(OR, 257). They patronize Henry as they once patronized Dean. In contrast
to his college buddies, Sal does not use Glass. Rather, almost as Mississippi
Gene might, he lends a hand seemingly without expecting anything in return
or without attempting to prolong the encounter. But there is an important
difference between Gene's tolerance and Sal's. Gene's seems based on a belief
that certain questions cannot be answered and Sal's, judging from his
encounter with Dean before leaving New York, on a temporary decision not
to ask certain questions. His clarity about Glass in effect presents Sal with a
problem. He is able to distinguish Glass from Dean because he has "no
dreams," and yet what redeems Dean and distinguishes him from Glass is
Dean's ability to dream, his imaginative vitality, his "strange saintliness." Sal's
dreamlessness allows him to see others as they are; yet what makes other
people humanly important to him are their dreams. And finally, Sal's
dreamlessness makes his own life temporarily tolerable; and yet dreams are
necessary if an alternative is to be found to the simple fatalism of Mississippi
Gene.

   Not surprisingly, it is Dean who ends Sal's passivity. Sal has planned a
trip to Mexico, and Dean buys a car to join him and do the driving. In
Mexico, Dean intends to get a quickie divorce from his third wife in order to
rejoin his second wife and most recent child. Sal reacts almost apocalyptically
to the news that Dean is on the way and imagines a figure of mythic
proportions.

> Suddenly I had a vision of Dean, a burning shuddering frightful
> Angel, palpitating toward me across the road, approaching like a
> cloud, with enormous speed, pursuing me like the Shrouded
> Traveler on the plain, bearing down on me. I saw his huge face
> over the plains with the mad, bony purpose and the gleaming
> eyes; I saw his wings; I saw his old jalopy chariot with thousands
> of sparking flames shooting out from it; I saw the path it burned
> over the road; it even made its own road and went over the corn,
> through cities, destroying bridges, drying rivers. It came like
> wrath to the West. I knew Dean had gone mad again. There was
> no chance to send money to either wife if he took all his savings

out of the bank and bought a car. Everything was up, the jig and all. Behind him charred ruins smoked. He rushed westward over the groaning and awful continent again, and soon he would arrive. (OR, 259)

Yet Sal is also aware that this vision does not coincide with the Dean others perceive.

He [Dean] stood and performed before Shephard, Tim, Babe, and myself, who all sat side by side in kitchen chairs along the wall.... Then Dean suddenly grew quiet and sat in a kitchen chair between Stan and me and stared straight ahead with rocky doglike wonder and paid no attention to anybody. He simply disappeared for a moment to gather up more energy. If you touched him he would sway like a boulder suspended on a pebble on the precipice of a cliff. He might come crashing down or just sway rocklike. Then the boulder exploded into a flower and his face lit up with a lovely smile and he looked around like a man waking up.... He had no idea of the impression he was making and cared less. People were now beginning to look at Dean with maternal and paternal affection glowing in their faces. He was finally an Angel, as I always knew he would become; but like any angel he still had rages and furies, and that night ... Dean became frantically and demonically and seraphically drunk. (OR, 262–63)

Sal sees Dean's mythic dimensions, both "demonic" and "seraphic," Dean's social dimension, and something of the extent to which Dean does and does not understand the interaction of the two. Sal sees Dean as he exists in time, suffering and as hung up as any character in the book, and Dean as he exists out of time, rising to his role and opening the possibilities of vision. Sal perceives and accepts Dean much as he perceives and accepts Henry Glass. But Dean is so compelling that Sal cannot, as he could with Glass, maintain his distance or equanimity, and Dean's arrival changes the trip to Mexico from a matter of casual sight-seeing into yet another quest. In setting out one final time with Dean, Sal puts himself in a situation where he must give in to vision and dream again.

Sal and Dean approach their journey to Mexico as if it will finally resolve the conflict between East and West. It isan attempt to get beyond the American patterns that have controlled the first three trips. At the end of part three, Sal admits that his repeated east–west crossings have made him feel "as though I were a traveling salesman—raggedy travelings, bad stock, rotten beans in the bottom of my bag of tricks, nobody buying" (OR, 245). But the new trip will be

> the most fabulous of all. It was no longer east–west, but magic *south*. We saw a vision of the entire Western Hemisphere rockribbing clear down to Tierra del Fuego and us flying down the curve of the world into other tropics and other worlds. "Man, this will finally take us to IT!" said Dean with definite faith. (OR, 265–66)

In fact, Sal feels the trip will be so "fabulous" that he can not "imagine" it. Nevertheless, it is clear that Sal and Dean approach it as an escape from their Americanness. "'Ah,' sighed Dean, 'the end of Texas, the end of America, we don't know no more'" (OR, 273). And while Laredo is "the bottom and dregs of America where all the heavy villains sink, where disoriented people have to go to be near a specific elsewhere they can slip into unnoticed" (OR, 274), when Sal and Dean look across into Mexico, they do so

> with wonder. To our amazement, it looked exactly like Mexico.... We were longing to rush right up there and get lost in those mysterious Spanish streets. It was only Nuevo Laredo but it looked like Holy Lhasa to us. (OR, 274)

And once they are in Mexico, Sal comments,

> Behind us lay the whole of America and everything Dean and I had previously known about life, and life on the road. We had finally found the magic land at the end of the road and we never dreamed the extent of the magic. (OR, 276)

The magic and the holiness Sal and Dean perceive in Mexico comes from the same source. They see Mexico as primitive. Its people live in a manner so old and fundamental that they are before history and timeless. To Sal, it is "the golden world that Jesus came from" (OR, 300), and "these vast and Biblical areas of the world" are

> the places where we would finally learn ourselves among the Fellahin Indians of the world, the essential strain of the basic primitive, wailing humanity that stretches in a belt around the equatorial belly of the world.... These people were unmistakably Indians and were not at all like the Pedros and Panchos of silly

civilized American lore ... they were great, grave Indians and they were the source of mankind and the fathers of it.... As essential as rocks in the desert are they in the desert of "history." ... For when destruction comes to the world of "history" and the Apocalypse of the Fellahin returns once more as so many times before, people will still stare with the same eyes from the caves of Mexico as well as from the caves of Bali, where it all began and where Adam was suckled and taught to know. (OR, 280–81)

In spite of the ambiguities of Adam's lesson in knowledge, to Sal and Dean the Mexican "Fellahin" is a positive figure. He is free from the dialectic of "East" and "West." He is neither restricted or oppressed by his society, nor is he isolated in his freedom. And his sense of the magical promises to heal the split between the reality of dream and the reality of Western culture.

According to Dean, even the Mexican border guards are "lazy and tender" and "n[o]t like officials at all" (OR, 274), and, as Dean eyes the girls they pass, he tells Sal,

"Oh, man, I want to stop and twiddle thumbs with the little darlings," cried Dean, "but notice the old lady or the old man is always somewhere around—in the back usually, sometimes a hundred yards, gathering twigs and wood or tending animals. They're never alone. Nobody's ever alone in this country. While you've been sleeping I've been digging this road and this country, and if I could only tell you all the thoughts I've had man!" He was sweating. His eyes were red-streaked and mad and also subdued and tender—he had found people like himself. (OR, 279–80)

However, these people are only partly like Dean, and the conflict Sal senses in Dean's eyes prefigures the failure of the trip. The Fellahin peasants suggest the source of Dean's energy and authenticity which is, in effect, preverbal just as the Fellahin precedes history, but the Fellahin peasants exemplify the primal in a calm and simple way that Dean, for all his atavism, can not. Dean belongs to a society which is historical and anything but primitive, and Dean's confused motivation for traveling to Mexico suggests the extent of his problem. He is both questing for some final and absolute version of "IT" and trying to resolve his tangled legal and social obligations, and Dean can no more separate his social life from his religious life than he can accept a marriage or do without one. Dean and Sal can recognize their source in the primitive but can no more return to it than Sal could return to childhood in part one.

Even could Sal and Dean become Fellahin, the world of the Fellahin also turns out to have its sorrows. In the "sun-baked town of Gregoria," Sal and Dean meet Victor, a Mexican "kid," who procures "'ma-ree-gwana'" and women for them. At first as Sal and Dean smoke "a tremendous Corona cigar of tea" with Victor and his brothers, they seem to be realizing their dream and entering the community of the Fellahin and the world of magic.

> It seemed the car was surrounded by brothers, for another one appeared on Dean's side. Then the strangest thing happened. Everybody became so high that usual formalities were dispensed with and the things of immediate interest were concentrated on, and now it was the strangeness of Americans and Mexicans blasting together on the desert and, more than that, the strangeness of seeing in close proximity the faces and pores of skin and calluses of fingers and general abashed cheekbones of another world. (OR, 283)

And as Victor and Dean try to talk without a common language, Sal experiences the entire encounter as an ecstatic vision.

> For a mad moment I thought Dean was understanding everything he said by sheer wild insight and sudden revelatory genius inconceivably inspired by his glowing happiness. In that moment, too, he looked so exactly like Franklin Delano Roosevelt—some delusion in my flaming eyes and floating brain—that I drew up in my seat and gasped with amazement. In myriad pricklings of heavenly radiation I had to struggle to see Dean's figure and he looked like God. I was so high I had to lean my head back on the seat; the bouncing of the car sent shivers of ecstasy through me. The mere thought of looking out the window at Mexico—which was now something else in my mind—was like recoiling from some gloriously riddled glittering treasure-box that you're afraid to look at because of your eyes, they bend inward, the riches and the treasures are too much to take all at once. I gulped. I saw streams of gold pouring through the sky and right across the tattered roof of the poor old car, right across my eyeballs and indeed right inside them.... For a long time I lost consciousness in my lower mind of what we were doing and only came around sometime later when I looked up from fire and silence like waking from sleep to the world, or waking from void to a dream.... (OR, 285)

But this ecstatic moment is quickly undercut. As Sal, Dean, and Victor look into the eyes of Victor's infant son to see "'the loveliest of souls,'" the child begins to cry.

> So great was our intensity over the child's soul that he sensed something and began a grimace which led to bitter tears and some unknown sorrow that we had no means to soothe because it reached too far back into innumerable mysteries and time. (OR, 286)

And then, when Victor takes them to the brothel, the visit, though performed without fear for appearances, is finally driven and frantic as much as it is orgiastic and celebratory. Even Mexican whores have their "grief," and Sal is left guilt ridden by the encounter. He has dispensed with a certain amount of American propriety only to encounter a more fundamental version of human suffering.

The visit to Gregoria suggests that the journey from Denver has involved an attempt to strip away old cultural and social identities. Sal and Dean, socially marginal even before the trip, attempt to communicate with Victor and his brothers at a level that precedes language and cultural distinctions, and in the brothel, Sal and Dean seek to become totally and only physical. They are not completely successful in either attempt, though Sal typically seems more aware of this in retrospect. After Gregoria, Sal and Dean move even farther from Denver and America both geographically and metaphorically. As they move south, night and jungle take from Sal and Dean even their awareness of themselves as human. It is not that Sal and Dean become simply physical, but, rather, they lose even the sense of their own bodies. Engulfed in the oppressive heat and insects, they merge with the jungle until

> I realized the jungle takes you over and you become it. Lying on top of the car with my face to the black sky was like lying in a closed trunk on a summer night. For the first time in my life the weather was not something that touched me, that caressed me, froze or sweated me, but became me. The atmosphere and I became the same. Soft infinitesimal showers of microscopic bugs fanned down on my face as I slept, and they were extremely pleasant and soothing. The sky was starless, utterly unseen and heavy. I could lie there all night long with my face exposed to the heavens, and it would do me no more harm than a velvet drape drawn over me. The dead bugs mingled with my blood; the live

mosquitoes exchanged further portions; I began to tingle all over and to smell of the rank, hot, and rotten jungle.... I opened my mouth to it and drew deep breaths of jungle atmosphere. It was not air, never air, but the palpable and living emanation of trees and swamp. (OR, 294–95)

This deathlike state is the polar opposite of Sal's vision in Gregoria where he loses "consciousness" in his "lower mind," though the "infinitesimal showers of microscopic bugs" is reminiscent of the "myriad pricklings of heavenly radiation." In the first case, one escapes consciousness by transcending the body in an ecstasy of light which is beyond the physical. In the second, one escapes consciousness by descending into the body and a darkness which is even physical in its radiation.

To the extent that the Mexican pilgrimage has religious dimensions, Sal has had a perception of absolute life and absolute death. He has died out of his old social identity and been reduced through a kind of death to a primal substance and process. The movement has been from life to death, and this prepares for the final phase of the quest, a return to life and the possession of "IT" and the end of the road. But the rebirth that follows the jungle night and the arrival in Mexico City are both finally ambiguous. At dawn as roosters "crow the dawn," though there is "no sign of dawn in the skies," Sal sees "an apparition: a wild horse, white as a ghost ... white as snow and immense and almost phosphorescent." The horse passes by Dean and the car "like a ship" and disappears into the jungle, leaving Sal to wonder, "What was this horse? What myth and ghost, what spirit?" (OR, 295–96). Sal offers no interpretation, though Dean has also "faintly" dreamed or seen the horse. The incident is one of the most puzzling in the book. One possible source of the explanation Sal fails to give may be chapter 42 of *Moby-Dick*, "The Whiteness of the Whale."

> Most famous in our Western annals and Indian traditions is ... the White Steed of the Prairies; a magnificent milk-white charger, large-eyed ... with the dignity of a thousand monarchs ... the elected Xerxes of vast herds of wild horses, whose pastures in those days were only fenced by the Rocky Mountains and the Alleghanies [*sic*]. At their flaming head he westward trooped it like that chosen star which every evening leads on the hosts of light. The flashing cascade of his mane, the curving comet of his tail, invested him with housings more resplendent than gold and silver-beaters.... A most imperial and archangelical apparition of that unfallen, western world, which to the eyes of the old trappers

and hunters revived the glories of those primeval times when Adam walked majestic as a god, bluff-bowed and fearless as this mighty steed ... in whatever aspect he presented himself, always to the bravest Indians he was the object of trembling reverence and awe.[12]

Whatever the precise import of the white horse, the dawn it announces should presumably lead to the climactic vision of "IT," and, as Sal and Dean leave the jungle, they appropriately begin to climb the mountain that leads to the high plateau and Mexico City. As they climb, Sal and Dean encounter "mountain Indians." These Indians make Victor and the people of Gregoria seem positively European by contrast. They are "short and squat and dark" and "shut off from everything else but the Pan American Highway" (OR, 297). Dean is "in awe" of these people even though he realizes that the "Highway partially civilizes" those by the road and that those in the mountains "must be even wilder and stranger." Finally, Sal and Dean stop to deal with some girls who sell "little pieces of crystal."

> Their great brown, innocent eyes looked into ours with such soulful intensity that not one of us had the slightest sexual thought about them; moreover they were very young, some of them eleven and looking almost thirty. "Look at those eyes!" breathed Dean. They were like the eyes of the Virgin Mother when she was a child. We saw in them the tender and forgiving gaze of Jesus. And they stared unflinching into ours. We rubbed our nervous blue eyes and looked again. Still they penetrated us with sorrowful and hypnotic gleam. When they talked they suddenly became frantic and almost silly. In their silence they were themselves. "They've only *recently* learned to sell these crystals, since the highway was built about ten years back—up until that time this entire nation must have been *silent*!" (OR, 298)

Dean then fishes a wristwatch out of his "old tortured American trunk" and trades it for a crystal.

> Then Dean poked in the little girl's hand for "the sweetest and purest and smallest crystal she has personally picked from the mountain for me." He found one no bigger than a berry. And he handed her the wristwatch dangling.... He stood among them with his ragged face to the sky, looking for the next and highest

and final pass, and seemed like the prophet that had come to them. (OR, 298–99)

The action is inherently allegorical. Dean attempts to give away his awareness of time and language for the timelessness and pure silence of the mountain Indian. And yet Dean can no more give away time with his wristwatch than the girl can assume Dean's awareness of history with it. Dean's prophetic status is ultimately ambiguous. His refusal to give into history is heroic and vicious, insightful and deluded.

> They watched Dean, serious and insane at this raving wheel, with eyes of hawks. All had their hands outstretched. They had come down from the back mountains and higher places to hold forth their hands for something they thought civilization could offer, and they never dreamed the sadness and the poor broken delusion of it. They didn't know that a bomb had come that could crack all our bridges and roads and reduce them to jumbles, and we would be as poor as they someday, and stretching out our hands in the same, same way. Our broken Ford, old thirties upgoing America Ford, rattled through them and vanished in dust. (OR, 299)

Yet this is as close to an ultimate vision of "IT" as Sal and Dean are to come. Like it or not, Sal cannot put aside his past of "old thirties upgoing America" nor the awareness of history, progress, and ultimate failure that that suggests to him. At best, Sal can only recognize that Dean is both prophet and fool: prophet for the awareness of primal vitality that he evokes in his most intense gesture, and fool for his refusal to recognize more clearly the way his allegiance to impulse and energy is gradually damning him. Like Huck sitting to his waist in the Mississippi and musing with Jim, Dean stands for the rejoining of man and nature and man and man outside of society; like Ahab almost admitting his doubts to Starbuck and himself, Dean stands for the ultimate conflict between the will and all else even at the expense of its own destruction. At best, Sal can only recognize the distinction between the grandeur of Dean's symbolic truth, that which makes him seem like a "God," even if a god torn between light and dark, and the pettiness of much of his actual life. Certainly it is something like this recognition that enables Sal to accept Dean's betrayal of him in Mexico City, when their stay in "the great and final wild uninhibited Fellahin-childlike city" they "knew" they "would find at the end of the road" (OR, 302) fails to provide a final vision. In Mexico City, Sal is soon "delirious and unconscious" with dysentery, and

Dean, divorce completed, within a few days feels the need "'to get back to my life'" (OR, 302) and starts back alone leaving Sal to fend for himself.

> When I got better I realized what a rat he was, but then I had to understand the impossible complexity of his life, how he had to leave me there, sick, to get on with his wives and woes. "Okay, old Dean, I'll say nothing." (OR, 303)

Dean is a "rat" and as much driven as the driver, but Sal is able to see that this does not negate the other side of the matter. Dean's intensity is the source of both his transcendence and his tendency to victimize those around him. Dean's "strange saintliness" does not negate his tendency to be a "rat," but it does redeem him from being merely a Henry Glass.

When Sal sees Dean the winter following their trip to Mexico, he realizes that Dean's doubleness is further complicated by the fact that the person most victimized by Dean is Dean himself. Having made his own way from Mexico City to New York, Sal takes up with a "girl with the pure and innocent dear eyes" that Sal claims he has "searched for and for so long" (OR, 306). When Sal writes Dean to tell him that they plan "to migrate to San Francisco," Dean makes his way to New York to drive them west. But Dean has not allowed Sal the time to save for the "jalopy panel truck" that was to haul them all to California, and Dean ends up going back as he came, alone riding in freight train cabooses with a borrowed railroad pass. The Dean that Sal sees in New York has been reduced by exhaustion and confusion and perhaps even despair to a point where he can express himself only through vague and disconnected phrases and gestures.

> He couldn't talk anymore. He hopped and laughed, he stuttered and fluttered his hands and said, "Ah—ah—you must listen to hear." We listened all ears. But he forgot what he wanted to say. "Really listen—ahem. Look...." And he stared with rocky sorrow into his hands. "Can't talk no more—do you understand that it is—or might be—But listen!" (OR, 306–7)

And when Sal sees Dean off, he thinks to himself, "Old Dean's gone," which seems as much a comment on what has become of Dean as it is on his having "rounded the corner ... and bent to it again" (OR, 309).

Dean's intensity and refusal to consider costs both redeems him and makes a shambles of his life and the lives of those close to him. And at the end of *On the Road*, Sal is left to try to make some sort of peace with his encounter with Dean, the road, America, and himself. In spite of the mawkish note introduced by Sal's sudden discovery of his one true love and the hint that "her innocent eyes" are the answer to all the failures of the book, Sal actually ends his story with a final recognition that there is probably no resolution to the conflict of "East" and "West" and that human experience is partial and a matter of conflict. At best, and Sal suggests it is enough to make life worthwhile, the imagination can place the fragments of time-bound experience within a timeless coherence that can be grasped symbolically by the imagination. The activity of the imagination does not allow escape from the sorrowful, but it allows a certain acceptance through the recognition of an absolute and the recognition that human experience itself is always a falling away from this absolute. In this sense, *On the Road* ends up being not so much "a lyrical Yae-saying outburst"[13] as an elegy for the inevitable failure that follows that "outburst."

Like that other American novel, *The Great Gatsby*, in which the narrator must make his peace with a larger-than-life, self-made hero who lives out his tawdry version of America's idealized past, *On the Road* ends with a lyric passage that evokes what has become a quintessentially American mixture of past and present, dream and nightmare, hope and nostalgia. Both passages evoke the original promise of the land. Fitzgerald dreams of "the green breast of the new world."[14] Kerouac sees the "raw land that rolls in one unbelievable huge bulge over to the West Coast." In both, a nightlike, deathlike "enchantment" competes with what seems the lost and perhaps illusory promise of America. Fitzgerald writes that Gatsby's "dream must have seemed so close.... He did not know that it was already behind him, somewhere back in that vast obscurity beyond the city, where the dark fields of the republic rolled on under the night." Kerouac describes "all the people dreaming in the immensity of [the land] ... just before the coming of complete night that blesses the earth, darkens all rivers, cups the peaks and folds the final shore in, and nobody, nobody knows what's going to happen to anybody besides the forlorn rags of growing old." And both passages end by blending past and present into a timeless sense of process. In *The Great Gatsby*, "we beat on, boats against the current, borne back ceaselessly into the past." In *On the Road*, we sense the merging of the generations, of Dean and Old Dean, his father. "I think of Dean Moriarty, I even think of Old Dean Moriarty the father we never found, I think of Dean Moriarty." In America, Sal learns, the child must be father to himself. This is his freedom and his ultimate burden. The father is "never found" and perhaps neither is the self.

In thinking of Dean Moriarty, Sal is clearly thinking of himself, "dreaming in the immensity" of "that raw land," and the presentness of the action in the final passage suggests that Sal will "sit on the old broken-down river pier" whenever "the sun goes down" as long as he is "in America," which, as Richard Brautigan notes, is "often only a place in the mind."[15] In this "America" that Sal discovers, the conflict of "East" and "West" finally translates into the contrast between the society of everyday life and the visionary society of one. Both are a state of isolation and suffering, but the visionary society of one, the true "West" of the "America" of the imagination, transcends and contains the actual society of the "East." The visionary America of one pays for its transcendence by its heightened awareness of its loneliness and suffering, and it is in turn rewarded by the timeless presentness visible in Sal's final vision as he looks out as "the sun goes down" and anticipates "the coming of complete night" which "blesses the earth," "folds the final shore in" and in death accomplishes the union of father and son, self and other, man and nature.

Short of "complete night," the closest possible approximation to union seems to be the community of comrades, and this too is finally more real in the timeless retrospect of the imagination and may be based on nothing more that the uneasiness of sons about the father. At the beginning of the trip to Mexico, Sal comments about himself, Dean, and Stan, a young Denverite who travels with them: "Here were the three of us—Dean looking for his father, mine dead, Stan fleeing his old one, and going off into the night together" (OR, 267). At best, the conflict with the father must simply be recognized and accepted, just as Sal must recognize and accept a phenomenon like the river that both divides and joins "East" and "West." The river, "the great brown father of waters" rolls "down from mid-America like the torrent of broken souls" (OR, 141), "washes" America's "raw body" (OR, 15), and is itself the "endless poem" (OR, 255).

The father cannot be escaped or replaced. He can only be acknowledged and that acknowledgment may partially heal and give one the recognition of the order of one's suffering, which in turn may allow one partially to recognize a kinship and from that kinship give speech to the paradoxical vision of suffering which in some way heals, as Sal attempts to do in his closing speech. At least, this is one way to understand the function of the various prophet-father figures that Sal encounters or imagines encountering throughout the book from the "old man with white hair" who is probably "walking" from "the Plains" toward Central City "with the Word" (OR, 55), to the old man who confronts Sal "one night just over Laredo border" as Sal is heading home from Mexico:

> I heard the sound of footsteps from the darkness beyond, and lo, a tall old man with flowing white hair came clomping by with a pack on his back, and when he saw me as he passed, he said, "*Go*

moan for man," and clomped on back to his dark. Did this mean that I should at last go on my pilgrimage on foot on the dark roads around America? (OR, 306)

The religious dimension of the encounter is perhaps made clearer by a letter of Kerouac's to Holmes dated 11–12 July 1950 and written from Mexico City where Kerouac describes walking home from the bullfights. He describes his remorse over the bull's death and how he contemplated walking to New York in penance. When Kerouac sees a pile of bricks lit oddly by the sun and shade, he says that he sensed that God was waiting there for him. As Kerouac stands at the bricks, he has a vision of a man who walks across the country communing with all he encounters until his death. In the letter, Kerouac refers to this figure as the saint of *On the Road*, and as in *On the Road*, this figure continually confronts those he encounters with the phrase "Whither goest thou?"[16]

And yet it is the religious import of the encounter with the old man that finally creates a problem for Kerouac and his reader at the end of the novel by raising the need for Sal to speak, not as the student he has been throughout the novel, but as the prophetic commentator Kerouac yearns to become but as yet cannot believe himself to be. The imagistic summing in the final description is formally more in keeping with the book, and yet the portentous encounters with the walking saints suggests the restlessness and confusion within the substantial achievement of the book.

NOTES

6. Kerouac's tendency to look at people in terms of literary classifications is suggested in the interviews with Kerouac's friends collected as *Jack's Book*. In one, Allan Temko, portrayed as Roland Major in *On the Road*, says, "I could never understand the fascination these people held for Kerouac, except that he thought they were America, and they are. He always thought that Neal [Cassady] was Huck Finn and Bob Burford [portrayed as Ray Rawlins in *On the Road*] was smart-aleck Tom Sawyer." Barry Gifford and Lawrence Lee, *Jack's Book: An Oral Biography of Jack Kerouac* (New York: St. Martin's Press, 1978), p. 64.

7. The dream of the "Shrouded Traveler" is shared by Kerouac and Allen Ginsburg. It appears in Ginsberg's "The Shrouded Stranger," in *Empty Mirrors: Early Poems* (New York: Totem/Corinth Books, 1961), pp. 60–62. The figure of the Shrouded Traveler is also incorporated into the figure of Doctor Sax in Kerouac's *Doctor Sax*. Whether the dream originated with Ginsberg or with Kerouac is unclear, but it seems to have passed back and forth between them as a collective possession as they shared and analyzed each other's dreams and writings in these years.

8. Greil Marcus, *Mystery Train: Images of America in Rock 'n' Roll Music* (New York: E. P. Dutton & Co., 1976), pp. 15–16.

9. Kerouac to Holmes, 24 June 1949, in *The Beat Diary*, ed. Arthur and Kit Knight (California, Pa.: TUVOTI, 1977), p. 128.

10. See John Tytell, *Naked Angels: The Lives and Literature of the Beat Generation* (New

York: McGraw-Hill Book Co., 1976); idem, "Revisions of Kerouac," *Partisan Review* 40, no. 2 (1973); Aaron Latham, *New York Times Book Review* (28 January 1973; 7); Leslie Fiedler, "The Eye of Innocence," in *The Collected Essays of Leslie Fiedler*, vol. 1 (New York: Stein and Day, 1971); and John P. Sisk, "Beatniks and Tradition," reprinted in *A Casebook on the Beat*, ed. Parkinson.

11. Fiedler, "The Eye of Innocence," pp. 491–92.

12. Herman Melville, *Moby Dick*, ed. Harrison Hayford and Hershell Parker (New York: W. W. Norton & Co., 1967), p. 165.

13. Kerouac, *On the Road*, Viking Compass edition (New York: The Viking Press, 1959), back cover.

14. F. Scott Fitzgerald, *The Great Gatsby* (New York: Charles Scribner's Sons, 1925), p. 182.

15. Richard Brautigan, *Trout Fishing in America* (New York: Dell Publishing Co., 1972), p. 116.

16. Kerouac to Holmes, 11–12 July 1950, letter held by Holmes.

ROBERT HOLTON

Kerouac Among the Fellahin:
On the Road *to the Postmodern*

We need studies that analyze the strategic use of black characters to
define the goals and enhance the qualities of white characters. Such
studies will reveal the process of establishing others ... so as to ease and
to order external and internal chaos. Such studies will reveal the process
by which it is made possible to explore and penetrate one's own body in
the guise of the sexuality, vulnerability, and anarchy of the other.

—Toni Morrison (52–53)

"It's the world," said Dean. "My God!" he cried, slapping the wheel. "It's
the world! We can go right on to South America if the road goes on.
Think of it! Son-of-a-bitch! Gawd-damn!"

—(*On the Road* 277)

I.

During the early postwar era, the pressures to conformity in middle-class
white American culture were enormous, and it should come as no surprise
that a reaction against that conformity—the Beat Generation—should arise
and attain notoriety. In some ways this response may now seem shortsighted
or dated, yet there are nonetheless aspects that remain contemporary,
especially in the light of recent discussions of postmodernism:[1] one of those
is the attempt to rethink the white American male subject in relation to the
racial diversity of the nation. While a sense of racial alterity had long been a

From *Modern Fiction Studies* 41, no. 2. © 1995 by the Purdue Research Foundation.

central topic of white American literature—examples from Freneau to Faulkner come to mind—one can argue that in Kerouac and the Beats a quite different manifestation of this American preoccupation appears. In Kerouac's Beat classic *On the Road* there is, on one hand, the expression of a radical desire to challenge the existing social order through a foregrounding of the conventions and limitations of racial identity; and, on the other hand, there is a misrecognition of those conventions and limitations so profound as to justify the claim that ultimately *On the Road* legitimates as much as it challenges the master narratives that postmodernism seeks to undo.[2]

As a young writer, Kerouac attempted to escape from the constraints of the bourgeois position which awaited him by seeking out a liberated discursive space in an exploration of American racial heterogeneity. However one assesses its literary strengths and weaknesses, Kerouac's *On the Road* has had an undeniable impact in ways that very few novels ever do. Enormously successful and influential, it contributed significantly to the alteration of postwar culture's universe of possibilities by making an image of white male subjectivity defined in terms of alienation, rebelliousness, intensity and spontaneity widely accessible—qualities repeatedly associated in the book with America's marginalized racial others. Given the endemic racial prejudice and oppression of the period, there would, however, seem to be a profound paradox entailed in Kerouac's search for freedom in the realm of injustice's victims, a paradox that calls into question the political and aesthetic presuppositions underwriting this strategy.

Alienated from the white mainstream, the Beats found models to emulate in all kinds of excluded groups, most notably perhaps African-Americans. In his influential 1957 essay "The White Negro," Norman Mailer asserted that "the source of Hip is the Negro" (313), adding that "The hipster ... for practical purposes could be considered a white Negro" (315). Allen Ginsberg's classic "Howl" begins with a vision of "the best minds of [his] generation," "dragging themselves through the negro streets at dawn" (126). In their virtual deification of jazz greats such as Charlie Parker, the Beats turned away from the aesthetic traditions of white America;[3] and in their adoption of a slang based on a style of "hip" African-American speech, they articulated a radically redefined relation both to the dominant white community and to the black community.[4] Even Malcolm X commented on this development, observing that during the 1940s "A few of the white men around Harlem ... acted more Negro than the Negroes" (George and Starr 191). While it was not, of course, unheard-of for American whites prior to this to accept the equality of African-Americans, outright emulation was unusual. Furthermore, rather than working for the integration of marginalized peoples into the American mainstream, in their discourse and their behavior the Beats expressed a desire to join the excluded others on the margins—not on the barricades. A peculiar reversal of Frantz Fanon's notion of black skin/white masks, this sense of racial alterity contrasted sharply with prevailing American ideologies.[5]

Throughout *On the Road*, Kerouac celebrates America's racial diversity. Mill City, for example, is described as "the only community in America where whites and Negroes lived together voluntarily," and, he adds, "so wild and joyous a place I've never seen since" (60). In California, Sal (Franco-American) and Terry, his Mexican-American lover, eat in a Chinese-American restaurant and spend a pleasant evening with an African-American family she knows (87–89). This passage seems to anticipate Lyotard's description of contemporary culture in which "one listens to reggae, watches a western, eats McDonald's food for lunch and local cuisine for dinner, wears Paris perfume in Tokyo and retro clothes in Hong Kong" (*Postmodern* 76); but Kerouac's depiction of this postmodern moment seems less depthless than Lyotard's "eclectic degree zero of culture" which is predicated on an evacuation of cultural depth. Whether African-American or Chicano, North American Indian or Asian, the imaginary racial other that Kerouac constructs and sometimes refers to as "the great fellahin peoples of the world" (98) offers him a discursive opening by means of which some of the structures of freedom and necessity that organize his subjects may be inverted. Adapting the term *fellahin* from Spengler, Kerouac employs it very generally to designate all those peoples—in North America and throughout the world—who appeared to him to be culturally situated outside the structures and categories, the desires and frustrations, of modernity.[6] Whatever their own problems, problems of which he seems for the most part unaware, Kerouac's fellahin appeared to exist in a more authentic, more real and vital space beyond the confines of a consumer culture which defined its subjects as those who "consume production and therefore have to work for the privilege of consuming, all that crap they didn't really want anyway ... all of them imprisoned in a system of work, produce, consume, work, produce, consume" (*Dharma Bums* 78).

For Kerouac, racial difference is conflated with escape from that prison. George and Starr note that this vision from the margins not only accepted difference, it valorized difference: in doing so the Beats were able to "ridicule the authorities, debunk the myths, expose the hypocrises, and, thus, delegitimate the culture of domination" (203–204). This postmodern desire for a heterogeneous, fellahin world, while scandalous at the time, offered the Beats a sense of renewed possibility, of release from conventional white middle-class desires. If this position provided them a vantage point which ultimately proved not only uninhabitable but also insufficiently aware of the real conditions of existence of the dominated groups, it did nevertheless afford for a time a much-needed disruptive critical perspective on the stifling affirmative culture of the period.

In their discussion of Kerouac, Deleuze and Guattari point out the importance of artists who know "how to leave, to scramble the codes, to cause flows to circulate.... They overcome a limit, they shatter a wall" (132–133). And, they continue later, "What matters is to break through the wall" (277). But which wall is *the* wall? Kerouac, a Deleuzian nomad, at least temporarily deterritorialized, does break through a wall, but other walls stubbornly remain. As Sal watches a sandlot baseball game, for example, he is touched by the peaceful scene: on the field, "heroes of all kinds, white, colored, Mexican, pure Indian." And in the stands a similar mix:

> Near me sat an old Negro.... Next to him was an old white bum; then a Mexican family, then some girls, some boys—all humanity, the lot.... Across the street Negro families sat on their front steps, talking and looking up at the starry night through the trees and just relaxing in the softness and sometimes watching the game. (180–181)

There is an idyllic, almost utopian quality to this all-American scene, but as Deleuze and Guattari note, cultural revolutionaries like Kerouac who choose the road of cultural flight are rarely able "to complete the process" (133). While the apocalyptic overtones of this postmodern formulation may be open to dispute—what, precisely, would it mean to complete the process?— the estimate of the limits of Kerouac's accomplishment is accurate.

For instance, while celebrations of diversity and difference are frequent in the novel, at times Kerouac attempts further transformations. At one point, Sal Paradise finds himself "wishing I were a Negro, feeling that the best the white world had offered was not enough.... I wished I were ... anything but what I was so drearily, a 'white man' disillusioned." He blames his sense of emptiness on the fact that "All my life I'd had white ambitions," and concludes by "wishing I could exchange worlds with the ... Negroes of America" (180). This longing—a sort of fantasized racial version of cross-dressing—tells us little, however, about that other world. A distant and indirect descendant of minstrel show blackface perhaps, a peculiar inversion of the earlier African-American concern with "passing," this desire comes up often in one form or another during the period. "Blackface whiteness," writes David Roediger, most often meant "respectable rowdiness and safe rebellion" (127) rather than any real cultural understanding. And, like the minstrelsy tradition described by Alexander Saxton, Kerouac's evocation of

African-American life combines aspects of critique and naïve escapism: a "ridicule of upper-class pretensions" (170), argues Saxton, is linked to a fantasy of "moral permissiveness" (171), and a nostalgia for a life of "simplicity and happiness" (173).[7] While Sal's desire to be black shares none of the overt and sometimes vicious racism of the earlier minstrel show tradition, it does in fact lead here to a revelation of a similarly extreme cultural misrecognition: as he gazes at the African-American family he is filled with a kind of envy for this "life that knows nothing of disappointments and white sorrows" (181). The suggestion seems to be that African-Americans are insulated from disappointment because they are lacking in aspiration, a notion that can be sustained only at a considerable distance from the actually existing African-American community. Nor could these fantasies of the placid fellahin survive exposure to the African-American literary culture of the time which included Richard Wright, Ann Petry, Chester Himes and Ralph Ellison, writers whose articulations of disappointment and frustration are, to put it mildly, unmistakable.

It is not difficult here to realize the limitations of Kerouac's naïve vision; and ultimately his predicament conceals more than it reveals about "the happy, true-hearted, ecstatic Negroes of America" (180). Nor is it hard to predict that his desire to avoid his "white sorrows" by changing racial/cultural worlds will not be realized. The transformation Sal desires is, then, an impossibility based on a misconception: a doubly obstructed road to heterogeneity. For all his desire to be black, the limits of his cross-cultural vision are all too often in evidence.[8] Kerouac's ethnic others rarely emerge from a sort of pastoral (or urban-pastoral) simplicity[9] and, as Kaja Silverman argues in her study of T. E. Lawrence's somewhat analogous "alignment with a series of Arab figures," this kind of "symbolic and imaginary identification [has] concrete political consequences ... since imaginary identification always carries meanings in excess of its fantasmatic use value" (337). Indeed, in light of the cultural limits of Kerouac's flight, and his eventual retreat to alcohol-fueled right-wing delirium, one might question whether Kerouac's work does not ultimately do far more to confuse the issues than to clarify them, more to augment than to destabilize the reified racial and gender categories of social identity. Still, to dismiss Kerouac entirely would be as simplistic as to elevate him to the level of cult hero, which many hagiographic Kerouac studies continue to do.

2.

Kerouac's deployment of the fellahin registers a concerted move away from at least some of the master narratives constraining early postwar culture. According to Allen Ginsberg, Kerouac took the term fellahin from Spengler's *The Decline of the West* (Gifford and Lee 38). Originally signifying Arabic peasantry, the term is extended by Spengler to include one of the three types in his historical "morphology of peoples" (169). The first stage, the primitive, refers to the predecessors of the world-historical cultures, the imperial cultures which make up the second term. The fellahin is the third term and refers in part to descendants of the primitives, those groups marginalized by civilization during its ascendancy who remain when a culture, having risen to world dominance, ends its trajectory with a gradual collapse. "[B]etween the primitive and fellah," he writes, "lies the history of the great culture" (362). In the aftermath of civilization, "The residue is *the fellah* type" (105) which occupies its ruins. Spengler thus sets up an opposition between the "historical peoples, the peoples whose existence *is world history*" on one hand, and the fellahin on the other, whose lives are postcivilization, posthistorical. Whereas the lives of the former are imbued with the meaning and depth legitimated and guaranteed by the imperial culture, "[l]ife as experienced by ... fellaheen peoples is just ... a planless happening without goal ... wherein occurrences are many, but, in the last analysis, devoid of signification" (170–171).

According to Spengler, a curious thing begins to happen when an imperial culture goes into decline: the intelligentsia, once leading the nation's historic climb from the local and primitive to world significance and imperial dominance, gradually become "the *spiritual leaders of the fellaheen*" (185). In their rejection of the metanarrative of national destiny, these "cosmopolitan" literary intellectuals too begin to accept that reality is "a planless happening without goal" in which the significance of events is not guaranteed. In their self-conscious relativist recognition that their national narrative or myth is in fact only one among many, neither unique nor divinely ordained, their existence becomes a "being without depth" (172–173). As the numbers of such intellectuals—"world-improvers" Spengler calls them dismissively, historical "wasteproducts" (185)—increase, so is the ultimate demise of the culture assured.[10] Spengler's conservative and pessimistic vision was enormously influential and can be found echoed in many cultural documents of the first half of this century.

Kerouac recognized himself in this description, but with a major difference. The image of the postimperial, postcivilization, postcolonial— indeed postmodern—depthless life of planless happening shared by fellahin and intellectuals that Spengler disparages, Kerouac, at least at the outset of his career, inversely admired and emulated. *On the Road* details a virtually plotless series of journeys across the continent, occurrences valuable not for their depth of signification but for their immediacy, their sense of thrilling surfaces. And as Fredric Jameson argues, "perhaps the supreme formal feature of all the postmodernisms" is "a new kind of ... depthlessness" (9). Rather than the careful construction of nuanced levels of symbolic resonance which give a multilayered sense of depth to modernist art, Kerouac experimented with what he called the "spontaneous prose method," an attempt to record both the mind's surfaces and America's surfaces on paper as directly and immediately (literally without mediation) as possible.

Kerouac's reversal of Spengler's valuation, if not his teleology, stems from his sense of the relation of surface and depth. The surest way to allow the emergence of the deepest contents of the mind, he argues in "Essentials of Spontaneous Prose," is to transcribe its surfaces as immediately and unobstructedly as possible.[11] The great model for such an art form is, of course, the improvisational jazz developed by African-American musicians—further confirmation for Kerouac that the fellahin margin rather than the imperial center is the site of authentic existence and true art. Thus fellahin culture, by virtue of its immediacy, its spontaneity, appears to afford access to a depth that the dominant culture increasingly voids.

Arriving in Cheyenne, for instance, Sal encounters a manifestation of postmodern history we have all become familiar with. The streets are crowded with people: in cowboy boots and ten-gallon hats, they "bustled and whooped on the wooden sidewalks of old Cheyenne." The saloons are crowded and gunshots are ringing out. Alas, it is "Wild West Week": tourists and businessmen are dressed up as cowboys, the guns shoot blanks, and history has become a parody of the past, a consumer spectacle without depth typifying postmodern historicity in one of its most banal forms. Except for one curious and repeated detail: scattered among these postmodern cowboys, the "fat burpers [who] were getting drunker and whooping up louder," are some Native Americans looking "really solemn among the flushed drunken faces ... a lot of Indians, who watched everything with their stony eyes" (33–35). In these, Kerouac's fellahin, there is a suggestion of impenetrable depth wholly absent from the general scene which, Sal says, "was ridiculous: in my first shot at the West I was seeing to what absurd devices it had fallen" (33–35). The fall he speaks of is the collapse of history into depthless postmodern parody. In a curious near-reversal of Spengler then, the fellahin "residue," whose evident alienation is strategically juxtaposed in order to highlight the superficiality of the event and to lend another dimension to Sal's parallel disillusion, seems to possess a kind of historical depth that the postmodern bourgeois subject lacks, and it is this that attracts Kerouac's imagination—if not to sound those depths, at least to reflect them.

One has the sense that there is a finite amount of reality in white America and that it is being consumed too rapidly by the culture industry, whose function it is to transcribe reality into depthless signifiers, simulacra. Soon, perhaps, reality will be exhausted and only empty signifiers such as Wild West Days will remain to remind people of their relation to a past whose specificity will have utterly disappeared.[12] This is the transformation of the real into the simulacrum that Baudrillard describes, a process in which the real is lost. It is, as Baudrillard suggests of postmodernity, a world strangely similar to the original but, he adds ironically, "even better" and "more authentic" (23). Kerouac, reacting against this postmodern tendency, locates the "real" in the fellahin, who have not experienced this loss presumably because they never identified with (or were excluded from) the narratives of white dominance that traditionally legitimized white versions of reality. The figure of the fellahin, then, is employed by Kerouac to represent a position that is neither wholly premodern nor wholly postmodern but more accurately extra-modern, thus making available a critical perspective outside the degraded culture of modernity.

The obvious problem with this notion is that it constructs others purely from the point of view of the alienated white male observer and never from the point of view of the others themselves—a fact that is never more apparent than when the privilege of the white subject is explicitly compounded by the privilege of masculinity. In a Mexican brothel, for instance, the necessity of restrained behavior that accompanies white middle-class respectability is transformed into its opposite, a carnivalesque indulgence in transgressive sexuality, alcohol and drug consumption—behavior that Sal associates with the freedom of lowered expectations supposedly experienced by the fellahin. That this space is constructed as freedom from a white male point of view, however, does not mean that it can be understood that way for anyone else, a point that emerges as Sal notes the sadness and despair of the young prostitute whose "awful grief" drives her to outrageous alcoholic consumption, who fixes "poor sunken lost eyes" on him as she begs for money and drinks (289–291). Yet his (un)critical analysis of the situation stops there, leaving her grief as an aesthetic or existential effect rather than one with more definite political or cultural reference. The description of the scene, the frequently noted skin colors of the "girls," place this narrative episode within the now-familiar racial and gender category of Orientalist discourse: Sal compares it to an "Arabian dream ... [including] Ali Baba and the alleys and the courtesans" (289).[13] As the white American men leave and the Mexican "girls ... gathered around the car," Sal reflects that they had "left joys and celebrations over hundreds of pesos behind us, and it didn't seem like a bad day's work." This postmodern quester wants the depth of real experience to be there, to be in evidence, but does not sound those fellahin depths himself. As Sal declares giddily elsewhere, "I was rushing through the world without a chance to see it" (205).

Similarly, when Sal and Dean finish a long night of drinking with a visit to the tenement apartment of an African-American man named Walter, they are very impressed by his wife's compliant behavior which contrasts markedly with the resistance to male dominance and irresponsibility articulated earlier that evening by the white women they know. While those white women are dismissed for their very vocal criticism of the men ("It wasn't anything but a sewing circle" [193]), the positive depiction of the black woman stands in marked contrast. She was "the sweetest woman in the world," says Sal, "She never asked Walter where he'd been, what time it was, nothing…. She never said a word" (203). In fact she never speaks at all, only smiles as they repeatedly wake her up with their drunken comings and goings, and their admiration grows in direct proportion to her silence and submissiveness. As they leave at dawn, Dean remarks, "there's a *real* woman for you. Never a harsh word, never a complaint…. This is a man, and that's his castle" (203). In this incident, as in the brothel incident, the multiple layers of dominance and submission—determined by race or gender—remain uninterrogated as Sal and Dean's admiration grows. The reduction to cliché of the significance of this event suggests in fact the degree to which the other is established not in order to investigate the complexity of social relations but precisely to limit that complexity and to act as a shield from it.

It is at least possible, then, that Kerouac locates depth in the ethnic or racial other in an attempt to maintain a distance between the personal and the political rather than traverse it. Unlike questions of race or ethnicity, which could in a sense be addressed from a safer distance, questions of gender seem to pose problems too difficult and too immediately threatening to address. For instance, to explore the depth in marginalized gay experience (with which he was intimately involved) would be to transgress a very powerful masculine taboo. Despite the very autobiographical—almost confessional—content of *On the Road*, and despite its importance to Kerouac and to a number of his male friends, gay sexuality is largely repressed in the book. One revealing reference occurs when Sal moves from discussing his erotic frustrations with women ("I tried everything in the books to make a girl") to the availability of gay men:

> There were plenty of queers. Several times I went to San Fran
> with my gun and when a queer approached me in a bar john I
> took out the gun and said, "Eh? Eh? What's that you say?" … I've
> never understood why I did that; I knew queers all over the

country. It was just the loneliness ... and the fact that I had a gun.
I had to show it to someone. (73)

The mixture of an explicit threat of anti-gay violence with barely concealed
desire, of the evident phallic imagery of the gun with a denial of
understanding, suggests the existence of a complex pattern of attraction and
repulsion that Kerouac apparently preferred not to investigate further.[14]
Similarly, to explore depth in women's experience would be to call into
question his own complex and fragile relationship to women, including not
only wives and lovers but also his mother (from whom he never managed to
separate) and daughter (whom he refused to acknowledge). Gender and
sexuality seem frequently to exist in Kerouac's life and work as a site of fear
and confusion and his resort to fellahin stereotype in many instances appears
as an attempt to ease those fears and reduce those complexities.

The fellahin, in Kerouac, thus becomes the sign of the real, a device
which allows him, a white male, a means of reflecting on himself—at times
even deflecting the difficulties of selfhood—more than it provides insight
into the experience of the marginalized other. Baudrillard speaks of a
postmodern sense of "mourning for the real" (46), and Sal's response finally,
as always, is sadness, a kind of nostalgia for the vanishing American "real"
which increasingly, he feels, can only be located in the fellahin. If, as Jameson
posits, "a history lesson is the best cure for nostalgic pathos" (156), this cure
by means of exposure to historical depth fails to penetrate the surface of
Kerouac's subject. Certainly in Kerouac, with his location of a nostalgia for
the real at the sign of the fellahin, the attribution and exploration of depth in
women, African-Americans, American Native people, Chicanos and so on
could only have been successfully accomplished at the cost of forcing a
political dimension to puncture the aestheticizing surface of the postmodern
white male subject—a step away from cultural fantasy Kerouac was not
interested in taking nor able to take. As Gifford and Lee put it, Kerouac's
position "was subversive without being political" (232). Yet this separation of
subversion and the political accepts not only a collapse of political resistance,
but also of the very depth Kerouac was at-tempting to preserve.[15]

Sal's encounter with Terry, a Mexican migrant fruit picker, provides an
interesting example of this problem of fellahin depth and postmodern
surface. Having been beaten by her husband, she has left him and is heading
to Los Angeles to stay with a sister. Her child has been left with her parents,
grape-pickers who live in a shack in a vineyard (81–82). Despite the levels of
social mediation implied in this brief narrative, Sal accepts it primarily as an
aesthetic surface—borrowed in part from Steinbeck to whom he refers
(90)—on which he can inscribe his own identity problems. During their time

together, there do occur genuine attempts to cross or at least gaze across the
ethnic barrier, attempts that recognize the real differences and depths of
culture; at other times the situation wholly dissolves into stereotype and
cultural fantasy. While picking cotton with her, for example, one of the
common American images of fellahin labor, Sal realizes just how arduous it
really is and how difficult to make a living at. Yet the responses he has to this
and to his fellow workers are notable: The "old Negro couple in the field,"
for instance, "picked cotton with the same God-blessed patience their
grandfathers had practiced in antebellum Alabama" (96), remarks Sal, an
observation leaving a great deal of history and ideology unpacked. At the end
of the day, he proclaims, "I looked up at the sky and prayed to God for a
better break in life and a better chance to do something for the little people
I loved." The condescension and cultural distance articulated here collapses
on the next page into something even odder. That evening, Sal's desire for
the real, for depth of experience, leads him to absorb, as if by osmosis, aspects
of another subjectivity: "Sighing like an old Negro cotton-picker, I reclined
on the bed and smoked a cigarette" (97). Later, following further osmosis, he
uses the phrase "we Mexicans" and adds that the other pickers "thought I was
a Mexican, of course; and in a way I am" (97). He does not make it clear
exactly in what way that is though, and his summation of the pastoral idyll
has a similarly peculiar ring to it: after a few days with Terry and her child in
the cottonfields, he declares, "I was a man of the earth, precisely as I had
dreamed I would be." His dreams have not so much been realized though, as
they have been overlaid as depthless cultural stereotypes on the backdrop of
his surroundings. A couple of weeks cannot make Sal a "Mexican," or "a man
of the earth" any more than it can make him "an old Negro cotton-picker."
Rather than offering a renewed sense of the authentic reality, this fascination
with the fellahin tends instead to obscure in nostalgia and cliché the real
historical conditions of their lives.

3.

There is, toward the end of the novel, an apocalyptic vision of a future
which can be taken to frame *On the Road*. While they travel through Mexico,
a powerful sense of cultural difference is manifest as Sal and Dean pass
through "[s]trange crossroad towns" and encounter "shawled Indians
watching us under hatbrims" (299). As these people reach out their hands,
begging for "something they thought civilization could offer," Sal reflects
that "they never dreamed the sadness and poor broken disillusion of it. They
didn't know that a bomb had come that could crack all our bridges and roads
and reduce them to jumbles, and we would be as poor as they some day"

(299). With a nuclear holocaust, the gap between civilized and fellahin would finally be closed. This is, in a sense, Kerouac's version of the conclusion to modernity as predicted by Spengler—but again with a twist. In Kerouac's rendition, the decline of the west is also a return to a unified source: "For when destruction comes to the world of 'history' and the Apocalypse of the Fellahin returns once more as so many times before, people will still stare with the same eyes from the caves of Mexico as well as from the caves of Bali, where it all began and where Adam was suckled and taught to know" (281). Albeit tragic, this is the fulfillment of Sal's desire to put an end to his white bourgeois life. Just as they begin there, all Kerouac's roads lead back to the fellahin. In *On the Road*, the road of modern western history leads inevitably to its own destruction—"bridges and roads" reduced to jumbles—and thence to ultimate union with the fellahin who, in the end, remain nonetheless misrecognized: a signifier of depth remaining unsounded, a unitary term masking a cultural multiplicity, a fantasy of freedom extrapolated from lives of marginalization.

In works such as *On The Road*, as well as *The Subterraneans* (in which he recounts a relationship with a woman whom he idealizes as half African-American, half Native American) and *Pic* (narrated from the point of view of an African-American child) Kerouac seems to be trying very hard—if naïvely—to reach out across boundaries of race and class, but is finally unable to get beyond his dreams of racial and class identity. Ultimately the effect is double: on one hand Kerouac draws the reader's attention toward the lives of marginalized people, to heterogeneous experience. On the other hand his inability to penetrate the stereotypes that frame his cognition of the marginalized other, his aestheticization of subversion, establishes very constricting limits for the understanding of those lives. In his recognition of the heterogeneity of human experience, Kerouac's road to the postmodern, like much contemporary postmodernism, runs alongside a postcolonial highway, but no junction had been constructed which could make available to him a point of view from the margins themselves. As Catharine Stimpson has written, there is much to learn from what the Beats could not say as well as from what they could: "Yet because of what they could not say or imagine, the Beats also caution us that those regulated by taboos, those whom history tightly nets, must speak for themselves. They must form their own communities of naming, and renaming" (392).

Given his retreat into an increasingly outspoken—even paranoid— right wing stance, it would be easy to dismiss Kerouac entirely as a man who in his youth was blinded by his romanticizing of the other and in his maturity was blinded by his fear of change. This would, however, be to overlook the Kerouac who in his life and writing did, for a while at least, challenge some of the orthodox boundaries constricting the categories of social cognition of his time. As a writer whose enormous influence over a (white? male?) generation extended beyond the literary to popular culture as well, Kerouac displays a combination of insight into the compelling need to break down the hegemonic structures of race and ethnicity and blindness to the lived experience of the marginalized people he looked to as a means of breaking them down. Whether one defines the postmodern with Baudrillard as the era of the depthless simulacra, or with Lyotard as the era of the breakdown of the grand metanarratives and the proliferation of heterogeneous discourse communities, or with Deleuze and Guattari as the era of the deterritorialized nomad, Kerouac's work provides a signpost indicating a route to postmodernity. The construction of a network of such roads allowing America's heterogeneous communities to communicate remains an ongoing project.

NOTES

1. While postmodernism has developed somewhat autonomously in the realms of literature and philosophy, Kerouac has been an influence both on the American postmodernist fiction of Thomas Pynchon—who remarks on the "centrifugal lure" of *On the Road*, "a book I still believe is one of the great American novels" (xvi)—and on the French postmodern philosophical theory of Gilles Deleuze and Felix Guattari (cited below).

2. In her discussion of gender, postmodernism, and the "pervasive misogyny" of the beats, Ellen Friedman has recently argued that Kerouac and the Beats, alienated from modern culture, looked backward to earlier versions of master narratives rather than forward and beyond them. "The master narratives," she maintains, "strangely, seem more alive in the beats' work than they do in works of modernity. They are the context of the beats' rebellion. The beats, in their very opposition, legitimate master narratives" (250).

3. As Dick Hebdige notes in his important study of subcultures, "by the mid-50s a new, younger white audience began to see itself reflected darkly in the dangerous, uneven surfaces of contemporary [African-American] *avant-garde*, despite the fact that the musicians responsible ... deliberately sought to restrict white identification (47).

4. Seymour Krim commented at the time that these whites, the Beats, were "pick[ing] up not only the fascinating American-Negro rhythm and notes [of jazz] ... but the spoken language as well." They absorbed the "improvisations and verbal inventions of the Negro" and incorporated them "in their language and in their *thinking*" (39–40).

5. The Beats, writes Barbara Ehrenreich, "were probably the first group of white Americans to believe that 'black is beautiful,' for blacks were, perforce, permanent outsiders, who ... creat[ed] their own language and art" (56). As Hebdige remarks, "This unprecedented convergence of black and white, so aggressively, so unashamedly proclaimed, attracted the inevitable controversy" (47).

6. While I recognize that such a vague and general term is of very limited use, if any, in describing so many different cultural formations, I have used it here in order to understand how it functions in Kerouac's discourse. Kerouac writes, for example, of the fellahin as "the basic primitive ... humanity that stretches in a belt around the equatorial

belly of the world" from Malaya to India to Arabia to Morocco to Mexico to Polynesia to Thailand and so on (280). In the earliest use of the term I am aware of, Kerouac speaks of the music of the international fellahin as "the world beat" (287).

7. Although Roediger and Saxton are both discussing the nineteenth century, their general points remain relevant. The most striking example of transracial identification is perhaps John Howard Griffin's *Black Like Me*, although his transformation was motivated by very different factors. Pop music is, of course, rife with this phenomenon: from Elvis (as Alice Walker's "1955" demonstrates) to Vanilla Ice, the imitation of African-American cultural forms animates the scene. An ironic comment on all this can be heard in Lou Reed's "I Want To Be Black."

8. Dick Hebdige, for example, writes of the "breathless panegyrics of Jack Kerouac (who carried the idealization of Negro culture to almost ludicrous extremes in his novels)" (47–48). And Simon Frith dismisses the concept of the White Negro with its valorization of the imputed rebelliousness and natural freedom of the African-American as "weirdly racist" (180).

9. Pierre Bourdieu asserts that "certain populist exaltations of 'popular culture'" constitute "the 'pastorals' of our epoch." Bourdieu suggests that such genres

> offer a sham inversion of dominant values and produce the fiction of a unity of the social world, thereby confirming the dominated in their subordination and the dominant in their superordination. As an inverted celebration of the principles that undergird social hierarchies, the pastoral confers on the dominated a nobility based on their adjustment to their condition and on their submission to the established order. (*Invitation* 83)

10. Such identification with the most dominated social group is an instance of the social dynamic Pierre Bourdieu describes whereby artists and intellectuals who have not found (or perhaps not sought) bourgeois acceptance tend to feel an affinity with other socially marginalized groups whose position is somewhat homologous. While having themselves the more direct connection to the dominant groups which is customary for the producers of "high culture,"

> intellectuals and especially artists may find in the structural homology between the relationship of the dominated classes to the dominant class and the relationship of the dominated fractions [of the dominant classes] to the dominant fractions the basis of felt and sometimes real solidarity with the dominated classes. (*Distinction* 316)

11. The spontaneous surface and the depth of the real are typically conflated. "Not 'selectivity' of expression but following free deviation (association) of mind into limitless blow-on-subject seas of thought," writes Kerouac. This is the way to "Blow as deep as you want—write as deeply, fish down as far as you want" ("Essentials" 744).

12. This process is evidently occurring on the literary as well as the popular level. At an early point in the book Sal Paradise—a writer himself—describes a short story by his friend Roland Major—another writer—about two men—presumably "arty types" themselves—who arrive in Denver but, ironically, are disappointed in it since there are arty types there already. "The arty types were all over America, sucking up its blood," laments Sal (41). Indeed, Sal's reality is often mediated by art: a town is seen as Saroyan's or Wolfe's; people imitate Hemingway and his characters; conversations are lifted from books and movies—*The Sun Also Rises* (78), Steinbeck's *Of Mice and Men* (90); being with Terry is described in terms of Joel Mc—rea and Veronica Lake in *Sullivan's Travels* and so on.

13. Orientalist imagery pervades the scene: they approach the bar "through narrow Algerian streets" (286); when it is time to go, they "still wanted to hang around with our lovely girls in this strange Arabian paradise" until Sal finally recalls that he is "in Mexico after all and not in a pornographic hasheesh daydream" (290–291). Although there has been much recent discussion of the term, current debate is still framed by Edward Said's Orientalism.

14. Gerald Nicosia discusses Kerouac's struggles with sexual identity at various stages in his life, including a "general tolerance ... [of] homosexuality as just another interesting lifestyle" (117), his own bisexual experiences (154–155), and, latterly, "a rage against homosexuals" (493).

15. In *One Dimensional Man*—a work published only slightly later whose title suggests an analogous sounding of depth and depthlessness in contemporary culture—Herbert Marcuse argued that "such modes of protest and transcendence" as the Beat movement "are no longer contradictory to the status quo and no longer negative" (14). In their loss of depth or dimensionality, such apolitical subversives "are no longer images of another way of life but rather freaks or types of the same life, serving as an affirmation rather than negation of the established order" (59).

Works Cited

Baudrillard, Jean. *Simulations*. New York: Semiotext(e), 1983.

Bourdieu, Pierre. *Distinction: A Social Critique of the Judgement of Taste*. Trans. Richard Nice. Cambridge: Harvard UP, 1984.

Bourdieu, Pierre, and L. J. D. Wacquant. *An Invitation to Reflexive Sociology*. Chicago: U of Chicago P, 1992.

Deleuze, Gilles, and Felix Guattari. *Anti-Oedipus: Capitalism and Schizophrenia*. Trans. Robert Hurley, Mark Seem, and Helen R. Lane. New York: Viking, 1977.

Ehrenreich, Barbara. *The Hearts of Men: American Dreams and the Flight from Commitment*. Garden City: Anchor-Doubleday, 1983.

Fanon, Frantz. *Black Skin, White Masks: The Experiences of a Black Man in a White World*. Trans. Charles Lam Marksman. New York: Grove, 1967.

Friedman, Ellen G. "Where Are the Missing Contents? (Post)Modernism, Gender, and the Canon." *PMLA* 108 (1993): 240–252.

Frith, Simon. "The Cultural Study of Popular Music." *Cultural Studies*. Ed. Lawrence Grossberg, Cary Nelson and Paula Treichler. New York: Routledge, 1992. 174–186.

George, Paul S., and Jerold M. Starr. "Beat Politics: New Left and Hippie Beginnings in the Postwar Counterculture." *Cultural Politics: Radical Movements in Modern History*. Ed. Jerold M. Starr. New York: Praeger, 1985.

Gifford, Barry, and Lawrence Lee. *Jack's Book: An Oral Biography of Jack Kerouac*. New York: St. Martin's, 1978.

Ginsberg, Allen. "Howl." *Collected Poems: 1947–80*. New York: Harper and Row, 1984.

Griffin, John Howard. *Black Like Me*. New York: New American Library, 1976.

Hebdige, Dick. *Subculture: The Meaning of Style*. London: Methuen, 1979.

Jameson, Fredric. *Postmodernism, or The Cultural Logic of Late Capitalism*. Durham: Duke UP, 1991.

Kerouac, Jack. *The Dharma Bums*. New York: Signet, 1958.

———. "Essentials of Spontaneous Prose." *boundary* 2 3.3 (1974/75): 743–745.

———. *On the Road*. New York: Viking, 1957.

———. *Pic*. New York: Grove, 1982.

————. *The Subterraneans*. New York: Grove, 1958.

Krim, Seymour. *Views of a Nearsighted Cannoneer*. New York: Excelsior, 1961.

Lyotard, Jean-François. *The Differend: Phrases in Dispute*. Minneapolis: U of Minnesota P, 1988.

————. *The Postmodern Condition: A Report on Knowledge*. Minneapolis: U of Minnesota P, 1984.

Mailer, Norman. "The White Negro." *Advertisements for Myself*. New York: G. P. Putnam, 1959.

Marcuse, Herbert. *One-Dimensional Man: Studies in the Ideology of Advanced Industrial Society*. Boston: Beacon, 1964.

Morrison, Toni. *Playing in the Dark: Whiteness and the Literary Imagination*. Cambridge: Harvard UP, 1992.

Nicosia, Gerald. *Memory Babe: A Critical Biography of Jack Kerouac*. Berkeley: U of California P, 1994.

Pynchon, Thomas. *Slow Learner*. New York: Bantam, 1985.

Roediger, David R. *The Wages of Whiteness: The Making of the American Working Class*. London: Verso, 1992.

Saxton, Alexander. *The Rise and Fall of the White Republic: Class Politics and Mass Culture in Nineteenth Century America*. London: Verso, 1990.

Silverman, Kaja. *Male Subjectivity at the Margins*. New York: Routledge, 1992.

Spengler, Oswald. *The Decline of the West. 1918–1922*. 2 vols. Trans. Charles Francis Atkinson. New York: Alfred A. Knopf, 1926.

Stimpson, Catharine R. "The Beat Generation and the Trials of Homosexual Liberation." *Salmagundi* 58–59. (1982–1983): 373–392.

DOUGLAS MALCOLM

"Jazz America":
Jazz and African American Culture
in Jack Kerouac's On the Road

In a 1995 review of Ann Charters's *The Portable Jack Kerouac* and *Jack Kerouac: Selected Letters, 1940–1956*, Ann Douglas comments that Jack Kerouac's work "represents the most extensive experiment in language and literary form undertaken by an American writer of his generation" (2). While Kerouac's poetics, articulated in "Essentials of Spontaneous Prose," have literary antecedents—he admired writers as different as William Carlos Williams, Thomas Wolfe, Ernest Hemingway, James Joyce, and William S. Burroughs—his literary experimentation was also modeled on his understanding of jazz improvisation. A number of Kerouac's biographers and critics, of course, have recognized this source; however; while their views differ on the value of the influence of jazz on Kerouac's work, they share the assumption that a direct transposition of theory and practice from music to literature can be accomplished in the fashion that Kerouac proposes. The purpose of this study is to examine Kerouac's poetics and his best known work, *On the Road*, which was initially typed on a roll of paper in one "250-foot single paragraph" (Weinreich 41), in the light of the various generic rules that distinguish jazz from other types of music. While jazz does play a significant role in the novel, its impact lies in the music's ideological, behavioral, and semiotic implications—in particular their roots in African American culture—rather than in the direct application of its formal rules.

From *Contemporary Literature* 40, no. 1 (Spring 1999): 85–110. © 1999 by the Board of Regents of the University of Wisconsin System.

Critical treatment of the jazz influence on Kerouac's prose and poetry has tended to explicate Kerouac's goals rather than to ask fundamental generic questions about what constitutes jazz and whether it might reasonably serve as a literary model. Mike Janssen, following other critics like Edward Foster and Bruce Cook, notes that the Beats "used the principal ideas of bebop playing and applied it [*sic*] to prose and poetry writing, creating a style sometimes called 'bop prosody'" (2). Robert Hipkiss is not entirely sanguine about the effect of jazz on the Beats' work: "The jazz idiom with which Kerouac and the Beats operated is ... in great measure responsible for his uninspired blowing as well as the occasionally ecstatic outbursts of poetic statement" (93). Malcolm Cowley, who persuaded Viking to publish *On the Road*, observes that the poems in *Mexico City Blues* demonstrate that "Kerouac's analogy with jazz is exact. Some of the choruses read like scat singing played back at slow speed, words 'blown' for their musical values or their primary link to the subject matter" (qtd. in Gifford 190). Gerald Nicosia reports that Kerouac's *Book of Blues* is "one of the most important poetic works in the second half of the twentieth century" and further can be regarded as "one of the best literary equivalents of musical blues" (412). In her discussion of *On the Road*, Regina Weinreich, who along with Tim Hunt examines the jazz influence on the novel in some detail, argues that Kerouac's "notion of improvisation informs the language of [his] writing at an exact technical level. Though Kerouac had neither the knowledge of a musician nor the critical vocabulary of a person learned in the subject of music, he clearly demonstrates a profound identification of the creation of music with that of literary works" (8–9).

What is striking about this commentary is how little formal terminology is employed by either the critics or Kerouac. Hipkiss, for example, notes that in articulating his poetics Kerouac "inevitably uses the vocabulary of jazz to illustrate what he is trying to do" (79). Yet in the passage from "Essentials of Spontaneous Prose" that follows, the so-called jazz vocabulary is colloquial and vague, as Kerouac exhorts his fellow writers to "blow-on-subject seas of thought, swimming in sea of English with no discipline other than rhythms of rhetorical exhalation and expostulated statement" (qtd. in Hipkiss 79). In his piece on Charlie Christian in *Shadow and Act*, a collection of essays from the 1950s and early 1960s, Ralph Ellison argues that jazz is much more than just musical technique and is, in fact, integral to African American culture, wherein each musician's improvisation "represents ... a definition of his identity: as individual, as member of the collectivity and as a link in the chain of tradition" (234). Ellison calls for "more serious critical intelligence" to be brought to the subject (240), and subsequent studies, like Amiri Baraka's (LeRoi Jones's) *Blues People*, Ben

Sidran's *Black Talk*, Albert Murray's *Stomping the Blues*, and Craig Hansen Werner's *Playing the Changes*, have built upon his central observation. In *Performing Rites: On the Value of Popular Music*, Simon Frith follows the same tradition and offers a cultural theory of musical genre that can help explain Kerouac's use of jazz in *On the Road* because it codifies the concept of genre to embrace elements outside of the strictly formal. Frith argues that music can be regarded "as a coded expression of the social aims and values of the people to whom it appeals" (62). The cultural code can be broken down into the various elements that constitute a musical genre, which Frith, adapting Franco Fabbri's theory, terms "a set of musical events ... whose course is governed by a definite set of socially accepted rules" (91). The formal and technical rule is obviously important, but Frith itemizes four others: the social and ideological, the behavioral, the semiotic, and the commercial. These genre rules, except for the commercial, which is concerned with "questions of ownership, copyright, financial reward and so on" (93), provide a useful tool for comparing jazz and Kerouac's simulation of it in his writing and in *On the Road* in particular.

The formal rules of jazz are of particular significance here since they would presumably be the model for Kerouac's improvisations. According to Frith, "the rules of musical form ... include playing conventions—what skills the musicians must have; what instruments are used, how they are played, whether they are amplified or acoustic; rhythmic rules; melodic rules" (91). Improvisation is the principal formal rule which distinguishes jazz from other types of music. Leroy Ostransky defines jazz as "a variety of specific musical styles [New Orleans, pre-swing, swing, bop, free jazz, and fusion] generally characterized by attempts at creative improvisation on a given theme (melodic or harmonic), over a foundation of complex, steadily flowing rhythm (melodic or percussive) and European harmonies" (*Understanding Jazz* 40). Composed works that have a jazz flavor, such as George Gershwin's *Rhapsody in Blue*, are not jazz because they lack the essential quality of spontaneous improvisation. "[J]azz," Ostransky laconically comments in *The Anatomy of Jazz*, "did more for Gershwin than Gershwin did for jazz" (26).

Although bop, the style of jazz that Kerouac tried to emulate, is different from swing, which preceded it, the two styles are nonetheless founded in a very similar concept of improvisation that is based on what in jazz is referred to as the chorus: "What musicians meant by the term *chorus* was simply that segment of a solo which used the entire thirty-two measure AABA chord progression or entire twelve measure blues progression. A soloist might take only a chorus or perhaps take ten to twenty choruses" (Gridley 41). "Chord progression" refers to the harmonic structure that underlies a melody; for instance, the traditional twelve-bar blues typically involves harmonic movement from a tonic chord, C major, say, to chords based on the fourth and fifth scale degrees of C major. The composed melody is written in notes derived from these chords and is usually played at the beginning and ending, the head and tail as they are known in jazz, of a performance. Between the head and the tail, the musician improvises on the tunes chord progression: "The chord progression to the tune is usually retained with exactness *throughout* the selection, even during the improvised solos, simply by repeating the entire progression ... over and over" (Coker 9).

In *Understanding Jazz*, Ostransky points out that the jazz solo may appear to be spontaneous but requires a high degree of skill and training. The improviser follows the chord progression of the notated melody and

> modifies and adapts, to his individual conception of jazz, melodic fragments, rhythmic patterns, and even entire phrases he has heard and admired. All these memories and impressions are assimilated and transformed into music that is fresh, and often, when it is coupled with the spirit of spontaneity, music that is new. The performer's task is to organize his material—however spontaneous his performance may seem—in such a way as to make it appear that the material is, in truth, his own.
>
> (60)

Even so-called free jazz, it is worth noting, is governed by rules that impose order on improvisation. In *Jazz Styles*, Mark Gridley observes that "even the most adventuresome, free-form improvisations are usually organized around tone centers, keys, modes, or shifting tone centers" (218). An untrained individual may attempt to improvise with absolute abandon, but whatever he or she produces will not be jazz or even music, for that matter, because it is excluded by physical, technical, and aesthetic rules.

"In a sense," writes Stephen Nachmanovitch in *Free Play: Improvisation in Life and Art*, "all art is improvisation. Some improvisations are presented as is, whole and at once; others are 'doctored improvisations' that have been revised and restructured over a period of time" (6). Jazz, of course, embodies the former type of improvisation and writing the latter. However, there is, as the tenor saxophonist Stan Getz makes clear, a close similarity between spoken language and jazz: "It's like a language. You learn the alphabet, which are the scales. You learn sentences, which are the chords. And then you talk extemporaneously with the horn" (qtd. in Maggin v). But while musical improvisation is like speaking a language, the musician alone understands its grammar; although clearly he or she is able to communicate to a listener, the listener is much freer than in language discourse to interpret the sounds autonomously. Moreover, the listener, unless a musician as well, cannot respond in a like fashion. Users of a particular language, however, understand its grammar and employ it verbally and in writing to communicate and to exchange specific ideas in an enormous range of contexts, of which literature is only one. As poststructuralists like Michel Foucault and Roland Barthes have pointed out, language is the chief means through which we as human beings bring signification to our lives, although the consequence is that "The individual is always already inscribed within a discourse that prescribes its own continuation, and his entrapment" (Patterson 261). Language texts are always compromised by a host of social and economic factors, but they are nonetheless structured by grammatical rules that are incomprehensible to those who don't understand a particular language. In "Miles Davis Meets Noam Chomsky: Some Observations on Jazz Improvisation and Language Structure," linguists Alan Perlman and Daniel Greenblatt argue that these rules are similar to those used in jazz improvisation: "Improvising musicians are in much the same position as speakers of a language.... Their improvisations are facilitated by their knowledge of the available harmonic and melodic possibilities and by their technical skill and imagination in combining and recombining these possibilities in novel ways" (182).

While writing generally follows grammatical rules—it is arguably even more reliant on them than speech since there are no visual or aural clues to meaning—literary writing is a privileged use of language whose chief purpose is not necessarily communication. In addition to the rules of grammar, it is governed by conventions pertaining to genre and to narration, plot, characterization, and so on. Literary writing, as Linda Hutcheon notes in *A Poetics of Postmodernism*, can even deliberately subvert itself so as to contest the surface intent of the language. Literature may be improvised, but before it is presented to an audience it is almost always "revised and restructured over a period of time." Written poetry that is read aloud is not improvised by jazz standards, since reading from an extant poem is conceptually the same as reading notated music. Even the poets of the oral tradition, much like improvising jazz musicians, did not make up their songs extemporaneously but relied heavily on stock phrases and chose "forms in accordance with their immediate need" (De Vries 8). The writer, therefore, perhaps even more than the jazz improviser whose language by comparison is much less precise, works within a highly sophisticated set of rules in order to convey meaning to his or her audience.

In "Essentials of Spontaneous Prose," written in 1953, Kerouac apparently instructs the writer to simply allow language to spill out without regard for rules, a practice which will, paradoxically, allow a deeper meaning to emerge:

Begin not from preconceived idea of what to say about image but
from jewel center of interest in subject of image at *moment* of
writing, and write outwards swimming in sea of language to
peripheral release and exhaustion.... Never afterthink to
"improve" or defray impressions, as, the best writing is always the
most painful personal wrung-out tossed from cradle warm
protective mind.

(58)

Although Kerouac mentions sketching in "Essentials of Spontaneous Prose,"
most critics have focused on its jazz references as the guiding principle for
his spontaneity. He refers several times to "*blowing* (as per jazz musician)"
and to "the vigorous space dash separating rhetorical breathing (as, jazz
musician drawing breath between outblown phrases)" (57). In a *Paris Review*
interview some years later, Kerouac explains this idea in more detail: "Jazz
and bop, in the sense of a, say, a tenor man drawing a breath and blowing a
phrase on his saxophone, till he runs out of breath, and when he does, his
sentence, his statement's been made .... that's how I therefore separate my
sentences, as breath separations of the mind" (qtd. in Weinreich 9).

Since Kerouac's claim here is used by Weinreich to demonstrate "the
equivalence of his writing and jazz at the technical level" (9), it needs to be
examined in more detail. Oddly, Kerouac's comments about saxophonists do
not take into account other musicians—pianists, bassists, guitarists,
drummers—whose instruments do not rely at all on breathing. It seems
peculiar that these musicians would be concerned with using their
vocabulary to construct musical phrases, while the sax player's musical
phrasing is limited by his or her breath. Larry Teal, in *The Art of Saxophone
Playing*, notes, in fact, that "methods must be devised to disguise breaks in
the tone line lest they detract from the total effect. The aim of good
breathing habits is to improve the meaning of a phrase, rather than lessen its
force" (92). An examination of transcribed solos from Charlie Parker
improvisations, albeit on alto rather than tenor sax, indicates that musical
phrasing was Parker's paramount concern, and that his breathing was
concealed in musical rests. A 1946 version of "Anthropology," which has an
AABA structure, is played in 4/4 time at a metronome setting of three
hundred beats per minute. In the B section of the first improvised chorus,
Parker plays the entire eight bars without a rest, the longest section without
a rest in the transcribed solo (Parker 11). Played at this speed, the eight bars,
broken down into thirty-two beats, would be performed in just over six
seconds, an insignificant time for a professional sax player.

Kerouac's conception of improvisation relies more on material support than it does on a musical vocabulary. Breathing punctuates his sentences, and the primary structure that controls his spontaneity is the physical dimensions of his writing surface. *On the Road*, for instance, was initially written on the legendary roll of paper so as to be composed in an unavoidably linear fashion. His jazz poems, Kerouac argues in the preface to *Book of Blues*, were "limited by the small page of the breastpocket notebook in which they are written, like the form of a set number of bars in a jazz blues chorus" (*Blues* 1). The claim that the physical limits of a roll of paper or the page of a notebook act as the chorus that limits his improvisation shows a misunderstanding of the harmonic function of the chorus in jazz improvisation and, for that matter, the purpose of grammatical rules in language use. To argue that the paper limits his spontaneity is like saying that the physical properties of a particular instrument limit one's improvisation. While it may be less difficult to play certain music on a saxophone, say, than on a trumpet, such a comparison has to do with an instrument's mechanics rather than with musical improvisation.

Both Tim Hunt and Regina Weinreich argue that jazz techniques, despite Kerouac's declaration of abandon, do order his prose. Hunt quite rightly notes, "Any jazz improviser, even the most inventive, a Lester Young or a Charlie Parker, comes to have not only his sound but phrases, rhythmic ideas, and ways of attack that are peculiarly and recognizably his own" (146). Such characteristics, however, are not structural like the chorus but are rather peculiarities of usage; the same could be said with equal validity of the writing styles of the authors Kerouac most admired. While Hunt mentions vaguely that the chorus is "roughly equivalent to the role of the 'image-object' in Spontaneous Prose" (146), Weinreich makes "the notion of repeated forms that become redefined and redeveloped through each rendition of the series" (43–44) central to her argument. Repetition, she argues, becomes Kerouac's organizing principle, since it "suggests a double movement in the act of composition, a movement that progresses and repeats at the same time.... Recurrence also marks the interior structure of Kerouac's very language so that the pattern of his whole career reflected in large the more microscopic structure of his language from book to book" (5). Although the chord progression, which this insight is based on, remains constant and is indeed repeated, the improvising musician is not melodically confined by the notated melody or by other musicians' improvisations; in other words, what emerges is far from repetitious. It was a practice of bop musicians, as I shall discuss later, to create new melodies based on preexisting chord progressions. Parker's "Koko," for instance, follows the chord structure of the standard "Cherokee," but the melody is completely different (Coker 13). Similarly, two novels might be founded on the same literary convention, the quest myth, for example, but be as different as *On the Road* and *Don Quixote*. The chord progression may be repeated, moreover, but the improvisation, whether of one or more choruses, is structured much like a literary narrative: "a solo should tell a story. This means it should have a clear exposition, development, climax, and release" (Sabatella 54).

Kerouac's justification for his advocacy of spontaneous prose is described by Robert Hipkiss as "the Romantic belief that the seat of truth is in the basic human emotions [which] makes of spontaneity a primary value. The Romantic writer believes the closer one comes to those emotions and the more purely they are communicated the more affecting will be his statement" (93). This spontaneous production of written language is similar to the technique of automatic writing designed to delve into the writer's unconsciousness that was developed during the nineteenth century and later practiced by a variety of different writers, among them the surrealists (Weinreich 3). The writer simply writes, not paying attention to spelling, punctuation, or syntax and not following any preset plan. Authorial intent alone, however, is not sufficient cause to treat a piece of writing as literature rather than, say, as a diary or a disconnected group of words. Such an approach also makes the writer more vulnerable to repeating cultural biases—as Ann Charters remarks about Kerouac's attitudes toward women and racial minorities in her introduction to *On the Road* (xxx)—rather than contesting them. Interestingly, Jung developed a similar method for unlocking the unconscious that he called active imagination, which he was adamant be conducted strictly for therapeutic purposes, not for artistic ones (Hillman 133).

Clearly, Kerouac's use of jazz as a means of structuring his prose was less formal than it was inspirational; indeed, it is possible that "Essentials of Spontaneous Prose" has caused more obfuscation than it has brought clarity. While beyond the scope of this study, there are compelling reasons to view Kerouac's prose, regardless of how it was composed initially, with its run-on sentences, its capitalizations, its eccentric punctuation, its poetic repetition of sounds, as developing out of the techniques of modernists like Joyce, Woolf, and Faulkner (Bartlett 125). Even Weinreich resorts to conventional literary terminology in her analysis of Kerouac's prose (46118). *On the Road*, moreover, is far less stylistically adventurous than later works and is usually regarded as representing a transition between Kerouac's conventional first novel, *The Town and the City*, and later ones like *The Subterraneans* and *Visions of Cody* (Bartlett 123). *On the Road* "was probably the most heavily edited of Kerouac's works" (French xii), and it shows considerable evidence of being shaped in the manner of a traditionally revised novel, of being "doctored," to use Nachmanovitch's term, rather than spontaneously created. Although it was not published until 1957, the final text is a thinly disguised portrait of a period in Kerouac's life that began in the late 1940s and ended in the early 1950s. It was originally typed on the roll of paper in April 1951, but on a later occasion Kerouac wrote it out by hand (Nicosia 355). After it was accepted, in order "[t]o restore the novel's freshness," Kerouac "typed up a final version directly from the 120-foot roll [*sic*]" (Nicosia 536). Finally, the novel was substantially edited by his publisher, Viking; Kerouac later charged that the published version was an emasculation of the 1951 book (Clark 152).

Kerouac was most attracted to jazz because of its ideological associations with African American culture, although as I shall discuss later he does use the behavioral and semiotic aspects of the music to reflect his characters' development. Kerouac and friends of his like Allen Ginsberg and William S. Burroughs typified the hipsters whom Norman Mailer, in his famous 1957 article "The White Negro," characterized as outsiders to American life who were treated by white culture as though they were black: "The hipster had absorbed the existentialist synapses of the Negro, and for practical purposes could be considered a white Negro" (341). In a contemporary response to Mailer's article, Ned Polsky comments, "The white Negro accepts the real Negro not as a human being in his totality, but as the bringer of a highly specified and restricted 'cultural dowry,' to use Mailer's phrase" (qtd. in Mailer, "Note" 369). However much he identifies with African Americans, Kerouac is more interested in the ideology of their "cultural dowry" than he is in the circumstances that produced it. Indeed, his primitivist view of black culture, one that shapes his use of jazz in *On the Road*, often misrepresents, exaggerates, and suppresses important elements of the music and the culture in which it originated.

In part 3 of *On the Road*, while listening to jazz in a Chicago club, Sal provides a brief but telling description of how bop developed out of the music's history. Bop emerged through the influence of innovative musicians like Charlie Parker, Dizzy Gillespie, and Thelonius Monk and by 1945 had pushed swing aside by offering listeners a completely different, more complex kind of jazz:

> Once there was Louis Armstrong blowing his beautiful top in the muds of New Orleans; before him the mad musicians who had paraded on official days and broke up their Sousa marches into ragtime. Then there was swing, and Roy Eldridge, vigorous and virile, blasting the horn for everything it had in waves of power and logic and subtlety—leaning to it with glittering eyes and a lovely smile and sending it out broadcast to rock the jazz world. Then had come Charlie Parker, a kid in his mother's woodshed in Kansas City, blowing his taped-up alto among the logs ... coming

out to watch the old swinging Basie and Benny Moten band that
had Hot Lips Page and the rest—Charlie Parker leaving home
and coming to Harlem, and meeting mad Thelonius Monk and
madder Gillespie—Charlie Parker in his early days when he was
flipped and walked around in a circle while playing. Somewhat
younger than Lester Young, also from KC, that gloomy, saintly
goof in whom the history of jazz was wrapped....

(239)

He begins this history by identifying the musicians in the novel's present as
"the children of the great bop innovators" (239), the inheritors of jazz
tradition.

Kerouac's conception of jazz history is conspicuous for being based on
individual stars rather than, say, the bands in which they played or the cities
in which their distinctive sounds originated. As Leroy Ostransky makes clear
in *Jazz City*, the musicians named by Kerouac derived their styles in major
part from the jazz communities in New Orleans, Kansas City, Chicago, and
New York. While he does mention Count Basie in connection with Kansas
City and Charlie Parker, there is no mention of Duke Ellington. Albert
Murray, who regards jazz as developing out of "blues-break riffing and
improvisation" (63), remarks that Ellington "achieved the most
comprehensive synthesis, extension, and refinement to date of all the
elements of blues musicianship" (214), and that his work is "by far the most
comprehensive orchestration of the actual sound and beat of life in the
United States ever accomplished by a single composer" (224). Although
Ellington played the piano, his genius manifested itself collectively in his
bands rather than as an individual performer. Kerouac also seems to elide the
New Orleans jazz from which Louis Armstrong emerged, perhaps because
unlike the styles that followed—pre-swing, swing, and bop—the innovation
of the individual performer was not as significant in New Orleans jazz, which
was founded on "collective improvisation" (Ostransky, *Understanding Jazz*
134). The characteristic which in Kerouac's mind unites the historic
musicians above all is their "madness"; the unavoidable implication is that
the music they create derives not from rational thought but from visceral
spontaneity. Hence Louis Armstrong springs like Adam from the "muds of
New Orleans" and literally erupts playing with the "mad musicians" of his
hometown. Roy Eldridge's music, although suggestive of "logic," comes in
"waves of power." Charlie Parker was "flipped" out of his mind, and Lester
Young is depicted as "the saintly goof."

Kerouac regards these musicians not so much as innovators of a
musical style—it is noteworthy that there is not one reference in the passage

to any formal musical advances—but as purveyors of a particular way of thinking, a vitalism which for him is the dominant trait of bop. Ted Gioia, in *The Imperfect Art: Reflections on Jazz and Modern Culture*, demonstrates that this way of viewing jazz, what he calls the primitivist myth, is central to how much of white culture has consistently viewed the music. Gioia traces the origin of this attitude back to the "idealization and theorization of primitivism in French culture" (21), which as early as Montaigne and Rousseau had elevated the idea of the "noble savage." Gioia discovers this attitude in the works of influential French critics Hugues Panaisse, Charles Delaunay, and Robert Goffin, whom he calls "the founding fathers of jazz studies" (28), and who helped shape jazz criticism in America. He finds it present in assumptions about jazz performers as disparate as Louis Armstrong and Ornette Coleman and notes that "its impact is all the more damaging, given that its influence is rarely stated openly. Rather ... it colors critical judgments while rarely submitting itself to critical scrutiny" (47). As though to confirm this connection between jazz and the Romantic tradition of primitivism, Kerouac makes a direct reference in his history to Coleridge's "Rimeof the Ancient Mariner." Roy Eldridge's "glittering eyes" echo the "glittering eye" of the Ancient Mariner as he stops a wedding guest to tell his story.

The chief ideological characteristic of jazz for Kerouac, the music's apparent "madness," derives not so much from bop itself as from white cultural assumptions about the music and about black culture. It is jazz's restless energy, bop being simply its most recent incarnation, that Sal Paradise discovers wherever he travels, and which comes to symbolize for him the America of his generation, what he calls "Jazz America" (204). In Chicago, at the beginning of the novel, for instance, Sal directly links bop and the aimless traveling of himself and his friends: "And as I sat there listening to that sound of the night which bop has come to represent for all of us, I thought of all my friends from one end of the country to the other and how they were really all in the same vast backyard doing something so frantic and rushing-about" (14). It is the "frantic and rushing-about" quality that Sal finds whenever he encounters jazz; significantly, he finds it played on both coasts, thus geographically embracing the nation. In New York, for instance, George Shearing plays while "a smile broke over his ecstatic face" (128), and later a black alto saxophonist in San Francisco "hopped and monkey-danced with his magic horn and blew two hundred choruses of blues, each one more frantic than the other" (202). In San Francisco, Sal also hears Slim Galliard, a madman, perform and at "wild jazz sessions at Jamson's Nook" thinks, "I never saw such crazy musicians. Everybody in Frisco blew. It was the end of the continent; they didn't give a damn" (177).

Even the records he and his friends listen to, like "The Hunt" by Dexter Gordon and Wardell Gray, have a "fantastic frenzied" quality (113).

Of course, Kerouac, as a young white male, was hardly alone in his fascination with jazz. Almost as soon as jazz became popular in the early 1920s, young men who considered themselves outsiders identified with jazz musicians' marginal social status in hegemonic white culture. While bop was more complex and the musicians more rebellious than their antecedents, the impulse of these young white men toward jazz had as much to do with ideology as it did with a particular style of music: "The white beboppers of the forties were as removed from the society as Negroes, but as a matter of choice," as Amiri Baraka puts it (188). This white identification with African American experience, moreover, was far from exclusive to the Beats. Lawrence Levine sees a correspondence to the Austin High gang in Chicago in the 1920s—made up of musicians such as Jimmy McPartland and Eddie Condon—who embraced New Orleans jazz and black culture with an abandon similar to that of the disaffected youth of thirty years later: "There was a direct line between this group of white jazz musicians in the 1920s and the alienated youth of the 1950s and 1960s whose rebellion owed so much, directly and indirectly, to aspects of Afro-American culture, particularly its music" (*Black Culture* 296). Ben Sidran explains this appeal by arguing that black music, by its very nature, is "revolutionary, if only because it maintained a non-Western orientation in the realms of perception and communication" (14).

Kerouac, as a French Canadian outsider whose first language was French (Charters 24), seems to use jazz to serve his purposes as an alienated white; as much and perhaps more than the music itself, it is the ideological implications of bop and its performers, as perceived by white culture, that attract him. Certainly, there is little evidence in *On the Road* that Sal Paradise recognizes that the spirit of jazz with which he identifies derives in good measure from the African American history of slavery and racial prejudice. In part 3 of *On the Road*, Sal walks through Denver "wishing I were a Negro, feeling that the best the white world had offered was not enough ecstasy for me, not enough life, joy, kicks, darkness, music, not enough night" (180). Earlier, while Sal is living with his girlfriend Terry in southern California, he picks cotton for a week or so as a way of earning some money. Sal has difficulty doing the work, but he notices an aging black couple who "picked cotton with the same God-blessed patience their grandfathers had practiced in antebellum Alabama" (96). What is interesting is how he seems to appropriate the experience, without demonstrating any understanding of the harsh world that would have produced such expertise: "But it was beautiful kneeling and hiding in that earth. If I felt like resting I did, with my face on the pillow of brown moist earth. Birds sang an accompaniment. I thought I had found my life's work" (96). He celebrates manual labor while seemingly utterly unaware of slavery. At roughly the same time as Kerouac was writing this scene in the early, 1950s, blues musician James Cotton was recording "Cotton Crop Blues" (Levine, *Black Culture*, 253).

Calling it a lament for "the loss of the Garden of Eden," James Baldwin commented insightfully on the Denver episode from *On the Road* several years after the novel's publication. After quoting the passage cited above, Baldwin remarks, "this is absolute nonsense ... objectively considered, and offensive nonsense at that.... And yet there is real pain in it, and real loss, however thin; and it is thin ... thin because it does not refer to reality but to a dream" (182). Black musicians, who often relied on white culture for employment, were usually less direct than Baldwin in their disparagement of such appropriative attitudes as Kerouac's. Instead, they would use music to engage in a subtle, often amusing commentary that white audiences would rarely understand. This tradition originated in antebellum America when slaves used music as a tool "to get around and deceive the whites" (Levine, *Black Culture* 11). Bop musicians often took advantage of the chorus's structure to augment this kind of ironic observation. For them, improvisation would mean creating something that was entirely different from the notated melody but still based on the same chord progression:

> For swing musicians, improvisation on "I Got Rhythm" meant a creation based on the melodic [notated] outline as well as the harmonic foundation; when a bop musician said "Rhythm"—an abbreviation—he spoke only of the harmonic foundation, a foundation that could serve for any number of original compositions. In Charlie Parker's recordings of "Bird Lore" and "Ornithology," for example, both numbers have their harmonic basis in "How High the Moon."
>
> (Ostransky, *Understanding Jazz* 203)

Bop musicians, like Parker and particularly Dexter Gordon, developed to a high degree the use of musical quotations as parodic devices. In *Dexter Gordon: A Musical Biography*, Stan Britt remarks, "Gordon's repeated recourse to brief excerpts from cornball pop standards, and even an occasional snatch of a classic, has been ... judicious in execution, and genuinely funny in impact" (126).

While Kerouac seems unaware of the music's cultural and historical associations, not to mention its irony, he does fashion a discourse based on jazz's appeal to marginalized white males. For him and his fellows, jazz and jazz musicians provided an insider's world of arcane knowledge that distinguished them from straight society. "Genres," as Simon Frith notes, "initially flourish on a sense of exclusivity; they are as much (if not more) concerned to keep people out as in" (88). At Sal's brother's house in Virginia, Dean plays "The Hunt" to the delight of his friends and the bewilderment of the other listeners:

> The Southern folk looked at one another and shook their heads in awe. "What kinds of friends does Sal have, anyway?" they said to my brother. He was stumped for an answer. Southerners don't like madness the least bit, not Dean's kind.
>
> (113)

Kerouac is knowledgeable about certain aspects of bop and frequently makes allusions that deliberately test his audience's understanding. At the beginning of the book, for example, he refers to bop being "somewhere between its Charlie Parker Ornithology period and another period that began with Miles Davis" (14). For the jazz cognoscenti, this reference would place the time between the 1946 release on Dial of Parker's "Ornithology" and the appearance of Davis's album *Birth of the Cool* in 1950 (Cook and Morton 1009, 324). Later, Kerouac elliptically refers to the death of a "bop clarinetist" who "had died in an Illinois car-crash recently" (236). This can only be Stan Hasselgard, who died outside Decatur, Illinois, in November 1948 (Collier 333). And making it clear to the reader that "these were his great 1949 days before he became cool and commercial" (128), Sal listens to George Shearing.

Kerouac's Romantic view of jazz also affects his presentation of the behavioral rules of the genre which, according to Frith,

> cover performance rituals in a widely defined sense. These are gestural rules [that] ... determine the ways in which musical skill and technique, on the one hand, and musical personality, on the other, are displayed.... Behavioral rules apply to audiences as well.
>
> (92)

Aside from a number of unnamed ones in New York, Chicago, and San Francisco, the two actual musicians whom Sal and Dean hear in *On the Road* are Shearing and Slim Galliard. They hear Shearing both in New York and later in Chicago, when he sits in with the band. On the first occasion, which takes place as part of an extended New Year's Eve party ushering in 1949, they go "to see Shearing at Birdland in the midst of the long, mad weekend"

(128). It is worth pointing out that Kerouac seems to be conflating a later performance with his desired chronology, since Birdland did not open until almost a year later, on December 15, 1949 (Russell 276). They see Galliard perform later in San Francisco. It is curious that Kerouac, who, Nicosia reports, saw such greats as Thelonius Monk and Charlie Parker perform—a Parker performance is described in *The Subterraneans*, and Kerouac wrote several choruses to Parker in *Mexico City Blues*—should use Shearing and Galliard as representative musicians, since neither one is central to the bop movement. Shearing, moreover, is white and English. What they do share, however, is a performance style that accentuates the appearance of musical possession, consistent with Kerouac's primitivist ideology.

At his Birdland performance, George Shearing seems actually to control the natural elements: "Shearing began to play his chords; they rolled out of the piano in great rich showers, you'd think the man wouldn't have time to line them up. They rolled and rolled like the sea" (128). Later, when Sal and Dean are in Chicago, Shearing "played innumerable choruses with amazing chords that mounted higher and higher ... and everybody listened in awe and fright" (241). On both occasions, the music prompts Dean to call Shearing a god: "There he is! That's him! Old God! Old God Shearing! Yes!" (128); "Sal, God has arrived" (241). Leonard Feather, who was Shearing's record producer in 1949 and a pianist himself, describes Shearing's technique at this time in more prosaic language: "By the time we were due to make the first MGM recordings on 17 February [1949], George had developed a new and unprecedented blend for this instrumentation. He would play four-note chords in the right hand, with the left hand doubling the right hand's top-note melody line, the guitar doubling the melody, and the vibes playing it in the upper register" (195). Kerouac, who as Weinreich notes had little formal foundation in music, sacralizes an effect that was created in an inspired but explicable manner. Shearing, moreover, is blind and like other blind pianists—Ray Charles, Stevie Wonder, and Marcus Roberts, for instance—seems to be wholly possessed by the music; the blind have no visual models to pattern their stage mannerisms on and to the sighted appear to be responding in an exaggerated way to the music.

Slim Galliard's performance in San Francisco is even more impassioned than that of Shearing. Galliard begins with verbal invention in which he attaches the three-syllable line "orooni" to everything he says. Then he plays Ellington's "C-Jam Blues" on the piano, after which "Slim goes mad and grabs the bongos and plays tremendous rapid Cubana beats and yells crazy things in Spanish, in Arabic, in Peruvian dialect, in Egyptian, in every language he knows, and he knows innumerable languages" (176). As with Shearing, Dean regards him as a divinity: "Now, Dean approached him, he approached his God; he thought Slim was God" (177). While he played on Charlie Parker's Savoy recordings, Galliard was most noted for his eccentricity, both musical and verbal. Early in his career, for instance, "he worked as a solo variety act, playing guitar and tap-dancing simultaneously: a bizarre combination which ... reflected Galliard's comedic view of life" (Carr et al. 178). Thus Kerouac seems to have selected both musicians because they are best suited to his Romantic notion of bop.

The behavioral aspect of jazz performance is one of the devices used by Kerouac to help shape the novel's narrative. *On the Road* involves the quest of Sal Paradise for transcendent signification in his life, what one critic calls the "Dionysian ideal" (Bartlett 122). "This can't go on all the time—this franticness and jumping around," he says to Dean. "We've got to go someplace, find something" (116). In part this frantic search is characterized physically through travel, but it is also apparent in their drug experiences, in their conversations, in their relations with each other and with women, and, of course, in jazz. Each of these circumstances reflects a definite shape that is characterized by increasingly frantic behavior which ultimately leads to a kind of deflation. Warren French, for instance, argues that "the repetition of the inflation–deflation pattern of the individual sections and the work as a whole" gives the novel much of its power (88). Each of the novel's first four parts concludes with Sal, after having set out in pursuit of truth— "somewhere along the line the pearl would be handed to me" (11)— returning home disillusioned. At the end of part 1, Sal has to beg money for the bus to get home. Part 2 ends with Dean and Sal parting: "It was a sullen moment. We were all thinking, we'd never see one another again and we didn't care" (178). Sal and Dean at the end of part 3 have been reduced to a state of debauchery in which they are almost swept away in the debris of a "horror-hole" theater where they have spent the night (245), and at the end of part 4, Sal, who is sick in Mexico City, is deserted by Dean: "When I got better I realized what a rat he was" (303).

In part 5, Sal meets Laura, agrees to settle down, and renounces Dean much as Peter renounces Christ after his arrest. They are on their way to a "Duke Ellington concert at the Metropolitan Opera" (308) and, because his friend Remi won't cooperate, are unable to give Dean a ride. It is noteworthy that this incident should take place as they are on their way to see Ellington. The African American culture from which jazz derived favored communal music which was participatory, unlike the Western tradition of classical music, which has sacralized the performer and proscribed audience involvement (Levine, *Black Culture* 203). In jazz clubs, audience and performers were not separated from one another; audience participation in the music was expected. Craig Hansen Werner explains that this attitude derives from the call-and-response patterning of African American sacred music and work songs, which allows listeners to be "understood as collaborators rather than an 'audience' in the Euro-American sense" (207). For Sal, however, this fracture in the rules of performer–audience separation governing white music is another indication of jazz's franticness. At the Shearing Birdland performance, for instance, the pianist "was conscious of the madman behind him, he could hear every one of Dean's gasps and imprecations" (128). Slim Galliard, after playing, actually sits with Dean and Sal: "I sat there with these two madmen" (177). The black audiences are also highly participatory: "it was a mad crowd. They were all urging that tenorman to hold it and keep it with cries and wild eyes.... A six-foot skinny Negro woman was rolling her bones at the man's hornbell, and he just jabbed it at her, 'Ee! ee! ee!'" (197).

The Ellington concert at the Met, however, suggests that by the end of the novel such wildness has been eliminated from Sal's life. Lawrence Levine argues that as the United States experienced an enormous influx of immigrants during the latter half of the nineteenth century, social elites used culture as a means of organizing and making sense of the newcomers: "the response of the elites was a tripartite one: to retreat into their own private spaces whenever possible; to transform public spaces by rules, systems of taste, and canons of behavior of their own choosing; and, finally, to convert the strangers so that their modes of behavior and cultural predilections emulated those of the elites" (*Highbrow* 177). What evolved was a hierarchical system of highbrow culture in which audiences, as well as readers and visitors to art galleries and museums, were taught "to approach the masters and their works with proper respect and proper seriousness, for aesthetic and spiritual elevation rather than mere entertainment was the goal" (146). The sacralization of culture was accompanied by a system of rules that, in the case of classical musical expression, for instance, prevented latecomers from immediately taking their seats, forced women to take off large hats, and frowned on applause after arias (190).

Ellington's performance in the early 1950s at the Metropolitan Opera, one of the bastions of highbrow culture, occurs roughly at the historical moment when jazz was being transformed from the lowbrow to the highbrow. Ellington's swing audience had mostly evaporated by then, and jazz, as David Hajdu, the biographer of Ellington's arranger Silly Strayhorn, notes, "was evolving into an elite music" (150); while it marked the direction of jazz for the remainder of the decade, bop attracted a much smaller audience than swing. "[E]xoteric or popular art," Levine comments, "is transformed into esoteric or high art at precisely that time when it in fact *becomes* esoteric, that is, when it becomes or is rendered inaccessible to the types of people who appreciated it earlier" (*Highbrow* 234). Ellington's Met appearance suggests that jazz has been accepted as highbrow culture, and that its performance is governed by regulations similar to those of classical music. The institutionalization of jazz at the conclusion of *On the Road* mirrors Sal's commitment to Laura and to a more conventional life. Although jazz and Sal have changed substantially by the end of the novel, Sal's attendance at the Ellington concert is consistent with his sacralization of jazz throughout *On the Road*. Characteristic of his Romantic instincts, Kerouac makes the music meaningful by discovering transcendent qualities in jazz improvisation. This process belongs to Frith's final category of genre, the semiotic. Its rules are

> essentially rules of communication, how music works as *rhetoric*; such rules refer to the ways in which "meaning" is conveyed.... How is "truth" or "sincerity" indicated musically? ... Rules here, in other words, concern musical expressivity and emotion.
>
> (91)

It is noteworthy that the way Kerouac invests jazz music with meaning is not exceptional but is, in fact, part of a broader historical phenomenon. "Romanticism, which has stimulated our aesthetic consciousness in so many respects," wrote John Huizinga in 1949, "has also been the chief promoter of an ever-widening appreciation of music as a thing of the deepest value in life" (188).

The sacralized quality of jazz for Sal and Dean clearly emerges in two incidents, in San Francisco and then in Chicago, when they go to jazz clubs. Both places feature many of the behavior characteristics, such as audience participation, of traditional jazz performance. In San Francisco, the crowd is anarchic—"Everybody was rocking and roaring" (197)—and in Chicago, the musicians are apparently maniacal, entirely taken over by the music: "The sad drummer ... completely goofed, staring into space, chewing gum, wide-eyed, rocking the neck with Reich kick and complacent ecstasy" (240). And yet the music is not entirely without order and meaning. A tenor saxophone player in San Francisco, for instance, sings "Close Your Eyes" in a way that expresses the "pit and prunejuice of poor beat life itself in the god-awful streets of man" (199); afterward, he sits in a corner and cries. Both he and an alto player in the same club possess a more mysterious quality: "the tenorman *had* it and everybody knew he had it" (197). The next day Dean remarks that the alto player was able to hold "IT" for longer than anyone he has seen. He explains that as the player improvises, suddenly "he *gets it*—everybody looks up and knows; they listen; he picks it up and carries. Time stops. He's filling empty space with the substance of our lives, confessions of his bellybottom strain, remembrance of ideas, rehashes of old blowing. He has to blow across bridges and come back and do it with such infinite feeling soul-exploratory for the tune of the moment that everybody knows it's not the tune that counts but IT—" Dean could go no further; he was sweating telling about it.

(206)

"IT" then appears to be some enigmatic aspect of the music that unites the musicians and listeners in a common purpose and apparently raises the moment to transcendent heights.

Stephen Nachmanovitch remarks that such a union is characteristic of all improvisation: "The time of inspiration, the time of technically structuring and realizing the music, the time of playing it, and the time of communicating with the audience, as well as ordinary clock time, are all one. Memory and intention (which postulate past and future) and intuition (which indicates the eternal present) are fused" (18). Nachmanovitch also remarks on the similarity between what is produced by improvisation and by Buddhism: "Buddhists call this state of absorbed, selfless, absolute concentration *samadhi*" (52). In *Mexico City Blues*, Kerouac, who according to Charters was "a self-taught student of Buddhism" (190), even compares Charlie Parker to Buddha (Nicosia 488). What Kerouac is intuitively recognizing in his celebration of "IT" is that order is, indeed, an important part of the jazz improvisation which appears to emerge out of nothingness. Anthony Storr makes a similar point: "Although both art and play have a necessary element of spontaneity, both are also concerned with order and with form" (116). It is the paradoxical balance of freedom and order, what Nachmanovitch calls "a harmony of opposite tensions" (12), not abandonment, that creates through improvisation the elevated spiritual moment described by Dean. Improvised jazz represents for Dean and Sal the epiphanal moment, a state of being that Kerouac was continually striving for in one way or another in both his writing and his life. The intuitive awareness of the need for an order to shape improvisation that is evident in Dean's description of how "IT" is produced can be likened to Ostransky's portrayal of jazz improvisation as a form of *bricolage* that unites disparate elements into a musical narrative.

Jack Kerouac's treatment of jazz in *On the Road* is consistent with what Christopher Miller calls Africanist discourse, the ways white Western culture has traditionally viewed Africa and, in this case, African Americans. Kerouac bases his argument for spontaneity in "Essentials of Spontaneous Prose" on his understanding of jazz improvisation, but he misunderstands and simplifies the formal rules that distinguish jazz as a musical genre. Jazz does influence *On the Road*, but it is largely through Kerouac's Romantic identification with the ideology of the African American jazz musician whose music is visceral and who has been marginalized by white culture. The behavioral aspects of the music are also significant in the novel, but again Kerouac views them largely through the eyes of white culture; the communal nature of the music and the exchange between audience and performer he regards as further evidence of the music's franticness rather than as characteristic of African American culture. Finally, Kerouac discovers epiphanal moments in improvised jazz, ironically, not because they are utterly free and abandoned but because their spontaneity is shaped by an underlying order. "[The] work suffers—or is at least peculiar," as Edward Said has noted in reference to a similar instance of appropriation, Verdi's treatment of Egyptian culture in *Aida*, "because of the selectivity of and emphases in what is included and, by implication, excluded" (122).

On the Road, as a narrative, shows an adherence to traditional literary form which is often at odds with the theoretical views espoused by Kerouac. The run-on sentence that ends the novel owes more to the modernist notion of stream of consciousness developed by writers like Joyce and Woolf than to jazz improvisation. While jazz does not formally hold up as a thoroughgoing structural model for the novel, it is important as an ideological, behavioral, and semiotic source for Kerouac's vision of America, even though his debt to African American culture is not acknowledged. *On the Road*, then, is a novel of contradictions. The Romantic ideology of primitivism through which Kerouac views jazz prevents him from recognizing the irony and self-reflection that is at the music's core. Moreover, the Romanticism through which he views his own life and those of his friends prevents him from achieving a postmodernist vision even though many of his materials—the autobiographical nature of the work and later the "Frisco: The Tape" section in *Visions of Cody*—point in this direction. The achievement of *On the Road*, finally, is that, like the early works of realism, it enlarges the scope of suitable fictional subject material to include alcoholics, junkies, and jazz musicians and fashions a distinctive prose style to depict their lives.

WORKS CITED

Baldwin, James. "The Black Boy Looks at the White Boy." *Nobody Knows My Name: More Notes of a Native Son*. New York: Dell, 1961. 171–90.

Baraka, Amiri [Leroi Jones]. *Blues People: Negro Music in White America*. New York: Morrow, 1963.

Bartlett, Lee. "The Dionysian Vision of Jack Kerouac." *The Beats: Essays in Criticism*. Ed. Lee Bartlett. Jefferson, NC: McFarland, 1981. 115–26.

Britt, Stan. *Dexter Gordon: A Musical Biography*. New York: Da Capo, 1989. Rpt. of *Long Tall Dexter*. London: Quartet, 1989.

Carr, Ian, Digby Fairweather, and Brian Priestly. *Jazz: The Essential Companion*. 1987. London: Paladin, 1988.

Charters, Ann. Introduction. *On the Road*. By Jack Kerouac. New York: Penguin, 1991. vii–xxx.

———. *Kerouac: A Biography*. 1973. New York: Warner, 1974.

Clark, Tom. *Jack Kerouac: A Biography*. New York: Harcourt, 1984.

Coker, Jerry. *Listening to Jazz*. Englewood Cliffs, NJ: Prentice, 1978.

Coleridge, Samuel. "The Rime of the Ancient Mariner." *The Norton Anthology of English Literature*. 5th ed. Vol. 2. Ed. M. H. Abrams. New York: Norton, 1986. 335–52.

Collier, James Lincoln. *Benny Goodman and the Swing Era*. New York: Oxford UP, 1989.

Cook, Bruce. *The Beat Generation*. New York: Scribner's, 1971.

Cook, Richard, and Brian Morton. *The Penguin Guide to Jazz on CD, LP and Cassette*. London: Penguin, 1994.

De Vries, Jan. *Heroic Song and Heroic Legend*. Trans. B. J. Timmer. London: Oxford UP, 1963.

Douglas, Ann. "On the Road Again." Rev. of *The Portable Jack Kerouac* and *Jack Kerouac: Selected Letters, 1940–1956*. *New York Times Book Review* 9 Apr. 1995. 2+.

Ellison, Ralph. "The Charlie Christian Story." *Shadow and Act*. London: Secker and Warburg, 1967. 233–40.

Feather, Leonard. *The Jazz Years: Earwitness to an Era*. 1986. London: Pan, 1988.

Foster, Edward Halsey. *Understanding the Beats*. Columbia, SC: U of South Carolina P, 1992.

French, Warren. *Jack Kerouac*. Boston: Twayne, 1986.

Frith, Simon. *Performing Rites: On the Value of Popular Music*. Cambridge, MA: Harvard UP, 1996.

Gifford, Barry, and Lawrence Lee. *Jack's Book: An Oral Biography of Jack Kerouac*. New York: St. Martin's, 1978.

Gioia, Ted. *The Imperfect Art: Reflections on Jazz and Modern Culture*. Oxford: Oxford UP, 1988.

Gridley, Mark C. *Jazz Styles*. Englewood Cliffs, NJ: Prentice-Hall, 1978.

Hajdu, David. *Lush Life: A Biography of Billy Strayhorn*. New York: Farrar, 1996.

Hillman, James. "Healing Fiction." *Jungian Literary Criticism*. Ed. Richard P Sugg. Evanston, IL: Northwestern UP, 1992. 129–38.

Hipkiss, Robert A. *Jack Kerouac: Prophet of the New Romanticism*. Lawrence, KS: Regents, 1976.

Huizinga, Johan. *Homo Ludens: A Study of the Play Element in Culture*. 1949. London: Temple Smith, 1970.

Hunt, Tim. *Kerouac's Crooked Road: Development of a Fiction*. Hamden, CT: Archon, 1981.

Hutcheon, Linda. *A Poetics of Postmodernism: History, Theory, Fiction*. New York: Routledge, 1988.

Janssen, Mike. "The Influence of Jazz on the Beat Generation." 1994. <http:wwwcharm.net/~brooklyn/Topics/JanssenOnJazz.html> 7 Apr. 1997.

Kerouac, Jack. *Book of Blues*. 1995. New York: Penguin, 1995.

C. "Essentials of Spontaneous Prose." *The Portable Beat Reader*. Ed. Ann Charters. New York: Viking, 1992. 57–58.

———. *Mexico City Blues*. New York: Grove, 1959.

———. *On the Road*. 1957. New York: Penguin, 1991.

———. *The Subterraneans*. New York: Grove, 1958.

———. *Visions of Cody*. New York: McGraw-Hill, 1972.

Levine, Lawrence W. *Black Culture and Black Consciousness: Afro-American Folk Thought from Slavery to Freedom*. New York: Oxford UP, 1977.C. *Highbrow/Lowbrow: The Emergence of Cultural Hierarchy in America*. 1988. Cambridge, MA: Harvard UP, 1990.

Maggin, Donald L. *Stan Getz: A Life in Jazz*. New York: Morrow, 1996.

Mailer, Norman. "Note to 'Reflections on Hip.'" *Advertisements for Myself*. New York: Putnam's, 1959. 359–71.

C. "The White Negro: Superficial Reflections on the Hipster." *Advertisements for Myself*. New York: Putnam's, 1959. 337–58.

Miller, Christopher. *Blank Darkness: Africanist Discourse in French*. Chicago: U of Chicago P, 1985.

Murray, Albert. *Stomping the Blues*. Da Capo: New York, 1976. Rpt..of *Stomping the Blues*. New York: McGraw-Hill, 1976.

Nachmanovitch, Stephen. *Free Play: Improvisation in Life and Art*. Los Angeles: Jeremy P. Tarcher, 1990.

Nicosia, Gerald. *Memory Babe: A Critical Biography of Jack Kerouac*. Berkeley: U of California P, 1994.

Ostransky, Leroy. *The Anatomy of Jazz*. 1960. Westport, CT: Greenwood, 1973.

C. *Jazz City: The Impact of Our Cities on the Development of Jazz*. Englewood Cliffs, NJ: Prentice-Hall, 1978.

———. *Understanding Jazz*. Englewood Cliffs, NJ: Prentice-Hall, 1977.

Parker, Charlie. *Charlie Parker Omnibook: For E Flat Instruments*. New York: Atlantic Music, 1978.

Patterson, Lee. "Literary History." *Critical Terms for Literary Study*. Ed. Frank Lentricchia and Thomas McLaughlin. Chicago: U of Chicago P, 1990. 250–62.

Perlman, Alan M., and Daniel Greenblatt. "Miles Davis Meets Noam Chomsky: Some Observations on Jazz Improvisation and Language Structure." *The Sign in Music and Literature*. Ed. Wendy Steiner. Austin: U of Texas P, 1981. 169–83.

Russell, Ross. *Bird Lives!: The High Life and Hard Times of Charlie "Yardbird" Parker*. 1972. London: Quartet, 1976.

Sabatella, Marc. *A Jazz Improvisation Primer*. 1996. <http://www.fortnet.org/~marc/primer/primer.txt.> 17 Apr. 1996.

Said, Edward W. *Culture and Imperialism*. New York: Knopf, 1993.

Sidran, Ben. *Black Talk*. 1971. New York: Da Capo, 1981.

Storr, Anthony. *The Dynamics of Creation*. New York: Atheneum, 1972.

Teal, Larry. *The Art of Saxophone Playing*. Seacaucus, NJ: Summy-Birchard, 1963.

Weinreich, Regina. *The Spontaneous Poetics of Jack Kerouac: A Study of the Fiction*. Carbondale: Southern Illinois UP, 1987.

Werner, Craig Hansen. *Playing the Changes: From Afro-Modernism to the jazz Impulse*. Urbana: U of Illinois P, 1994.

ALEX ALBRIGHT

Ammons, Kerouac, and Their New Romantic Scrolls

A. R. Ammons and Jack Kerouac share much beyond the coincidence that both typed some of their best work on scrolls. Both Ammons's *Tape for the Turn of the Year* (1965) and Kerouac's *On the Road* (1957)[1] sought an immediacy in their composition that would transcend traditional approaches to their genres—taking them and their readers into "the seething poetry of the incarnate Now." Both used the scrolls on which they typed to help force into being the seamless compositional style they hoped would free them from the poetry of "perfected bygone moments" and of the "glimmering futurity,"[2] a style that would arise out of the moment but that could flow like time itself. Yet, even as Ammons and Kerouac try in their spontaneous composition to tap into an eternally flowing *now*, their heroes try valiantly to stop time and to understand it in its many implications, to "accept Time absolutely."[3]

Tape and *Road* are more conservative versions of experiments Ammons and Kerouac conducted with composition on scrolls. *Tape* is a tighter, more controlled version of Ammons's critically maligned volume, *The Snow Poems* (1977); both seek to depict the commingling flows of tape, time, and thought, product, process and poem, and both use the moment's atmospheric conditions, its weather *right now*, as metaphor fraught with a multiplicity of meanings. *Visions of Cody* (1972) was the book Kerouac felt came closest to fulfilling the promise of the compositional method he first called "sketching"

From *Complexities of Motion: New Essays on A. R. Ammons's Long Poems*. © 1999 by Associated University Presses, Inc.

and, later, "spontaneous prose," a method Ammons freely admits having employed in most of his long poems and many of his shorter ones, but with much more critical success, generally, than Kerouac has yet to attain.

Ammons himself is the hero of *Tape*, the poem he composed on an adding-machine roll between 6 December 1963 and 10 January 1974, using each day's date as the poem's dividers. As others have noted, his is a mock-epic journey that leads him to an acceptance of his limitations, his mortality, despite his desire that things be different: "I wish I had a great / story to tell," he writes, but then, as if to set out the true Sisyphean nature of his quest, he says why he wishes this: "the / words then / could be quiet, as I'm / trying to make them now—/ immersed in the play / of events" (T, 8). Impossibly, the hero wishes to "get / right up next to the / break between / what-is-to-be and / what-has-been and / dance like a bubble / held underwater by water's / pouring in" (T, 19). He wonders why "can't we break loose / and live" (T, 8), and he implores us, like Whitman, to remember our bodies: "let's touch, patiently, / thoroughly" (T, 202); "To touch my person to some one else's is about as much as I can stand."[4] Although Kerouac's persona, Sal Paradise, narrates *Road*, the Neal Cassady-based character Dean Moriarity is its hero, the one who talks "about every detail of every moment that passed," and who knows that the only thing to do is go with the energy of a jazzman's solo: that's the only way to know time (OTR, 114, 121–22, 184–85, 194–96).[5]—assady/Moriarty becomes, for Kerouac, the perfect physical embodiment of what he and Ammons sought: release "from mental / prisons into the actual / fact, the mere / occurrence—the touched, / tasted, heard, seen" (T, 99).

Both *Tape* and *Road* are revolts in compositional mode and in theme against the currency of their days. "Poetry & prose had for long time fallen into the false hands of the false," Kerouac writes;[6] Ammons demands to "let a new / order occur / from the random & / nondescript" (T, 17). Both play off the notions of their central metaphors to demonstrate that, while we like to think the road goes on forever and the tape of our days will keep uncoiling indefinitely, both will end; all we really have to treasure is in front of us right now, for we cannot know what lies in our future, if, even, we will have a future. Thus the heightened interest on intensely feeling what Lawrence called that "quivering momentaneity,"[7] with blowing the moment up like a bubble so that we can luxuriate in its fullness, allowing our imagination full and free range into a timeless and eternal-seeming now, where we have time to touch "patiently, thoroughly."

Ammons and Kerouac, like Whitman and Emerson, Lawrence and Charles Olson, seek original thought, "the essence of genius, of virtue, and of life, which we call Spontaneity or Instinct."[8] In their respective approaches to a spontaneous poetics, Ammons and Kerouac flaunt the traditionally held notion that true literary art is created through carefully considered revision; and they both glory in the celebration of the quotidian as the essential key to understanding the sacred, or mystic. In their quest to bring to their new romanticism a heightened realism, one that rides a "moment- / to-moment crest" (T, 31) "running from one falling star to another till I drop" (OTR, 8) both Ammons and Kerouac explore their similar aesthetics, expressed by Kerouac as "the essentials of spontaneous prose."

*   *   *

Despite Kerouac's blustery claims to the contrary, spontaneous writing did not originate with him. Robert Hipkiss points out that Blake claimed that his "Milton" was written effortlessly, the transcription of a voice speaking to the poet, and that André Breton and the surrealists had experimented with automatic writing and free association.[9] John Tytell notes the automatic writing experiments of William James and Gertrude Stein at Harvard.[10] But such questions—did the author revise or otherwise *think* about word choice?—detract from the texts at hand, from what, ultimately, we are left to deal with: the printed words on the page, in the order that an author has placed them. Tim Hunt has demonstrated that Kerouac—despite the legend—was a careful revisionist with much of his work; *On the Road*, in fact, is but one of five very different versions of what Kerouac came to call his Road manuscript.[11] Donald Reimann notes that Ammons, in *Tape*, did not always go with whatever flow of words he found himself in, but instead made a number of aesthetic choices that "produced a work of art rather than a collage of random jottings."[12] Still, both authors used their scrolls to shape and to pace their respective manuscripts, forcing on their writing a rush of motion that delineates over and over again the infinite range of moments that comprise the continuums of our lives. Kerouac's legendary teletype roll afforded him the nonstop pacing and long rambling "sentences" that he sought as the format for plunging headlong into the spontaneous composition of his narrative; Ammons's roll of adding machine tape gave him the seamlessness he sought for his narrative, and in its boundaries prescribed for him the slim lines of his song. Ultimately, it is their unique commingling of form, format, and subject to emphasize theme that best unifies them.

Reimann also traces the history of using physical materials to shape a poem back to Homer and up through Gertrude Stein; he suggests that in *Tape* Ammons uses "form and content to echo the poem's theme: humanity must be content to go with the flow and to renounce—or downplay—systems and structures, rational constructs, in favor of untutored reality."[13]

To perceive an untutored reality, what Emerson distinguished as intuition as opposed to tuition, gets us back to experiencing life beyond language and interpretation, to the immediacy of vision. "[R]elease us from mental / prisons into the actual / fact, the mere / occurrence," Ammons writes in *Tape*. "[L]et's not make up / categories to toss ourselves / around with" (99).

Kerouac claims to have invented the idea of a spontaneous bop prosody in order to rewrite the first draft of *On the Road*, which was composed in April 1951 on a very long teletype roll. He told Allen Ginsberg that the idea, which he originally called "sketching," came to him on 25 October 1951;[14] but letters recently published indicate he was developing his "finally-at-last-found style & hope" earlier in the month.[15] Charters also credits Neal Cassady, both in a famous lost letter and in his rough attempts at beginning his own autobiography, as helping Kerouac solidify his poetics.[16] Robert Hipkiss believes that Kerouac, in *Vanity of Duluoz* (1967), claims a 1944 origin point for this new style. He suggests, as others do, that precedences for spontaneous prose are to be found in Charlie Parker's bop, Jackson Pollock's action painting, and Dylan Thomas's organic verse.[17] Regina Weinreich credits John Clellon Holmes with suggesting to Kerouac that he fill his "head (and page) with everything you can think of, in its natural order."[18] Gerald Nicosia cites Kerouac's explanation that his new "notion of writing as Reichian release" was also an attempt to combine "Dostoyevsky's confessional method in *Notes from the Underground*" with William Carlos Williams's "measured pauses of speech."[19] Wherever its origin, the first draft of Kerouac's "Essentials of Spontaneous Prose" was composed at the request of Allen Ginsberg and William Burroughs just after Kerouac had written *The Subterraneans* on a teletype roll in three nights in 1953.[20]

Philosophically, the idea of getting outside one's consciousness and into a stream of time, or life, that is beyond interpretation and language, had intrigued Kerouac since his first introduction to Buddhism, at least as early as 1950, although his readings several years earlier of Whitman and Emerson had acquainted him with ideas on spontaneity. He sees its aesthetic origins expressed by Buddha, "2,500 years ago as 'The Seven Streams of Swiftness': 'If you are desirous of more perfectly understanding Supreme Enlightenment, you must learn to answer questions spontaneously.'" He also sees precedent in Mark 13:11: "Take no thought beforehand what ye shall speak, neither do ye premeditate: but whatsoever shall be given you in that hour, that speak ye: for it is not ye that speak, but the Holy Ghost." And he notes that both Mozart and Blake often felt "twas the 'Muse' singing and pushing."[21] Ammons's *Tape*, of course, is addressed to his muse, and the poem itself can easily be read as one long, continuous attempt by the poet to reconnect with that muse, to get back in "the river of going" (T, 191).

Kerouac also was intrigued by Lao-Tse, whose notion that "Nothing that can be said in words is worth saying" is central to Ammons's philosophy. (Ammons uses Lao-Tse's words as the epigram of his essay, "A Poem Is a Walk.") But before we can so easily dismiss the work, then, of one who has labored some fifty years with words as being "not worth saying," we should know too that Ammons sees poetry as "maybe one way of / coming home" to "silence, / restfulness from words" (T, 87). For Ammons, "nonverbal assimilations" are the "things that really draw us" to poems (SM, 47). He has acknowledged being influenced by Whitman and Emerson but has also pointed out that "my source is the same as theirs."[22] And Kerouac shares all of these influences—Lao-Tse, Blake, Whitman, Emerson, the Eastern notions of transcendence. And like Ammons, he never had much interest or trust in the American academy. Ammons wonders, for example, "what it is about critics that enables them to know so much about poetry when they obviously don't have the faintest idea how it comes about" (SM, 31); Kerouac writes: "I hadn't learned anything in college that was going to help me to be a writer anyway and the only place to learn was in my own mind...."[23] Kerouac's dissatisfaction with Columbia University and its formalized traditions—coupled with his introduction into the hipster scene in New York in the late 1940s—led him to explore the notion of a spontaneous poetics that could reflect individual, untutored genius. As published in the last issue of the *Black Mountain Review* (1957), "Essentials of Spontaneous Prose" offers a way of explicating the compositional method Ammons has used in *Tape* and other poems, which helps place Ammons firmly in the, company of the Beats and of those who are sometimes identified as the Black Mountain College poets, as both Alan Holder and Donald Reimann have suggested but not fully explored.[24]

Although loosely defined, the Black Mountain College poets are generally seen to have worked under Charles Olson's influence, and his 1950 essay "Projective Verse" is this group's aesthetic pronouncement.[25] Whether Olson influenced Kerouac or vice versa is not clear; most likely, they were influenced in like ways through mutual friends and ideas that were gaining currency after World War II. Hipkiss says Kerouac obviously used some of the ideas being discussed by Olson, Robert Duncan, and Robert Creeley, a core of the writers who dominated Black Mountain College in the early 1950s.[26]

In "Projective Verse," Olson makes three main points preceded by his assertion that "composition by field" is a new method of writing poems, contrasted with the "old" base of "inherited line, stanza, over-all form." He asserts that (1) "a poem is energy transferred from the poet who got it, by way of the poem itself to ... the reader"; (2) "form is never more than an extension of content"—an idea he credits to Creeley; and (3) [The poet should] "USE USE USE the process at all points.... Move, instanter, on to another." Olson also argues that the syllable (born from the "union of the mind and the ear"), not "rime and meter" or "sense and sound" should be allowed "to lead the harmony [of the poem] on." He credits Edward Dahlberg with having first instructed him that "One perception must immediately and directly lead to a further perception," which, he says, "means exactly what it says ... keep it moving as fast as you can, citizen" (PV, 148–49). D. H. Lawrence, Holder has pointed out, was anxious for "another kind of poetry: the poetry of that which is at hand: the immediate present ...," to find the "inexhaustible, forever-unfolding creative spark."[27] Duncan adds: "We begin to imagine a cosmos in which the poet and the poem are one in a moving process." He thanks projective verse for showing him that one could "derive melody and story from impulse not from plan," and he quotes Whitehead, "The present contains all that there is."[28]

The reliance of Black Mountain poets on an objectivist aesthetic has led to the occasional charge that they in general and Olson in particular are too cold and removed from nature. Yet Olson begins the conclusion of "Projective Verse" with a description that fits Ammons and his poetry perfectly:

> It comes to this: the use of a man, by himself and thus by others, lies in how he conceives his relation to nature, that force to which he owes his somewhat small existence.... [I]f he is contained within his nature as he is participant in the larger force, he will be able to listen, and his hearing through himself will give him secrets objects share. (PV, 156)

Ammons listens keenly—no American poet has so persistently sought to deduce the mystery in mundane objects of nature—and his poems reveal that "nature's message is, for / the special reader, / though clear, sometimes written / as on a tablet underwater" (SP, 241). That message, when things are clear, bright, sunny, and their edges distinct, might be that "nature goes so far to make us / one of a kind / and treat us all alike" (SP, 170); it might be a simple reminder that "the flawless evidence favoring / death leaves us / unconvinced / and we're ready / on no evidence / to believe we live forever" (SP, 249); or it might be an extended lesson on how to "absorb the margins: / enlarge the range: / give life room" so that we might "widen / the band / of acceptance (T 191)".

Olson is most important to understanding Ammons in his discussions of man himself as an object in a poem, and of objectivism as the "getting rid of the lyrical interference of the individual as ego, of the 'subject' and his soul, that peculiar presumption by which western man has interposed himself between what he is as a creature of nature ... and those other creations of nature which we may ... call objects," himself included (PV, 156).[29] Projective verse, or composition by field, yields a relationship between poet, object, and poem that cannot be delineated; Duncan adds: "We begin to imagine a cosmos in which the poet and the poem are one in a moving process...."[30] Boundaries blur, as Ammons suggests repeatedly in the natural imagery of *Tape*, much like Steven Schneider has suggested in reminding us that what we once thought of as "solid" and fixed in science, even in space-time, is both permeable and fluid. No longer does science so much recognize discrete particles as it does levels of excitation of abstract underlying fields.[31] And, to borrow from Ammons's metaphorical warehouse, from a distance, the edges of these fields blur—in seeing the one, we lose sight of the many, although they are still there—and we think, then, that what we're seeing is solid, in much the same way we think of ourselves as solid and fixed, though we know that we are not.

Ammons writes of "the circles of reach," how they expand in our lives to a certain point in a "widening circle," then begin contracting, "the gradual / shrinking" (T, 92–93). In *The Snow Poems*, he watches from his distance the action of objects in the "field" of his neighbor's lawn, where a chained dog tests the limits of his range. Ammons compares the worn ground the dog can reach with the "unworn ... untouchable / other" (SP, 26), a boundary as real as that separating life from death, or an object from the words that describe it. But in other cases, what we believe to be peripheries are in fact the "moment-to-moment edge of growth"; given enough distance, these peripheries will blur "into nothingness" (T, 113, 104).

Kerouac, too, is intrigued with peripheries—the point where things "disappear"—in *Road*, although in his field nature rarely stands as predominately as man will, and he will usually stand for loss. Leaving New Orleans, for example, Paradise wonders, "What is that feeling when you're driving away from people and they recede on the plain till you see their specks dispersing?—it's the too-huge world vaulting us, and it's good-bye" (OTR, 148). Leaving a friend in Tucson, Paradise says, "It was sad to see his tall figure receding in the dark just like the other figures [we've left] in New York and New Orleans: they stand uncertainly underneath immense skies, and everything about them is drowned. Where go? what do? what for?" (158). As they leave Montana, Paradise and Moriarty watch a friend "recede ... till there was nothing but a growing absence in space ... that led all the way back to my home" in the East (252). Like Ammons, he sees how the "periphery / vanishes into nothingness / the stabilizer" (T, 104).

But where Olson is helpful for contemplating a philosophy behind Ammons's imagery (and for explaining, too, what Vendler has noted as his lack of adjectives), Kerouac's spontaneous poetics is better suited for exploring Ammons's actual method of composition, not just in *Tape for the Turn of the Year*, but in much of his poetry. Ammons has said, "I was in South Jersey at the time [1963] of *T[ape] for the T[urn] of the Year*, and I don't know if I was aware of the automatic-extemporaneous writing of Kerouac. I guess I was beat, but not Beat."[32] Yet, consider how closely the two writers explain what Kerouac called the first of his nine essential steps, "the set up." Kerouac says that the poet must first have an "image-object ... set before the mind either in reality ... or in memory" (ESP, 69). Ammons ascribes such a beginning to his long poems, including *Tape*: "When I found a single image that could sustain multiplicity, I usually could begin to write" (SM, 102). Over his career, the most powerfully realized of these images have been the adding machine tape, the earth as seen from outer space, snow, and a garbage dump.

But the image that most dominates Ammons's poetry goes back to his experience in the navy, at age nineteen, of looking from the bow of a ship to a distant horizon at

> the line inscribed across the variable land mass, determining where people would or would not live, where palm trees would or could not grow.... The whole world changed as a result of an interior illumination: the water level was not what it was because of a single command by a higher power but because of an average result of a host of actions—runoffs, wind currents, melting glaciers. I began to apprehend things in the dynamics of themselves.... (SM, 95)[33]

That line of water's level, of course, is the dominant image of the title poem of Ammons's second collection, *Expressions of Sea Level*; it and its variations will inform much of the rest of his poetry, including *Tape*, *The Snow Poems*, *Garbage* (1993), *Brink Road* (1996), and many of the individual poems he's published along the way: "into the salt marshes the water comes fast with rising tide: / an inch of rise spreads by yards / through tidal creeks, round fingerway of land: ... is there a point of rest where / the tide turns: is there one / infinitely tiny higher touch / on the legs of egrets ..." (ESL, 31).

In addition to giving him an image to contemplate for a lifetime, the question of where and when the sea levels neatly wraps up for Ammons two interrelated themes that permeate his work: (1) our natural boundaries are not truly fixed once we see the edges of their growth (or decay, a sort of "growth" towards nothingness), which we cannot see if we distance ourselves too far away—distance, we might say, makes the edge seem solid; and (2) we should seek the appropriate "zones" where each of us "do best in" (T, 53). These leave us with the notion that nature, especially its weather, affords us a limitless supply of metaphors with which to explore "centers & peripheries / in motion, / organic, interrelations" (T, 112). In *Tape*, Ammons considers these questions in "the slow accretion of hard rock"; sunshine and shade alternating; the line between surf and shore; and the transformation of water into ice, to name but a few (T, 14, 24, 175, 149, 171).

Olson says in "Projective Verse" that "objects which occur in every given moment of composition (of recognition, we can call it)" must be treated as they occur in the poem, and not by ideas outside the poem. They "must be handled as a series of objects in field in such a way that a series of tensions (which they also are) are made to hold, and to hold exactly inside the content and the context of the poem which has forced itself, through the poet and them, into being" (152). Ammons is playing directly in Olson's field when he begins the third day of *Tape* with this declaration of fact derived from a *negative* field: "the way I could tell / today / that yesterday is dead / is that / the little gray bird / that sat in the empty / tree / yesterday is gone" (T, 11). *Tape*, throughout, is a series of "tensions" observed by the poet in the moments he witnesses passing: "can a lip quiver with / more need / ... than now?" (T, 87). Ammons continues to combine the weighted object with fluid moments captured, frozen and examined, on December 28, noting parenthetically "(just now, the / thorns / are black / against the wall)" (T, 117). And, over and over, we are made to wait, tensely, to see what happens next: Will the water turn to ice? Will the leaf turn over? Will the sun drop behind a cloud, obliterating thorn's shadow—the object itself? In Ammons's tape, we see levels of tensions, too, in the pull of tape through typewriter, "the centers & peripheries / in motion, / organic" (T, 112).

Kerouac's "procedure," the second essential, recommends writing with the "undisturbed flow from the mind of personal secret idea-words, blowing (as per jazz musician) on subject of image" (ESP, 69). *Tape* is, essentially, one long jazz blowing on the search for idea-words that will get the poet back in touch with his Muse, where "only the lively use of language lives" (176). Each day's notations contain undisturbed flow, although on some days the flow gets disturbed, as all flows ultimately must—too many intervals break up the road, Ammons writes in *The Snow Poems* (19)—but all this is just coming / out of my head" (T, 47).

Ammons told an interviewer in 1984 that "my first drafts would indicate that my best poems ... come almost as they are" (SM, 42). He explains that he attempts to write a complete poem at a first sitting—"I try to let that happen spontaneously"—and adds:

[I]n the long essay poems and in *The Snow Poems*, and earlier in the *Tape for the Turn of the Year* ... I tested my ability to say it right the first time in a long poem.... [T]hat is an exaggerated test to place on oneself but if it does come right somehow it has a ... necessary quality to it that seems inevitable; it seems that there was something taking place in the mind and there was no difference between that and what happened on the page and so it just became itself. (SM, 43)

Realistically, the simultaneous describing of imagery or thought as it flashes by in a flickering moment is, of course, impossible. The lightning Ammons observes in *Tape* on December 8 flashes and is gone ("just flashed") before the poet can finish typing the word (15). Still, Ammons finds himself "running to catch up: to / be at the / crest's break, the / running crest, / event becoming word" (T, 37). To help indicate that flow in the artifice of story-on-paper, Kerouac's "method" suggests "no periods separating sentence-structures" but offers dashes as alternative. He composed his first Road scroll with dashes only; he remarks in *Vanity of Duluoz*, "Insofar as nobody loves my dashes anyway, I'll use regular punctuation for the new illiterate generation."[34] Ammons has been luckier with his colons: nobody changes them to periods for him, and critics can talk about how democratic they are, how they fit—like Kerouac's dashes—with the flow of his poems, indicating for us the "measured pauses which are the essentials of our speech" and "divisions of the sounds we hear" (ESP, 69). Olson, however, goes after more than mere punctuation marks: "Do not tenses, must they not also be kicked around anew, in order that time, that other governing absolute may be kept, as must the space-tensions of a poem, immediate, contemporary to the acting-on-you of the poem?" (PV, 152). Ammons doesn't so much kick verb tenses around as kick them out on occasion, allowing particular phrases special emphasis without verbs, separated on either side by colons: "a spinning of diameter into / nothingness: exclusions: lepers on their islands..." or "raining: / at the borderline & / promise / of snow" (T, 59, 150), for example.

Ammons has also been much luckier with critical reception to his spontaneous poems. Weinreich and others have noted how the main controversy over the quality of Kerouac's prose has "always been centered around the basic tenets of his writing philosophy, especially those that preclude the writer's essential control: revision."[35] Truman Capote's oft-repeated charge—that's not writing, that's typing—could easily be leveled against *Tape* and other Ammons poems, by the poet's own admission; but although occasional critics have commented negatively on Ammons's "doodling," most have agreed that *Tape* is an important poem. Kerouac suffers, perhaps, from his insistence on thumbing his nose at the literary establishment; Ammons, on the other hand, has operated for much of his career from within the academy, so his taunts are not as threatening. Ammons, like Kerouac, seems to have "gotten sick and tired of the conventional English sentence which seemed to me so ironbound in its rules." Kerouac came to detest what he saw as the "shameful" process of revision; to revise meant that the writer was ashamed of what had just been written. He saw craft and revision as antithetical to art, as "laborious and dreary lying," the "sheer blockage" of the spontaneous mental process that might allow the writer to "finally say something we never heard before." He made these proclamations over and over in the last years of his desperate career, and they are what he is remembered for, not his recognition of the "delicate balancing point between bombast and babble."[36] Ammons, on the other hand, has written his lyrics as well as his long poems in his own doggedly individualistic fashion; he's made few statements on poetics, the most prominent of which are collected in *Set in Motion*. He has opted for the spontaneous and original but has done so quietly, all the while garnering increasing critical acclaim.

As if to emphasize that his lessons in technique are really variations on the same notion, three of Kerouac's essentials, "Scoping," "Lag in Procedure," and "Timing," reiterate the importance of "following free deviation (association) of mind into limitless blow-on-subject seas of thought with no pause to think of proper word," and "no revisions" (ESP, 70). Both *Tape* and especially *The Snow Poems* (as well as *Road* and much else of Kerouac's work) have been assailed by critics for their inclusion of material deemed, by the critics, as being extraneous. *Tape* includes "verbal doodling ... from time to time to feed the empty page";[37] *The Snow Poems* contains "mental garbage ... graffiti."[38] Vendler, although generally impressed, complains that in *Tape* "there is also a trust that everything you do, like everything the weather does, has its part in the configuration of the whole."[39] These complaints basically attack Ammons for his lack of revision; yet, for him, these, "doodlings" are an integral part of the whole, and an essential part of spontaneous poetics. Of *Tape*, he has admitted, "The material itself seemed secondary; it fulfilled its function whether it was good or bad material just by occupying space. In many ways the arbitrary was indistinguishable from the functional" (SM, 102). Both *Tape* and *The Snow Poems*, then, are exercises in a "free association of mind" as Ammons explores the myriad ways of figuring out "time and how to note it down" (OTR, 69); both are riddled throughout with time indicators and expressions of what is happening *right now* in front of the poet; that event-object is the (sometimes floating) center of each poetic sequence and the start of another experiment in spontaneous poetics of free-associational responses.

Using a tape to compose *Tape* was, of course, intended to allow Ammons as close an access as possible to "the going tension / that holds us, / suspends, rises, & falls, / the going on" (T, 177). In that suspension, we can meditate, go back in memory, forward in dream, or we can watch wide-eyed as "a drop forms at the / icicle-tip, tapers, pulls / free, rounds-up ... / breaks free ... / the precise event ... / when it hits the ground" (T, 171). That Ammons, too, could not have been working toward the moment when his tape ends unless it had been for his typewriter seems on the surface, perhaps, pointless to mention; but in 1950 Olson believed that the typewriter had advantages that had not been used "sufficiently." He found it ironic that this machine would lead "directly on toward projective verse and its consequences"; but he saw that, "due to its rigidity and its space precisions, it can, for a poet, indicate exactly the breath, the pauses, the suspensions of syllables, the juxtapositions even of parts of phrases, which he intends. For the first time the poet has the stave and the bar a musician has had" (PV, 154).

One of the most evocative examples of Ammons's movement in *Tape*, through streams of consciousness triggered by poetic images associating freely in his mind, is December 17th's entry. It begins with the retelling of Sisyphus's story. In Ammons's version, he quits his task, throws down his rock, and lets "out a / cry of joy that / rang through the / valley / mixing with stone-thunder" (77). Using "rang" to suggest perhaps a cash register, he segues, with a couple of cents marks as an indicator of a break in the text, into an extended rumination on Christmas trees that shifts from an indictment of commercialized holiday customs ("everything different / now & sort of loused up"), into a poignant recollection of childhood Christmases: "we had no electricity but / we had pine-cones & / colored paper & / some tinsel: it / was beautiful enough: / it was very lovely: / and it's lost." Out of the reverie comes a crashing reality: "now, a tree from / somewhere—maybe Vermont— / got by handing over / two or three green / pcs of paper." A line of dollar signs follows, breaking the text before the poet asks, "do you hear me, Sisyphus, / durn you? do you hear me / groan: / like: / wow." (T, 79–81) "Wow!" Kerouac echoes in *Road*, over and over again: "the only Word I had was Wow!" (38).

Kerouac's "Center of Interest," the seventh of his essentials, suggests that the poet "begin not from preconceived idea of what to say ... but from jewel center of interest in subject of image at moment of writing" (ESP, 70). As noted, Ammons has needed that "jewel center of interest," one that can "sustain multiplicity," in order to begin his long poems especially. Although the roll of tape is one literal center of interest for Ammons, *Tape* is more about the subject of poetry, so much and so intensely that at one point, on December 15, he writes of the poem as subject having become object: "My poem went for a ride / today: I / backgutted it all / the way out / of the typewriter, / rewinding the roll, / stuck it in a paper / bag, then in the / glove compartment: / we all went to York, Pa. / to visit relatives." By the time he's then writing, 10 p.m., he's returned to Ithaca and "reinserted & rewound: / I'm beat" (T, 70–71). Ammons's physical tape also has, as a center of interest, its own center, "organic, in motion," with peripheries constantly-at least when the poet writes-in flux. "look! / there's the red ink rising from the / floor," Ammons writes as his tape nears its end; and we see then that the poem arises out of—is created from—the consumption of the tape, which rises like a Phoenix, only to be relegated once again into "trash," into the "unity of its / conflicts" (T, 10).

Ammons most differs from the literalness of both Kerouac's and Olson's poetics in one key way. They both insist on a poetic "line" as related to the natural motions of speech and pauses; Ammons, in *Tape* and *The Snow Poems*, uses the vertical linearity of his medium to go beyond *suggesting* a flow to *becoming* flow itself. He is, then, using "line" in a an even newer way, one that suggests *time's* flow and pauses, not speech's.

Ammons is fond of using the numerical stating of time's present as though he is taunting his readers with the duality inherent in a Western mind trying to think in Eastern concepts. He told one interviewer, "I have tried to get rid of the Western tradition as much as possible" (SM, 105); but time's marking is one tradition he cannot escape. Helga Nowotny notes that "[s]ince the 1880s, psychologists had been in search of the duration of the present," and that William James's formulation of 1890—that time is 'a stream of thought'—showed the present to be more like a 'saddle-back' than a knife's edge, having as each moment has 'a certain breadth of its own' ... from which we look in two directions." Time is more than just a fleeting moment, because it is "dense enough to perceive more than just one event, to hear more than just one melody" simultaneously. She also discusses how Western culture developed its systems of uniform time measurement, culminating in 1884 with the international time conference that established the world's twenty-four time zones.[40] Herbert Rappaport believes that the Western mind sees time as a line, with a past, present, and future, so that we can be led forward into "progress." He sees in our insistence that time is linear and not circular "inherent anxieties" that account "for much of the stress of modern Western society." Non-Westerners, he asserts, are able to experience time as circular, in waves that do not "lose" time to the past but simply move events "to another point in the cycle."[41]

Ammons discusses how he started *Tape* in a 1996 interview: "I had been thinking of having the primary motion of the poem down the page rather than across.... Soon after I started ... I noticed resemblances between it and a novel. The point, like and unlike a novel, was to get to the other end; an arbitrary end would also be an 'organic' end" (SM, 101–2). Ammons calls the "tape itself" the "hero" in his novelistic poem (SM, 192). The unrolling poem itself—its "endless unfolding of words," as Whitman said—is also a dominant image of the text, which continually addresses variations on "the circles of reach / ... always / the widening circle" as well as "the gradual[ly] shrinking" one (T, 92–93). But circles for Ammons are also containers, barriers that he wants to transcend into a wholeness: "Absorb the margins," he urges (T, 91); observe "the moment-to-moment edge / of growth" and "let centers / proliferate / from / self justifying motions!" (T, 113, 116).

If, as Ammons suggests, the tape itself is the hero of *Tape*, then the story's climax, say, would occur simultaneously to the tape as hero, the tape as object-subject, and the poet; throw in "reader," who's *there* at the same time as the rest of them, and that's potentially one heck of a simultaneous orgasm. But Ammons teases us with climaxes: at the mid-point, he says "I admit / I've shot my load" and pleads for a second chance: "give / me a second wind: / it's there, I'm sure / of it, somewhere in the / mind—another valve to / open: / let it open & / fill this tape / plentifully up" (T, 101).

The last of Kerouac's nine elements of spontaneous poetics, "Mental State," urges, "write excitedly, swiftly ... in accordance (as from center to periphery) with laws of orgasm ... Come from within, out" to the "relaxed, said" (ESP, 70). Much of *Tape* is addressed directly to the poet's seductive Muse; on December 11, he asks her, "who are you / anyhow? some kind of a / prickteaser?" But things work out well for them: a couple of weeks later he urges her to "come again / and make your will in me...." After the mid-point "climax," Ammons proclaims, "the volcano shoots & / rests, gathering" (101). Later, on the last day of *Tape*, he notes that "somehow in taking / pleasure / from yr body, / I have given you / my heart: / I care now / more for you than for / the pleasure you give / me: you, your total / self, my anchorage: / the universe shifts its / center: / it turns about you" (T, 198).

Climaxes, of course, are pivots, and in his eighth essential Kerouac suggests in addressing the "structure of your work" that in your "mindflow" you arrive at the "pivot, where what was dim formed beginning becomes sharp-necessitating ending and language shortens in race to wire of time-race of work" (ESP, 70). Ammons, from a "dim-formed beginning," sees his tape as an "epic" task, the tape moving almost imperceptibly at its beginning. By New Year's eve, nearly a month into it, he finds the empty tape is still imposing, frightening: "the unconscious will / have to act out / several more shows / before the marginal red / ink / warns it's time / for a new tape" (T,

145). But the pivot arrives; the red ink rises from the floor. Ammons searches for pivotal points, too, in much of his imagery; he especially likes getting inside the bubble of the pivotal moment and watching it equivocate, *not* change: On December 10, he awaits the turn to winter, which "seems about to, but hasn't / quite decided how to / happen" (T, 24); on January 1, it's "raining: / at the borderline & / promise / of snow" (T, 150); and he spends a couple of pages anticipating the moment that a leaf might finally turn over (T, 170–72). We never find out if the leaf turns; it's left flapping in time, pinned *there* to a rock in the poet's back yard, in a tension that's lasted long past leaf's decomposition.

Kerouac's last stage—"mental state"—also defines this idea of writing as one that uses a new language, one that conscious art would censor. Ammons, too, is "looking for a level / of language / that could take in all / kinds of matter" (T, 142–43), because "only the lively use of / language lives" (T, 176). Olson, like Kerouac and Ammons, is also intrigued by the untapped potentials of language. He says that "*all* parts of speech suddenly, in composition by field, are fresh for both sound and percussive use, spring up like unknown, unnamed vegetables in the patch, when you work it, come spring" (PV, 153). Ammons has already been generally credited with adding scientific language to contemporary poetic language, yielding in the process Steven Schneider's book, which discusses Ammons's use of anatomy, archaeology, astronomy, behavioral optometry, biology, botany, chemistry, ecology, geology, relativity, quantum physics, statistics, and zoology, not just in terms of language but also Ammons's use of scientific metaphors. Schneider also discusses "rheomode" (from the Greek meaning "to flow"), a new language proposed by Larry Dossey, "to be consistent with physics' understanding of reality."[42] Such a language might approximate the flow that Ammons and Kerouac sought to re-create in their scrolls, although Kerouac's, with its traditional paragraphing and punctuation imposed by editorial dictum, loses some of its intended flow and much of its experimental nature. Ammons's use of language, especially his sentence and phrase constructions, is a much closer approximation of how poetry in "rheomode" might be composed, in a truly new language that operates at associational levels that break down the subject/verb and subject/object dualities inherent in how we learn to use our existing language.

What Ammons achieves in *Tape for the Turn of the Year* is what Kerouac sought, as the ideal, in his spontaneous poetics, which are, for Kerouac, best demonstrated in the highly experimental *Visions of Cody*. For *Road*, despite its compositional method, is still a retelling of a very linear narrative, out of the narrator's past. *Cody*, on the other hand, employs verbatim tape recordings and lots of sketching to "restructure time and space beyond" the "fiction" of traditional narrative form.[43] The result is a circular, rather than linear design, which approximates how we actually experience time as it flows: moments are blown up into larger significances, time sometimes slows down in them and at other times speeds up. In each moment's "saddle," we are sometimes able to "dwell in the ongoing, onbreaking wave" in a "symmetry of actions" that gets us into the "effortless harmony of things" (SM, 21). Ammons captures a multiplicity of such moments in both *Tape* and *The Snow Poems*.

*   *   *

"There's no news like snow news."

—A.R. Ammons

"Hast thou entered into the treasures of the snow?"
—Job 38:22

The Snow Poems, as Steven Schneider points out, met with "almost unanimous disapproval" when it was published in 1977.[44] Today, it is long since out of print and virtually impossible to discuss for other reasons as well. Helen Vendler and Michael McFee have offered its most sympathetic readings, Vendler suggesting that it "needs to be lived in for days, reread after the first reading has sorted out its preoccupations and methods, and used as a *livre de chevet* if its leisurely paths are to be followed in their waywardness." Vendler recognizes, it seems, how *The Snow Poems* echoes Ammons's essay "A Poem Is a Walk." And she hears the poet's "voice reasonable in loss" evidence of an "eviscerated Ammons, doggedly writing down the weather day after day ... Beckett-like, hard on himself as ice." Yet, Vendler still chides him for his excesses, finding parts of the book "annoying," evidence of the poet's "distracting habit of doodling on the typewriter."[45]

Both McFee and Vendler have, like others, remarked on the compositional, prosaic, and thematic similarities between *The Snow Poems* and *Tape*, which was much more generally praised (and remains in print). McFee refers to *The Snow Poems'* "testy reception" as being evidence of readers' general inability to appreciate "being spilled on their fine-fannies." He calls it "anti-formalist," but it is also anti-*poetry* and he goes on to make an excellent case for the rereading of *The Snow Poems* that Vendler recommends, referring to it along the way as audacious, contentious, garrulous, moody, unpredictable, and "even more radical" than *Tape*. McFee uses Ammons's descriptions of *The Snow Poems*, taken from its early pages (17–18), to refer back to it as a puzzler, sleeper, a tiresome business that nobody can make any sense of, a shindig, fracas, uproar, high shimmy uncompletable. McFee also sees, like Vendler, how *The Snow Poems* "shows us the dark side of Ammons's radiant sublimity."[46]

Yet, despite the near polar critical responses to *Tape* and *The Snow Poems*—*Tape* seems generally well-liked despite its doodling, while complaints about the doodling seem to dominate critical views of *The Snow Poems*—they are simply different versions of the same notion, as Ammons so frequently has tried to establish in his poems' images, and they are these different versions in a multiplicity of ways. When seen together, they show that looking at the one, or the few, loses the perspective of the larger view, the many, and the larger view, conversely, loses the focus of the closer one. And they must be looked at together, for *The Snow Poems* is a *Tape* from a larger perspective than *Tape*'s clearly delineated plot—I'm going to type this poem till the tape runs out—and time markers: *Tape*, of course, is divided into thirty-three sections according to the consecutive days of its composition, from 6 December 1963 to 10 January 1964, and it talks often of one year's ending, another's beginning. *The Snow Poems*, however, is the larger chronicle of *season*'s change, as well as of one man's change at middle-age. These are the larger contexts, then, of *Tape*'s specific one: not just one calendar year changing (and not just one book coming out, either, for *The Snow Poems* presages in both theme and imagery *Garbage*, "Ridge Farm," and *Glare*, Ammons's most recent book-length poem), but one man's epochal, pivotal move cast against the larger backdrop of the march through the ending and beginning of yet another cycle of life. These are the ways Ammons's images work best: in multiplicities, impossible to pin down precisely, one wheel within another, centers moving about and peripheries crossing into planes that surprise us. It's a wearisome move, annually, the agony of waking up seeds' dormant forces, the release of nature's flows, both in life-giving energy and life-giving water turned loose from frozen snows, moment by moment, drop by drop; and it's wearying to suddenly find one's self old, and to realize that the "crest due ... to arrive" has already "arrived or isn't coming, not / ever coming" (SP, 2).

Tape has dates to signify its neat and orderly march through linear time, a notion as comfortable to Western minds as stanzas. But what does snow, the weather, care for such time? It holds time—at least linear time, as we know it—in abeyance. And in *The Snow Poems*, the poet holds us, too, in the tense circle of becoming that doesn't always become either snow, or poem, but sometimes dissipates into thin air, or doodling.

Ammons has said: "[Poems] are not written to be studied or discussed, but to be encountered, and to become standing points that we can come to and try to feel out, impressionistically, what this poem is recommending" (SM, 58). Yet, we continue to study and discuss them. But with *The Snow*

Poems, Ammons has finally accomplished writing a poem we can't easily discuss without, it seems, first dismissing it. (He's also said, of course, that he'd prefer silence to poems, yet he's continued to write them, because "I can't do anything else" [T, 58]; critics, it might be said, operate under the same imperative.) Few critics thus far have been very forgiving of Ammons's excesses in *The Snow Poems*, which will grow increasingly offensive to policers of correct speech—what to do, say, with poems titled "Things Change, the Shit Shifts," images of "hairpie dinners," wishes of "better laid than never or up," aphorisms such as "sores run / scabs / stay put" (SP, 4, 73, 154, 182). What can we make of a poet who says, elegaically, that a poem is a walk, but then turns around and says that "on the walk a fart worked its / way loose" (SP, 177)? He would be a hard poet to talk about in classrooms, especially if other passages make those above look rather tame—wildness in language that gets, as Whitman said of himself, "hankering, mystical, gross, and nude." Which, of course, is the point: Ammons is putting up, in *The Snow Poems*, to back up all his poetics-talk: "Our experience of poetry is least injured when we accept it as useless, meaningless, and nonrational" (SM, 19), and "Nothing that can be said about it in words is worth saying" (SM, 20).

The Snow Poems is a flaunting of critical intrusion—verbal intrusion—into the experience of encountering a poem. Ammons's general disdain for critics is plain from both his prose and poems, especially *Tape* and *The Snow Poems*, which contains a truly violent attack on contemporary criticism in the form of the quotidian narrative arranged, at its beginning, in six regular stanzas of tercets. "I cut the quince down the other day into so / many stalks it all made a big bundle / upon the lawn high as my head I'd say" it begins (9), in an ironic deconstruction of "The Quince Bush." While cleaning his yard, he's cleaning up the landscape of his poems, taking away the symbol we've wanted to play with: "quince" suggestive of Stevens, quince as leafless but thorny as it blossoms. The experience of dismantling his quince leads him to "whiff ... eighty times, / the universal smell of rotten meat" that a dead blue jay has brought to the scene of the poet's walk in "Here I Sit, Fifty in the." Here, significantly, as the poet sits in the bubble of turning that critical age, that pivot, the regular stanzas cease, and the poet will not go back to them for the remainder of the book. Immediately after we've been hit with the smell of death, the stanzaic structure of the narrative disintegrates: "I do not, can not, will not / care for plain simple things / with straightforward fences round them" (9).

The act of the poet cutting down—literally deconstructing—the predominant image of several of his poems is one of protest; but over the stench of death, and after he has gotten out of the straightforward fences of stanzas, he finds "a live jay lit on the pearlimb (pearl imb) / over the dead jay

/ ... shrieked ... / a scolding for dying / or grief trying to make itself heard" (SP, 10). We might wonder if the "jay" of "Sight Seed" might be the same jay of "Winter Scene," the one that can turn a winter's bare branches blue. But we can be sure that the dead, stinking jay is equivalent to what Ammons thinks of theory. This version of Ammons's attack on theory and interpretation is much harsher than *Tape's* playful observation: "look: it's snowing ... / without theory / and beyond help ... / I see black & / white ... / if I were / looking with the snow, / I'd see all white" (T, 100). But it remains consistent with other notions: "Writing about the stone cannot replace the stone" (SM, 32), and "the only representation / of the sea's floor / is the sea's floor itself" (T, 184).

So it would seem natural that critics might not like the larger view of things, the harsher one that *The Snow Poems* represents, but one that's needed to understand *Tape's* larger contexts more forcefully, beyond the intellectualizing *Tape* allows us. *The Snow Poems* pushes us into a much more brutal confrontation with the ideas we are more comfortable with in *Tape's* niceties. Still, both poems recommend—insist—that we pay attention to the weather. *Tape* does it in its controlled fashion, but *The Snow Poems* explores it in its intensity in ways organically different from *Tape's* successful use of the adding machine tape to "grow" itself. Where *Tape* seeks to become "a long / thin / poem / employing certain / classical considerations" (1) on an adding machine tape the poet has purchased at a hardware store, *The Snow Poems*, in its first poem, "Words of Comfort," announces that it will be "a drone, narrative, longer than mourning" (SP, 1). We don't know how long this dirge is going to go on, and we're thrust uneasily into a world that's "misty drizzling" (SP, 1). Sometimes, it will seem, we'll find ourselves in a sort of perverse Hallmark-Cards writers' workshop, where aphorisms might sound churchy but just as likely will be as earthy as the "whiff of earthworm" (22).

But whereas the task of *Tape* proves doable, not Sysiphean after all, the original task of *The Snow Poems* proved impossible:

> I had meant to write a book of a thousand pages.... I wanted to say here is a thousand pages of trash that nevertheless indicates that every image and every event on the planet and everywhere else is significant and could be great poetry, sometimes is in passages and lines. But I stopped at 300. I had worn myself and everybody else out. But I went on long enough to give the idea that we really are in a poetically inexhaustible world, inside and out. (SM, 66)

Both *The Snow Poems* and *Tape* reiterate Ammons's dominant metaphors taken directly from the atmosphere that we live in (though *The*

Snow Poems has a lot more time, and thus weather, to play with, for the poet to watch): the settling into levels, or zones, that belies the illusion of distinctness, of fixity, and proves flux and flow, growth and decay. Weather itself becomes—as the poet wishes it to become—a perfect metaphor for proving the inexhaustible source of poetry about us. It controls not only the elements that we take for our symbols, the objects in the world about us, obscuring, rearranging, sculpting what we see, but also us, when we're not too removed from it. Schneider quotes one critic of *The Snow Poems*, who said, "We talk about the weather when we are self-conscious or embarrassed, when we are looking for distractions, and when we want to break the awkward silence of having nothing at all to say."[47] She was probably not a farmer, and self-depracatingly Ammons might say to her, in his courtly fashion, should they meet, "people who have a life / to live don't notice weather" (SP, 93). But under his breath, he'd just as likely say, "when we / have nothing / significant / to say / spelling it / right matters" (SP, 65).

This is the kind of critical attitude that no doubt troubles poets such as Ammons, whose experience is so radically different from that of most academics. He has said plainly, "I had wanted to stay a farmer.... I love the land and the terrible dependency on the weather.... [M]y life and my family and people around me depended on weather and seasons and farming and seeds and things like that" (SM, 60, 105). Yet, the assertion of the individual critic's view—in this case the bold cliché quoted above, assuming that "we" talk of weather only when "we" have nothing to say—as a universal one denies the individual experience that Ammons seeks in his poetry. For him, clearly, weather has lots of meaning, import, and whether we learn to appreciate it or not, we should, it seems, at least give him credit for being passionate in his weather obsessions and, perhaps, look a second time at what he *does* with weather, which sometimes, for *some* people, might be the *only* thing worth talking about, despite what the occasional critic might believe.

Still, good intentions don't necessarily make good poetry, as *The Snow Poems'* critics should all be quick to agree, though clearly they'd not be of one accord in defining "good." But that, for Ammons, would seem to be how he'd prefer things to be, for *The Snow Poems* was written as an affront to critical dissecting of poetry. McFee calls it "anti-formalist," but it's really more anti-poetry, at least in the sense of how poetry is taught and discussed in universities. Olson, the Black Mountain poets, and the Beats—Kerouac and William Burroughs especially—fall outside the realm of *how* we learned to think about literature. In their push for the spontaneous and the new, they have dug new critical furrows yet to be fully explored. Ammons is clearly playing in their collective "fields."

As if giving example of Kerouac's insistence that we not pause to think of "proper" words, Ammons at one point in *The Snow Poems* writes "whiff of earthworm / (I almost said earthroom)" (22–23). Critics have generally disregarded *The Snow Poems* because of such "doodling," which Ammons took to a new level by including "his second thoughts in the margin" of some poems.[48] What he has also done in these instances, where lines run in parallel columns, is create a tension within the physical body of his poem that is constant, what Olson had sought in the use of objects in his. Ammons also suggests in his special arrangement of text blocks on the physical page the cut-up methods and permutated sentence experiments of William S. Burroughs and Brion Gysin, both of which employ "the principle of randomness" and seek, creation of art through "the success of its own accident."[49] Like Ammons, Burroughs is intrigued by "how word and image get around on very ... complex association lines." Burroughs calls "The Waste Land" the first "great cut-up collage," notes that Tristan Tzara did similar work, and that Dos Passos uses the same idea of incorporating the artist's collage method into writing to produce "The Camera Eye" sections of U.S.A. "Cut-ups," he explains, "establish new connections between images, and one's range of vision consequently expands."[50]

Ammons also goes beyond the literal, linear reading we yearn to give to words on a page when he employs in the physical arrangement of text-blocks a kind of concrete poetry that represents, in its visual display on the page, the flow of rivers, the play of tides, and the breakup of geological forces. Schneider notices a similar technique in "Ridge Farm," with its text blocks "resembling the irregularities of topology on a ridge."[51] But when we've been trained to seek in writing coherence and flow of logic, not image and association, it's difficult to maintain the distance required to "look" anew at a printed page, to drop back for a moment and study how Ammons, for example, displays "Hard Fist" in *The Snow Poems* (44–47), a section representative of both the collage, or cut-up, technique and the topographic display.

Ammons's *The Snow Poems* is a rugged version of *Tape*, more graphic and mournful and tragic. In *Tape*, the poet recognizes, finally, that "it's as brave to accept / boundaries, / ... & do the best you can" (T, 201); its ending is final, with the curl of its tape: "so long" (T, 205). *The Snow Poems*, on the other hand, ends enigmatically, on-goingly, an obvious fragment and thus, again, more difficult to discuss. Given the extent and range of the poet's word play throughout, its last line, the single word "we(l)come" might translate as "we'll come," "well, come," "we/I come," or "welcome," as an ironic response to the critical "thank you" the poet knows he will not receive.

Given past criticisms of *The Snow Poems*, it may not return to print anytime soon. Both it and *Tape* are important poems to consider together because they provide a core for seeing virtually all of Ammons's work as one vast poem about his own personal poetic sense of wonder and exploration. Willard Spiegelman has already noted that the differences in Ammons's long poems and his lyrics are quantitative only, that otherwise his poems, "from the very beginning" have not changed or developed, "formally or technically, in any significant ways.[52] Although both books have been discussed as diaries, Ammons has not yet been looked at as an autobiographical poet, perhaps because the poetry of his autobiography is not of days of momentous import; future biographers will find little of significance to report, based on the facts of the poet's life, as revealed in his poems. Kerouac, on the other hand, is most easily dismissed, when he's dismissed, by charges that he writes autobiography, not literature, that he has no aesthetic at work beyond the spewing of words on a page. Kerouac's are certainly bigger stories, his characters grander than a store clerk chanced to meet, their narratives more pressing and frantic than a casual walk to a brook, or the gentle play of sunshine and shade on a wall. Ammons, who employs the same aesthetic but doesn't talk about it nearly as much, remains firmly ensconced—at least with his shorter lyrics—in those arbiters of American lit, the college textbooks, as he has for the last twenty-five years.

Still, Kerouac's *On the Road* is an important book for what it says about the boundaries of America; critics have yet to notice, for example, how the main characters find the "wilderness" of modern America to be in its roads, which—like jazz—afford for them the same access to an eternal now that Emerson found in the woods. They bounce off the "walls" of America like Melville's Bartleby looking for a place to be, some thing to do. Nor have they caught yet what seems an essential part of Kerouac's story, the home his narrator always returns to when things collapse into sadness, as they always do at their ends. Ammons, in *Tape*, might be writing that alternate version, "*Off* the Road." He says, for example, that his "story is how / a man comes home / from haunted / lands and transformations" (T, 9). He doesn't need the "going" of Kerouac's road, because he has already felt "the bitterness of fate: / what it means to / drive away from the / house" (60).

Both Kerouac and Ammons are working with variations of what M. M. Bakhtin referred to as the road chronotope, which "permits everyday life to be realized" within its narrative. Bakhtin's idea of "chronotope" comes, as he explains it, from science, indicating for us the temporal and spatial relationships that are artistically expressed in literature. Like Einstein's theory of relativity—and rheomode—it indicates for us that space and time are inseparable, that time is the fourth dimension of space. Bakhtin's discussion is clearly directed to classical forms of literature, but his definition of "adventure-time" in novels (whose traits he also sees in drama and epic poems) seems perfectly suited as descriptive of both Ammons's and Kerouac's work: Moments of adventure time occur when the normal course of events is interrupted, providing an opening for the intrusion of nonhuman forces, which then take the initiative. The temporal marker, for Bakhtin, is inseparable from the spatial marker. In using the chronotope of the road, the writer permits everyday life to be realized within his narrative; choice controls the path he will take. However, once on the path, chance encounters predominate. The *Tape for the Turn of the Year* and *The Snow Poems*, like *Visions of Cody*, combine elements of what Bakhtin, using Dante's *Inferno* as example, calls a "vertical chronotope," which is a world outside of time's flow, with one where spatial and temporal coordinates define human fates. Bakhtin's "road" is formed when time fuses with space and flows in it; it is "both a point of new departures and a place for events to find their denouement."[53] Both Kerouac and Ammons sometimes take that new departure into a bubble of time that holds itself, for a while, outside the flow, in vertical time.

Ammons in his poems and Kerouac, in *Vision of Cody* especially, demonstrate that the notion of a "denouement" might not so easily apply to life as it does to literature. Ammons suggests, in the process, that if we can break our conditioning to expect in literature the neat containers and resolute endings we never get in life, *Tape* and *The Snow Poems* will reveal to us, if we read openly and freely enough and translate the "lessons" of our reading into the daily "walks" of our lives, how to be less rigid in our thinking, more considerate of differing points of view, less likely to see things from the hierarchical and polar views of Western philosophy. We might, along the way, even learn how to water bees. Ammons might be talking to the critic in us all when, after giving us an elaborate lesson in this arcane procedure, he writes near the end of *The Snow Poems*:

> if people who can think of
> nothing to do would
> water bees
> they would find themselves
> working with the principles
> of the universe ... (260)

NOTES

1. Ammons, *Tape for the Turn of the Year* (Ithaca, N.Y.: Cornell University Press, 1965), referred to in the text as T; Kerouac, *On the Road* (New York, N.Y.: Viking, 1965), referred to in the text as OTR.

2. D. H. Lawrence, "Preface to the American Edition of *New Poems*" [1919], in *Poetics of the New American Poetry*, ed. Allen and Tallman (New York: Grove, 1973), 71, 70.

3. Walt Whitman, "Song of Myself," in *Leaves of Grass* (New York: New York University Press, 1965), 910.

4. Ibid., 915.

5. Moriarty says over and over, "God exists, we know time" (115); Ammons, for example, recommends throwing "yourself / into the river / of going" (T, 119).

6. Kerouac, "The Origins of Joy in Poetry" [1958], in *Good Blonde & Others* (San Francisco: Grey Fox, 1993), 74.

7. Lawrence, "Preface," 71.

8. Ralph Waldo Emerson, "Self-Reliance" [1841], in *The Complete Essays and Other Writings* (New York: Modern Library, 1950), 637.

9. Robert A. Hipkiss, *Jack Kerouac: Prophet of the New Romanticism* (Lawrence: Regents Press of Kansas, 1976). 80.

10. John Tytell, *Naked Angels: The Lives and Literature of the Beat Generation* (New York: McGraw-Hill, 1976), 17.

11. Tim Hunt, *Kerouac's Crooked Road: Development of a Fiction* (Storrs Conn.: Archon, 1981), 106–21.

12. Donald Reimann, "A. R. Ammons: Ecological Naturalism and the Romantic Tradition," *Twentieth Century Literature* 31, no. 1 (Spring 1985): 35.

13. Ibid.

14. Ann Charters, *Kerouac* (New York: Warner, 1974), 139, 124.

15. Kerouac, *Selected Letters: 1940–56* (NewYork: Viking, 1995), 325.

16. Charters, *Kerouac*, 147; Hunt offers the most thorough narrative of the scroll draft of *On the Road*. Kerouac himself over the next years enjoyed rewriting the circumstances of its composition, and combined with others' claims, time's passing, and memories' reconstructions, the exact circumstances are probably impossible to reconstruct—even the scroll's length is debated. Ginsberg first used the term "spontaneous bop prosody" to describe Kerouac's method, which Kerouac first described as "sketching" in 1951 as he tried to transform his first *Road* manuscript from a traditional narrative into a "thickly layered multidimensional conscious and unconscious invocation" of Cassady's character. His friend, the painter Ed White, said to him, "Why don't you just sketch in the streets like a painter but with words?" (Tytell, *Naked Angels*, 143), a description that would seem to fit perfectly what Ammons does in *Tape*, except that he sits in his study instead of the street. After Sputnik in 1957 (and the resultant coinage by the media of the term "beatnik"), Kerouac sometimes used the term "Space Age Prose," because "when the astronauts are flowing through space and time they too have no chance to stop and reconsider and go back" (Kerouac, "The First Word" [1967], in *Good Blonde & Others*, 190).

Cassady's 23,000-word letter, sometimes known as the "Joan Anderson letter," was shared by Kerouac with several of his friends and ultimately lost. Kerouac received the letter on 30 December 1950 and immediately proclaimed it "the greatest story" every written by an American, the beginning of an "American Renaissance." He compared it favorably in the process to Dostoyevsky, Joyce, Céline, Proust, Dreiser, Wolfe, Melville, Hemingway, and Fitzgerald. (See also Gerald Nicosia, *Memory Babe: A Critical Biography of Jack Kerouac* (Carbondale: Southern Illinois University Press), 336–38.) The portion of Cassady's autobiography published as *The First Third* (San Francisco: City Lights, 1971) includes a few letters and fragments.

17. Hipkiss, *Jack Kerouac*, 86, 78.

18. Regina Weinreich, *The Spontaneous Poetics of Jack Kerouac* (Carbondale: Southern Illinois University Press), 112

19. Nicosia, *Memory Babe*, 453.

20. Jack Kerouac, "Essentials of Spontaneous Prose," hereafter cited in-text as ESP.

Charters, *Kerouac*, 189. *Good Blonde & Others* collects Kerouac's various statements on poetics, which also were published in the *Evergreen Review* (1956), the *Chicago Review* (1958) Grove Press's *The New American Poetry* (1960), *Writers Digest* (1962), and *Escapade*, the men's magazine (1959–60, 1967).

21. Kerouac, "The First Word," 189–90.

22. Reimann, "A. R. Ammons," 24.

23. Kerouac, *Vanity of Dulouz* [1967] (London: Quartet, 1974), 130.

24. Holder, *A. R. Ammons* (Boston, Twayne, 1978), 161; Reimann, "A. R. Ammons," 35.

25. Charles Olson, "Projective Verse," in Allen and Tallman, *Poetics of the New American Poetry*, New York: Grove, 1973. Hereafter cited in text as PV.

26. Hipkiss, *Jack Kerouac*, 80. Other writers at Black Mountain College in the early 1950s were Fielding Dawson, Michael Rumaker, and Jonathan Williams. Donald Allen's anthology *The New American Poetry: 1945–60* defines the Black Mountain writers as those who had published in Creeley's *Black Mountain Review* and the journal *Origin*, begun by Cid Corman in 1951. Mary Emma Harris points out: "Although there is often a common point of view shared by Black Mountain artists, writers, dancers, and musicians, there is not a Black Mountain style" (*The Arts at Black Mountain* [Cambridge: MIT Press, 1987], 245). As a result, many writers who studied or taught at BMC are not generally included in the group known as "Black Mountain writers": Russell Edson, Elaine Gottlieb, Francine du Plessix Gray, James Leo Herlihy, Jane Mayhall, Hilda Morley, M. C. Richards, and José Yglesias, among others.

27. Lawrence, "Preface," 70.

28. Robert Duncan, "Towards an Open Universe," in *Poetics of the New American Poetry*, ed. Allen and Tallman, 217, 224.

29. Kerouac, it could be argued, sees his narrator, Sal Paradise, and Moriarty/Cassady primarily as subjects who act on objects such as cars, women, drugs. Occasionally, the objects seem to be doing the acting, but always in conjunction with one or the other of the main characters, never alone, "in a field." Action in *Road* is, in a sense, the object, and the narrator of this action delights in "lyrical interference" of the individual who witnesses and records.

30. Duncan, "Towards an Open Universe," 28.

31. Schneider, *A. R. Ammons and the Poetics of Widening Scope* (Madison, N.J.: Fairleigh Dickinson University Press, 1994), 194, 201.

32. A. R. Ammons, Letter to author, 30 Oct. 95.

33. Waggoner has successfully reclaimed "visionary," attaching it to its roots in "vision," and he includes Ammons in his catalog of contemporary poets who write visionary poems and whose "[i]maginative, interpretive perception, both subjective and objective," shape and dominate their point of view (*American Visionary Poetry* [Baton Rouge: Louisiana State University Press, 1982], 3, 12). Schneider also uses "visionary" as a way of describing one who sees "better or farther, deeper or more truly, than we," and adds that the "visionary poet is not 'mystical'" (71–72). Yet, I would suggest that Ammons is "visionary" in both senses of the term. Ammons uses his acute physical vision to see, in multiplicities, a unity that seems to apply, for discussion's sake, to what R. M. Bucke called "cosmic consciousness," a term no longer discussed in literary studies. But Ammons's description of this singular experience—both in prose and in its repeated employment as image in his subsequent poetry—fits neatly with how Bucke defined the "intellectual illumination" and "transfiguration" that cosmic consciousness affords. (*Cosmic Consciousness* [New York: Dutton, 1901]. See page 79, especially, for the eleven common traits.) Ammons's "vision" might well have been highlighted by a "subjective light" that allowed him to see more clearly—or deeply—what he had looked at before; the experience

afforded him both moral and intellectual illumination; his poems have often indicated his sense of immortality, and the loss of his fear of death and sense of sin. The experience of his awakening was sudden, and it came upon a man of impressive intellectual, moral, and physical maturity. Many of his poems can be read as examples of what Schneider calls "vision therapy," allowing us "to see better and understand more" (72).

34. Kerouac, *Vanity of Dulouz*, 1.

35. Weinreich, *Spontaneous Poetics*, 3.

36. Kerouac, "The First Word," 188–89, 191.

37. Holder, *A. R. Ammons*, 110.

38. Schneider, *A. R. Ammons*, 157. Schneider, who is quoting DeRosa, does an excellent job of summarizing the critical reception to *The Snow Poems* (155–66).

39. Vendler, *Part of Nature, Part of Us: Modern American Poets* (Cambridge: Harvard University Press, 1980), 331.

40. Nowotny, *Time, The Modern and Postmodern Experience* (Cambridge: Polity, 1994), 21, 24–27.

41. Herbert Rappaport, *Marking Time* (New York: Simon and Schuster, 1990), 173. The point of Rappaport's book, interestingly, is to demonstrate how to use, in the treatment of psychological disorders, his RTL (Rappaport Time Line), which is constructed by patients in therapy on a 24" piece of adding machine tape.

42. Schneider, *A. R. Ammons*, 192.

43. Weinreich, *Spontaneous Poetics*, 58–61.

44. Schneider, *A. R. Ammons*, 166

45. Vendler, *Part of Nature*, 369.

46. Michael McFee, "A. R. Ammons and The Snow Poems Reconsidered," *Chicago Review* 33, no. 1 (Summer 1981): 33, 36–37.

47. Schneider, *A. R. Ammons*, 190.

48. Waggoner, *American Visionary Poetry*, 172.

49. Charles Olson, *The Special View of History* (Berkeley, Calif,: Oyez, 1970), 48. Olson spoke of the importance of accidents to the "creation" of art as well as life in a series of lectures delivered in the last days of Black Mountain College and collected in 1970. The best explanation of the Burroughs/Gysin experiments with word collages is in *The Third Mind* (New York: Viking, 1978).

50. Burroughs, *The Third Mind*, 3–4.

51. Schneider, *A. R. Ammons*, 190.

52. Willard Spiegelman, *The Didactic Muse* (Princeton: Princeton University Press, 1989), 112.

53. M. M. Bakhtin, *The Dialogic Imagination* (Austin: University of Texas Press, 1981), 84, 94, 120, 157, 243–44. Dante's world is "vertical," not horizontal, because there is no past or future, only an eternal now, a single time where all is simultaneous.

JAMES T. JONES

The Place Where Three Roads Meet:
Pic, On the Road, *and* Visions of Cody

> ... attractions and hostility toward members of both sexes are inherent in
> the triangular structure of the Oedipus complex.

Nowhere is the process of revision more revealing than in the composition of Kerouac's most famous novel, *On the Road*, which went through five distinct versions, the last three of which were eventually published as *Pic*, *On the Road*, and *Visions of Cody* (Hunt 98). After struggling with writing and editing his first published novel for almost four years, Jack built up a new kind of athletic stamina that he used to focus his continued attention on this major work for nine years (1948–57), even as he completed six other books. His persistence in the face of repeated rejections from publishers suggests that he viewed his road novel as the most important book of his career. In the various versions of his travels, he takes events that in Sophocles's play happen before the main action and so are described only in retrospect by Oedipus and an old family retainer, the only two surviving witnesses to the murder of Laius, and makes them the focal point of the drama. In the process, he wrote himself out of the imitative style of *The Town and the City* and into his own voice, making "the manuscript history of *On the Road* ... the history of Kerouac's development as a writer" (Hunt 78).

In the first two versions of the story, Kerouac tried to expand the

From *Jack Kerouac's Duluoz Legend: the Mythic Form of an Autobiographical Fiction*. © 1999 by the Board of Trustees, Southern Illinois University.

description of postwar American Bohemia he had given in *The Town and the City* (in fact, he once referred to *On the Road* as the second novel in the Martin trilogy [SK 7]), and his later title for these drafts, *The Beat Generation*, suggests a sociological rather than a literary treatment. Years later, trying to make the best of the publicity that followed the publication of *On the Road*, Jack also used the title *The Beat Generation* for a play that served as the basis for the plot of *Pull My Daisy*, Robert Frank and Alfred Leslie's avant garde film about an incident that occurred in Neal and Carolyn Cassady's Los Gatos, California, home in 1955 (Hunt 107; described in Cassady 2.64–66), though the title was eventually co-opted by Hollywood for the name of a "Beatsploitation" film. The third version, which Kerouac left unfinished until just before he died (Gifford and Lee 159), tells the tale of a true outsider, an eleven-year-old black boy, Pictorial Review Jackson, who is rescued from his abusive relatives by his brother, Slim.

The foremost critic of the various versions of Kerouac's road story, Tim Hunt, observes that *Pic*, as the novella came to be called, is Kerouac's least autobiographical work. However, like eleven-year-old Mickey Martin's first literary venture, *Mike Martin Explores the Merrimac*, *Pic* is based on *Huckleberry Finn* (Hunt 102), converting the image of Huck sneaking out of the Widow Douglas's window to meet Tom in the first chapter of Twain's novel into the title of chapter 6. In light of recent scholarship about the African-American origins of Huck's character, Kerouac's use of the story seems prescient. But though an important river scene does occur in his cross-country journey, Pic's real river is the road. Kerouac also imported into this text one of his earliest stories, the episode of the prophet on Times Square, written for a group of his literary peers in Lowell in 1941; a chapter about a cookie factory, which had been edited out of *The Town and the City*; and the first appearance of the Ghost of the Susquehanna, which he repeated in *On the Road* and *Visions of Cody*. In addition, the setting of the opening of the novel pays homage to Kerouac's growing interest in the South, specifically North Carolina, where his sister had moved after the war to raise a family and where Kerouac was to spend a good deal of time during the composition of his road story. Further, the title character comes from the miniature baseball game Kerouac describes in *Doctor Sax* (Isaacs 16-C), and his last name serves to connect him with the identity of his author. So while the characters of *Pic* bear no resemblance to identifiable figures in Kerouac's life, the story itself still has an autobiographical ring.

The most interesting feature of the novella, indeed, is its clear connection with the Oedipal themes of the Duluoz Legend. For while his readers may find Kerouac's use of African-American dialect disconcerting, even offensive, they will certainly see the connection he is trying to make between the legend of his own life and the curse under which the character Pic lives his early years. This curse is not Original Sin, as Gerald Nicosia has suggested (696), but something far more specific. In fact, Pic's father, Alpha Jackson, had for some unexplained reason blinded his father-in-law (160), the "serpentine" Grandpa Jelkey. At one point, the cyclopean maternal grandfather inspects Pic with "one great big yaller eye" as unseeing as the other, which is entirely missing. Grandpa Jelkey functions as a combination Oedipus and Tiresias, bearing his blindness as the result of some incident presumably involving his daughter, the elder Jackson's wife, and also serving to announce the curse on his son-in-law's family. Even though Pic's Aunt Gastonia, his mother's sister, tries to shield him from both her father-in-law's and her husband's wrath, insisting, "'It ain't his fault what his father done to your eyes'" (135), in the end Pic must flee the place of the curse with the aid of his older brother, Slim (whose given name is John), a zoot-suited, jive-talking hipster musician, who wants to take his little brother to New York City. When Uncle Simeon threatens to brain Slim with a shovel, Gastonia drives home the pervasive nature of the curse by warning him: "'[D]on't come here fetchin no chile from outen my roof and learn him the ways of evil like you done learned from your pappy ... you no better'n your pappy ever was and no better'n no *Jackson* ever was'" (144, italics in original). Here, it seems, the brother, who also bears the Oedipal curse, must function as the shepherd who rescues the son from the house of the curse, thereby delivering him to his fate by a more circuitous and painful route. Kerouac's character names—which are generally ironic—suggest here that the author has identified himself with both the older brother and with the family (Jarvis 226).

After Slim kidnaps Pic, Pic begins to address his narrative specifically to his paternal grandfather, whose death at the outset of the novel forced Pic to move in with his aunt's family. Though Pic (like Sal Paradise) harbors a mysterious fear that he has forgotten to do something before leaving (*Pic* 156), the brothers' bus ride to New York City presents a lighthearted version of Kerouac's own move from the town to the city, the source of so much confusion in the earlier episodes of the Legend. On the road north, Slim shows Pic a photo of his wife, Sheila, telling him, "'[S]he'll be your new mother now'" (159). Slim also summarizes their father's crime, explaining that Alpha's wife, their mother, had died insane after their father was released from prison. The older brother insists that their father, wherever he may be, "'was a wild *man* and a *bad man*'" and concludes ominously, "'[Y]ou and me come from the *dark*'" (160, italics in original). As the brothers leave their curse behind, Slim tries to teach Pic American history starting with the Civil War, and as they move from country to town to city, Pic also travels forward an entire century in time. Arriving in Harlem, Pic likes Sheila at first sight and she blushes when he speaks to her (180).

When Sheila discovers she is pregnant, the new family decides to move to California, where Slim has spent most of his time since leaving North Carolina, to stay temporarily with her sister Zelda until they can find a permanent home. To save money, Slim and Pic hitchhike to the coast, while Sheila takes a transcontinental bus. The trip west, though sketchy and incomplete, features a few symbolic scenes. Even before they leave the city, Slim and Pic encounter a Salvation Army street meeting, where a ninety-year-old hobo also bound for California, threading his way through the crowd, shouts prophetically, "'*Go moan for man*'" (212, italics in original). Meanwhile, the street preacher foretells the televising of the Second Coming and advises everyone to "'live as best you can and be hereinafter kind to one another'" (216). On the road in New Jersey, the brothers spot the old hobo again, and this time he reminds Pic of Jesus (220). At the Susquehanna River in Pennsylvania, another hobo, confused about his own course, mistakenly leads them back towards New York City instead of on to Pittsburgh. After they discover they have taken the wrong road, Slim determines that the hobo must have been "some kinda ghost of the river" (229). Outside Pittsburgh, Slim and Pic take refuge in a Catholic church, where the priest invites Pic to sing in the choir and offers them a job with room and board, the last fully developed scene in the book. A single page of narrative takes the Jackson boys the rest of the way to the West Coast, where Sheila rewards them with a big dinner, followed by a Freudian dessert (Hipkiss 8), in Pic's words, a "cherry banana spoon ice cream split" (236).

Though the brothers encounter only a ghost of their father on the road where they take the wrong fork, Pic nevertheless has an allegorical significance (Nicosia 695). The brother serves as both rescuer and guide in the protagonist's travels, and if their shared Oedipal curse condemns them to wandering both before and after the death of the father, it also provides them with a bond of love so strong it forges a new family, one in which the brother's wife also mothers his sibling. Perhaps this allegory appealed to Kerouac's third wife, because when he undertook to finish the novel in the last months of his life, Stella objected to the original ending, in which Slim and Pic were to have met and joined up with Dean Moriarty and Sal Paradise, the corresponding characters in *On the Road*. That unpublished version of *Pic* would have given the story an effect similar to that of *The Town and the City*, in which the actions of the older brothers mirror the actions of the younger brothers, and clarified its connection to the Duluoz Legend. As it stands, they reach their goal of the nurturing wife and mother with too little difficulty.

The next version of Kerouac's road adventure took a form that symbolizes both his demand for speed of composition and his continuing quest for spiritual renewal. Though the conservation department of the New York Public Library has definitely determined that it is typed on a yellow teletype roll, as Kerouac informed Charters while she was compiling the first bibliography of his works (*Bibliography* 19), many Kerouac fans still believe that the manuscript of *On the Road*, written in three weeks in April 1951, is constructed of long sheets of rice art paper taped together end-to-end to a length of 120 feet, perhaps because of Kerouac's own published description of it (*BD* 77). This postmodern scroll bears a striking resemblance to the Dead Sea Scrolls, the ancient New Testament manuscripts discovered in 1947 that electrified the Christian world throughout the 1950s. Apparently, one impetus for its composition came from Jack's reading of the manuscript of *Go*, a realistic novel about Beat life written by his friend and rival John Clellon Holmes (Turner 119). Kerouac's new "spontaneous prose" was inspired by the stream-of-consciousness letters of Neal Cassady, an intelligent, street-wise, fast-living young man from Denver. Born in 1926, the same year that Gerard died (Kerouac makes the connection explicit in *VC* 97), Cassady had come east in the fall of 1946, hoping to enroll in Columbia University under the sponsorship of a Denver alumnus he had met. He was introduced to Jack as someone who might help him learn to write, and for the next decade, Kerouac served as literary tutor while this surrogate younger brother taught him how to live. The novel that immortalizes Neal in the character of Dean Moriarty covers the period from 1947 to 1951, and its origin coincides with the latter stages of editing *The Town and the City*. In fact, the protagonist of the later novel, Sal Paradise (whose name derives from a comment about "the sad American paradise," reported in *The Town and the City*, made by Allen Ginsberg [*T&C* 369] and whom Kerouac explicitly identifies as a version of Jack Duluoz [*SD* 321]), is just about finished with "one of the best chapters of the book" when he goes out for his first night out with Dean (6). The completion, acceptance, and publication of the half-finished manuscript that Sal leaves lying on the desk in his room at his aunt's house in New Jersey provide the background for the action of *On the Road* (11–12).

The first sentence of the published version of *On the Road* varies significantly from the first sentence of the scroll version, in that it substitutes the breakup of the narrator's marriage for the death of the narrator's father as the controlling circumstance for his first meeting with Dean. In Oedipal terms, this substitution shows that Kerouac was at once aware of the connection and also unwilling to invent a fictional pretext that disregarded it. This brother-figure, like Slim Jackson, enters the scene to rescue Sal

Paradise, who, like Pic, is living with his aunt. Ostensibly in search of pure kicks, Dean actually leads Sal on a search for Dean's father, a pitiful wino and jailbird. At the same time, he also provides a continuous series of lessons in how *not* to be a successful husband and father. Sal's aunt sizes Dean up at a glance, deciding that he is a "madman" (6), and in the only passage in the novel in which she speaks at length, Mrs. P chastises him for fathering children and leaving them to fend for themselves, essentially repeating his own father's abandonment of his family (253). As Sal learns to see Dean as a flawed saint, a "HOLY GOOF" (194), rather than a perfect hero in the course of their adventures, he grows more confident of his own desire for a wife and family (116), yet the novel concludes with only a promise of the satisfaction of that desire.

Indeed, Sal Paradise's romantic view of marriage makes it realistically unattainable. As Dean tantalizes him with the prospect of sharing two of his wives, Sal struggles to recover from an unspecified illness brought on by the "miserably weary split-up" with his own wife. Between his father's death in April 1946 and his first meeting with Neal Cassady, Kerouac did in fact suffer from the first of many bouts of phlebitis, dangerous blood clots in his legs that threatened to incapacitate or even kill him, while his first wife, Edie Parker, was arranging to have their marriage annulled in Detroit. Sal's dilemma gives him the feeling, common to many victims of incest, "that everything was dead" (3). Though his relationship with Dean seems to promise new life in the form of reconciliation with a lost father and the sharing of his brother's wife, it actually leads him farther from his dream, and Sal's hopeful tone at the end of the novel belies the damage done by his Oedipal situation.

Many of the minor characters and most of the episodes of *On the Road* expose Kerouac's preoccupations with his brother, his father, and his mother. For instance, on his very first failed venture on the road, in which he mistakenly travels north in order to follow U.S. Route 6 all the way across the country, he is set straight by a man traveling with two women. This stranger's situation prefigures Sal's triangular relationship with Dean and Marylou and announces the Oedipal theme. His false start makes Sal realize that he must take "various roads and routes" (13) to appreciate the process of his journey, and henceforth he becomes more attentive to the deeper meaning of his human encounters, making almost every person he meets a messenger to unfold a part of his fate. This recalls the myth of Oedipus by making Sal's revelation a progressive affair rather than a single specific moment, a process that is still operating in *Satori in Paris*, the last installment of the Duluoz Legend. His ability to see the repeating patterns in his experience will create self-knowledge. Sal's stumbling block lies in his very sensitivity, so that practically every encounter on the road can be seen as an omen, every stranger a prophet. If Kerouac puts a Puritan spin on self-knowledge by viewing even the smallest incident in life as providential, he also invokes Freud's method in *The Psychopathology of Everyday* Life, determining that his true danger lies not in the Oedipal curse, but rather in the likelihood that his supersensitive self-consciousness will drive him mad.

In his first trip west alone, Sal Paradise suffers a serious loss of identity (*OTR* 17) parallel to the one parodied by the narrator in section two of Book One of *Vanity of Duluoz,* perhaps to indicate that the precondition for self-knowledge is to eradicate the most basic assumptions about one's own nature. After Sal recognizes that his "whole life was a haunted life," he is able to cross "the dividing line" between his past and his future (17). A fellow hitchhiker, Eddie, makes off with Sal's shirt, carrying part of Sal's identity with him. This character, connected by Carlo Marx to Dean, whom he refers to pointedly as "Oedipus Eddie" (48), turns up in Denver after Sal has made contact with his gang there. Eddie, however, has joined his girlfriend, and when he and Sal land jobs at a wholesale produce market, only Eddie shows up for work (47). Sal is too busy with his journey of self-exploration to settle down, and his irresponsible male attitude toward marriage may have been one of the features of *On the Road* that delayed its publication (Ehrenreich 55).

On "the greatest ride in [Sal's] life" on the way to Denver on the back of a truck driven by two young farmer brothers from Minnesota (24), almost everyone already has a traveling companion, including Mississippi Gene and his "charge," a sixteen-year-old kid. Sal pairs up with a suspicious-looking character on his way to Montana to visit his father. Slim is one of four characters by that name in the novel, including one Duluoz first met in the Navy psychiatric ward during the war, here called Big Slim Hazard, short for William Holmes Hazard, similar to the name given the Burroughs character in *Vanity of Duluoz.* Of course, Slim is also the nickname of Pic's older brother. Mississippi Gene, coincidentally, is acquainted with Big Slim, and Gene himself reminds Sal of one of his other Bohemian friends in New York (28). At Cheyenne, Sal gets off the truck with the new Slim, Montana Slim (whose given name turns out to be a commonplace Richard), to investigate Wild West Week, a travesty of frontier life staged by the local Chamber of Commerce. Together they pick up a couple of girls, and when Sal's date rejects his romantic notions of the plains and tells him she wants to go to New York City, he feels he has "broken up the purity" of his entire trip (35). After making a "strange request" that Sal mail Slim's "tenderly polite" postcard to his father (34), Slim disappears. Two more uneventful rides take Sal into Denver, leaving the Oedipal reader with the impression that nearly every encounter in the novel will fit the pattern of two brothers looking for love on their way to find the father.

In Denver, Sal discovers that his gang has split into factions engaged in "a war with social overtones" (38). This scenario repeats earlier ones in the Duluoz Legend, such as the contrast between Jack's Lowell friends and the Bohemians in *The Town and the City*, in which a wholesome, small-town, adolescent brotherhood is contrasted with a corrupt, urban, adult one. In *On the Road*, the narrator makes it obvious that the good brothers (and sisters) come from the middle class, while the bad ones represent the lower class. The Dionysian Dean and Carlo have been ostracized by their upwardly mobile friends, and like some modern Natty Bumppo, Sal finds himself torn between civilized stability and semi-civilized excitement. Sal rooms for awhile with Roland Major, an imitative short-story writer, whose function seems to be to connect Kerouac's novel with Hemingway in some fashion. The critic Regina Weinreich, indeed, places *On the Road* in the genre of elegiac romance, in which the squire from the traditional quest romance becomes the central character in the Modernist novel. And in fact the relationship between Sal and Dean replicates the relationship between Jake Barnes and Robert Cohn in Hemingway's first novel, *The Sun Also Rises*, as well as that between Nick Caraway and Jay Gatsby in Fitzgerald's classic, *The Great Gatsby*. When Sal chooses to cast his lot with Dean, then, he breaks with his own middle-class ambitions and stakes out a new literary territory for his novel as well. Ironically, Major has just finished a story "about a guy who comes to Denver for the first time" (41). This guy, Phil, is surprised to find "arty types" out West, unlike his companion, "a mysterious and quiet fellow called Sam" (41). Sal's friend has unwittingly fictionalized their relationship in a way that anticipates Kerouac's own adaptation of the Modernist romance.

In short order, Carlo reveals to Sal just what kind of adventure he's in for in Denver. Dean is sleeping with both his wife, Marylou, and his new girlfriend and future wife, Camille. While Dean lives up to his role as what one critic has called a "phallic totem" (Tytell 62) by letting Camille draw him in the nude, "enormous dangle and all" (*OTR* 44), Sal gets stuck with a mousy waitress, Rita Bettencourt, and when he tries to practice on her Dean's belief that sex is the "one and only holy and important thing in life" (4), he fails miserably and Rita only yawns (56). In stark contrast to his brush with high society in Central City on the arm of the beautiful sister of a friend at the gloomy opera *Fidelio* (Beethoven's story of the triumph of a faithful Spanish wife in rescuing her husband from prison, from which Kerouac probably took the jailer's name, Rocco, giving it to Sal's brother in the novel), Sal's encounter with Rita ends with him lying on the grass with a bunch of hobos—whose lifestyle takes on mythic significance in the Duluoz Legend—who make him "want to get back on that road" (57). He is not yet ready for the humdrum life

Rita sees in store for herself. Carlo, meanwhile, is deriving intense pleasure from the moments he can steal with Dean between his assignations with the two women. In his basement apartment, which Sal likens to the "room of a Russian saint" (47), probably Father Zosima in *The Brothers Karamazov,* Carlo keeps busy writing rhapsodies to "Dean as a 'child of the rainbow' who bore his torment in his agonized priapus" (47–48). Apparently, in order to emulate his brother-figures, Sal must become either a super-stud or a homosexual. The route of ordinary married life seems closed off to him, and even when he recovers his shirt from Eddie just before leaving Denver, "the whole enormous sadness" of his identity is tied up in it (58).

On the way to San Francisco to meet yet another brother-figure, Sal passes through Dean's birthplace, Salt Lake City, "the least likely place for Dean to have been born" (59), and this fleeting reference serves as a transition to assure the reader that Sal's encounter with Remi Boncoeur will repeat and expand the details of the sibling rivalry. And indeed, among Remi's first instructions to Sal is the order "not to touch Lee Ann," his girlfriend (62), whose name resembles that of Neal Cassady's first wife, Luanne. The special significance of this taboo lies in the autobiographical connection Sal details in his introduction of Remi (who reappears in the first section of *Lonesome Traveler*), a character based on Kerouac's prep school buddy Henri Cru, who dated Edie Parker until Jack stole her away from him. According to the Kerouac biographies, Edie often used her relationship with Hank, as she called him, to make Jack jealous, and though Sal insists that Remi never blamed him "for taking off with his girl," Remi is obviously wary that the same situation will repeat itself. Sal believes that their past sharing of the same woman "always tied us together" (61), and when he sees Lee Ann sunbathing in the buff, he fantasizes about jumping "right in her" (73). Although the two men are supposedly awaiting a ship they can sail out on, Remi invents a scheme to keep them busy in the meantime. Sal is supposed to write a screenplay, which Remi's step-father will then help them sell in Hollywood. All the writer can come up with is "some gloomy tale about New York" (63), but Remi insists that he choose a subject that illustrates "the human-interest things of the world" (72). Remi and Sal's meeting with Remi's step-father turns into a fiasco when Sal gets drunk and flirts with the old doctor's young wife. At the same bar, Roland Major turns up, also drunk, and he and Sal end the evening "carrying on with the Hemingway imitation," Sal playing Sam to Roland's Jake. Sal's failure to complete the triangle with Remi and Lee Ann prompts him to decide to make his "trip a circular one" (78), and he ends his stay in San Francisco by climbing a mountain, where he has a vision of a young man holding hands with his girl, wondering aloud all the while, "'O where is the girl I love?'" (79).

This episode leads directly to one of the best-known passages in all of Kerouac's writing, a section that was published separately in 1953, four years before the release of the novel. "The Mexican Girl" presents the same scenario as the three novels Kerouac wrote during the latter stages of revising *On the Road*, that is, *Maggie Cassidy*, *The Subterraneans*, and *Tristessa*, all of which concern the rivalry of brother-figures and the intervention of a father-figure in their love for the same woman. Here the woman, Terry (presumably short for Teresa, suggestive of Saint Therese of Lisieux) is a married Mexican American with a child, and Sal's two-week relationship with her represents his first successful attempt at being a responsible husband and father and so escaping the orbit of Dean's gravitational pull. Nevertheless, the usual brother- and father-figures still intrude. After resolving their mutual fear of each other—Sal taking Terry for "common little hustler" (*OTR* 82), and she taking him for "'a goddam pimp'" (83)—they make love in a cheap hotel. In Terry's hometown, Sabinal, Sal imagines himself a character in Steinbeck's *Of Mice and Men*, another story about the difficulties of brotherly love and rivalry for a woman. While Sal waits, Terry rounds up her brother, "a wildbuck Mexican hotcat with a hunger for booze" (whose given name, like Montana Slim's, is Rickey), his buddy, Ponzo, who "had eyes for Terry," and her seven-year-old son, Johnny (91). Here again, instead of an exogamous mate, Kerouac finds for his character a woman with a child who bears his own name. After Sal rents a tent for himself, his baby, and his "baby boy" (94), he and Terry make love while Johnny looks on, anticipating a similar scene in *Big Sur* and recalling the suggestions in *Doctor Sax* that Kerouac himself may have witnessed his parents' lovemaking. Despite Terry's insistence that Johnny won't mind because he's asleep, Sal notices that "Johnny wasn't asleep and he said nothing" (94).

After a futile attempt to support his new family by picking cotton, Sal hears that Terry's husband is "out for" him, at the same time that some Okies tie a Mexican man to a tree and "beat him to a pulp with sticks" (97). Besides his fear of violence, Sal feels the pull of his own life calling him back, and he rationalizes that Terry must return to her family for the sake of her child. Terry's father calls her a whore, but her mother prevails upon him, as the mother "always does among the great fellaheen peoples of the world" (98). Sal sings Billie Holiday's "Lover Man" as he watches the family scene from the bushes. Meanwhile, Rickey has stolen Ponzo's woman, Big Rosey (also the nickname of the oldest Martin daughter in *The Town and the City*). Terry and Sal make love for the last time in a barn beneath a hovering tarantula, and the next morning the owner, Farmer Heffelfinger, tells him of his suspicion that Terry is illegitimate because of her blue eyes (100–01). Sal's naive venture into ersatz married life concludes by revealing that his life is poisoned by the multiple threat of incest, sibling rivalry, and violence from the father, but ironically, he is saved by his aunt (101), identified in a later book as "MA" (*BD* 5), who sends him money for the bus.

On his way home to his aunt after his first circular odyssey, Sal encounters the same old hobo who misled Pic and Slim on their trip west, whom Kerouac now identifies as the "Ghost of the Susquehanna" (103). Sal reckons that the ghost is about sixty years old; he leads the young man to a nonexistent bridge over "a terrifying river" (104), recalling the Watermelon Man episode in *Doctor Sax.* Even though Sal soon discovers the ghost is leading him in the wrong direction, he also realizes that he has revealed that all wilderness is not reserved for the West. He returns with the knowledge that the true wilderness exists at home: he asks rhetorically, "'Isn't it true that you start your life a sweet child believing in everything under your father's roof?'" Eventually, however, Sal avers, "you are wretched and miserable and poor and blind and naked, and with the visage of a gruesome grieving ghost you go shuddering through nightmare life" (105), language that would not be out of place in Sophocles's *Oedipus at Colonus.* Obviously, the Ghost of the Susquehanna is the ghost of the father who makes a ghost of the son. As Sal returns inevitably like the "Odyssean logs" floating down the Mississippi from Montana (103), he describes his home as a "place to lay my head down and figure the losses and figure the gain" (106). For the only time in the novel, his aunt calls him by his full first name, Salvatore (Savior), and reveals that Dean has visited her, "talking ... as she worked on a great rag rug woven of all the clothes in my family for years" (107). Like Penelope, Mrs. P has apparently been weaving to keep the rival suitors at bay, stalling them until her nephew/son/husband returns. On his desk, the savior finds his "half-finished manu-script" and settles down to write as the head of his original household, safe in the knowledge that Mr. P is already dead.

A little over a year lapses before Dean finds Sal at his brother Rocco's home in Testament, Virginia, and this time he has come to involve his friend in another three-way love affair. According to Sal, Dean has matured, but his behavior still contrasts sharply with that of Sal's earthy Southern relatives. For the first time, too, Dean is identified with Doctor Sax by virtue of his maniacal laugh (115), with the suggestion that perhaps the next journey may involve a confrontation with evil. Despite Sal's urge to marry a married woman named Lucille in order to reach some sort of destination (116), he allows Dean, who has abandoned Camille and returned to Marylou, to tempt him back on the road. Leaving his aunt to spend New Year's Eve alone, Sal—like Pic—begins to feel haunted about some decision he has forgotten to make regarding the Shrouded Traveler, his name for the ghost of his father (124). Nevertheless, Sal takes Dean to a party in the city, where Marylou flirts with him just to make Lucille jealous, but Sal reiterates his willingness to marry Lucille and care for her baby daughter if only she will get a divorce from her abusive husband (125). Perhaps what Sal has forgotten is that his encounter with the Shrouded Stranger was meant to remind him that he is not fated to marry Lucille, even though she is married and has a child, but someone much closer to him. Kerouac has embedded the confusion that followed Joan Haverty's pregnancy and the breakup of their marriage in Sal's relationship with Lucille. A brief interlude at the Long Island estate of Rollo Greb prefigures the long scene in *The Subterraneans* in which Mardou and Leo spend the weekend with Austin Bromberg (*Sub* 117–26), suggesting that some rivalry over a woman is about to occur on the road.

Sal rejects his mother's warning that he is wasting his time with Dean, because he senses that Dean is the messenger of his true fate and that his arrival, like the arrival of the messenger in *Oedipus the King*, announces "the moment when you know all and everything is decided forever" (129). Sure enough, before they even leave New York, Dean asks Sal to "work" Marylou so he can see what she's like with another man (131). In short order, the three of them end up in bed together in "the deathbed of a big man" in Carlo's apartment (which Duluoz identifies in *Visions of Cody* as the bed his father died in [341]), but Sal cannot perform in Dean's presence because he is "trying to decide something in the night and having all the weight of past centuries ballooning in the dark." In case any question remains as to the nature of his decision, he projects his feelings onto Dean, who "had never seen his mother's face." Sal analyzes his friend's behavior pattern with women in Oedipal terms: "Every new girl, every new wife, every new child was an addition to his bleak impoverishment" (132). Finally, Sal asks, "Where was his father?" The implication of this scene is that the absence of the father—regardless of whether he has been murdered, died of natural causes, or is simply missing—causes and perpetuates the compulsive behavior in both brothers. Almost in the same breath as he announces, Gerard-like, that "'everything is fine,'" Dean proposes bigamy to Marylou, happy to escape "'frosty fagtown New York'" (134), and Sal is once again forced to choose between heterosexual excess and homosexuality. Ironically, on their return trip to the "Biblical" town of Testament, they encounter a Jewish hitchhiker named Hymen Solomon, an allegorical figure presumably placed in Sal's way to admonish him of the wisdom of choosing a virgin for a wife.

On the route west, the trio stops to visit Bull Hubbard, the William S. Burroughs character, and at his home in Algiers, across the river from New Orleans, Sal is confronted by two atypical examples of married life. On the one hand, Bull, a heroin addict, and his wife, Jane, a benzedrine addict whose death by the hand of her husband is discussed in the tape section of *Visions of*

Cody, have "one of the strangest" relationships between husband and wife, something "curiously unsympathetic and cold between them" (146). On the other hand, Ed Dunkel, who has been riding with Dean and the others, is now reunited with his wife, Galatea. Unlike the fabled creation of Pygmalion, this Galatea has no intention of allowing herself to be molded to suit someone else's needs. After Dean had used up all her money to start their trip, soon after her wedding to Ed, Galatea abandoned them, going south to stay with Bull and Jane until her errant husband passed through on his way back west. And though Ed has apparently been unfaithful to her by going out with Lucille's sister (126), they reconcile and stay on in New Orleans, leaving Sal to ponder their relationship, as well as Bull and Jane's, as he continues his trip with Dean and Marylou.

Before they leave New Orleans, Sal and Bull also spend a symbolic day at the races. With a story about the father of Bull's friend Dale and the image of Bull's son, Ray, curled up asleep in his father's lap, in the background, Sal and his mentor set out for the Graetna racetrack. This scene recalls both young Jackie Duluoz's and young Mickey Martin's childhood interest in horse racing, and predictably, Sal has an experience that reminds him of his father. He finds a listing in the racing form for a horse named Big Pop, which wins, paying fifty to one. Bull criticizes himself for failing to heed what he calls Sal's "vision," explaining that Sal's father, an old fan of the horses himself, was probably communicating with him from beyond the grave. Further, Bull speculates that "[w]hen a man dies he undergoes a mutation in his brain that we know nothing about now" (153–54), giving Sal a reason to believe that his father still exists in some other realm of being. The net effect of Sal's visit to New Orleans is summed up in his meditation on the ferry crossing the Mississippi, which immediately follows Bull's diagnosis that Dean is suffering from "compulsive psychosis dashed with a jigger of psychopathic irresponsibility and violence," a Freudian evaluation that might be applicable to any Oedipus. Bull goes on to call Dean's ailment "his ideal fate." Crossing the Mississippi reminds Sal of Big Slim Hazard and of Mississippi Gene, and he suddenly realizes "that everything I had ever known and would ever know was One" (147). While the tone of this statement may sound positively Platonic to the unwary reader, its purport is also Oedipal. Sal has come to a place on the road at which he begins to perceive that all the characters in his "sad drama" (148) represent the members of his original family circle.

Leaving New Orleans, Sal has an "apparition" in which an old black man is "praying or calling down a curse" (157). This omen introduces a Gothic sequence reminiscent of Doctor Sax, replete with a "mansion of the snake" and an illegible "manuscript of the night" (158), reminding the reader of the Duluoz Legend that Dean's motives and language, like Sax's, are inscrutable. Yet, like the evil in Kerouac's fantasia of adolescence, the evil in Dean's behavior neutralizes itself, or, as he says, Sax-like, "'Everything takes care of itself'" (159). So when Dean, Sal, and Marylou disrobe in the car and a passing truck driver catches a glimpse of "a golden beauty sitting naked with two naked men" (161), it now seems like innocent fun, though in *Visions of Cody* she is applying cold cream to their privates (340). Sal sleeps through Sabinal, scene of his affair with Terry, and when Dean unceremoniously dumps him and Marylou in San Francisco, leaving them to fend for themselves, he consoles himself and her by retelling his own myth of Doctor Sax, assuring her that in the end "when the snake dies great clouds of seminal-gray doves will flutter out and bring tidings of peace around the world" (172). Sal has lost faith in Dean's road, and when Marylou also abandons him, he also realizes "what a whore she was" (*OTR* 172).

Sal's sudden and unexpected solitude provokes a second vision, this time a maternal one. Walking down Market Street, he passes a fish-and-chips joint where the proprietor reminds him of his mother in a past life. In this life "two hundred years ago in England" Sal himself was a criminal who had just returned from jail to haunt his mother's "honest labors." In present time, he is "frozen with ecstasy on the sidewalk." Once again he loses his identity and becomes disoriented, confusing Market Street with Canal Street in New Orleans and Forty-second Street in New York, all of which lead to water. He imagines his "strange Dickensian mother" begging him not to return to haunt her. "'You are no longer like a son to me,'" she tells him, "'and like your father, my first husband'" (172). Her new husband, she explains, is a "'kindly Greek'" and she adjures her lost son to "'[r]eopen no old wounds, be as if you had never returned and looked in to me.'" Naturally, her prayer reminds her "mean-minded son" of his father, "the Big Pop vision" (173). Kerouac wrote to Cassady about the vision in early 1951: "Of course I always felt like an orphan because my brother, who came before me, died to 'save me,' as it were, for my mother's arms (here I'm acquiescing to the pre-established musings of any Freudian mysterious-reader)" (*Letters* 281, parentheses in original). With Buddhist reasoning about the "stability of the intrinsic Mind," he assuages the terror of this new vision of his mother as Jocasta, but he is nearly scared to death. Yet he doesn't die. Instead he is brought back to life, not by the sounds of Easter hymns like Faust, but by the aroma of food wafting from San Francisco's myriad restaurants. Back in his skid row hotel, Sal concludes, "I was too young to know what had happened" (*OTR* 173). But though the character claims not to understand, Kerouac—and by this stage in the unfolding of the Duluoz Legend, the reader—is aware of the significance of this vibrant scene. He has weathered the triangular test of his latest trip with his brother-figure as guide, only to find his mother at the end of the road. And though she warns him of the danger of returning to her, he has not yet found the means to overcome his fate. So he gets on a bus, thinking he'll never see Dean, the "pagan mayor" of San Francisco (175), again, and rides cross-country to his aunt.

Dean and Sal's next-to-last trip together in the spring of 1949, described in part three, seems ill-fated from the start. Though Sal, having finished his book and had it accepted for publication, envisions himself "in Middle America, a patriarch" (179), his longing for exciting companionship lures him into a reunion with Dean. In San Francisco, Camille, now pregnant with Dean's second child, fears Sal as "the strange most evil angel" (183) who has come to disrupt her happy home. She accurately calls Dean a liar for breaking his promise to provide for their family and throws both men out of the house. Having now begun to disrupt family life like Dean and sensing that their fate is wound together (189), Sal proposes to spend the money from the advance on his book to take Dean to Italy. Though the two pledge themselves buddies unto death, two omens overshadow their departure. First, standing next to Camille and Dean's apartment, they see a Greek wedding, "probably the thousandth time in an unbroken dark generation" (190), suggesting both a link to Oedipus's incestuous marriage and an ambiguous hint that Sal will fulfill his fate even as he tries to escape it by traveling with his brother. Next, Galatea Dunkel reappears in the form of a Sybil, "long hair streaming to the floor, plying the fortune-telling cards" (192). While Sal tries to defend Dean by making him into a crazy Christ-figure, the Holy Goof, Galatea excoriates Sal's brother-figure for his irresponsibility. Sal rationalizes, "Now his disciples were married and the wives of his disciples had him on the carpet for the sexuality and the life he had helped bring into being" (194). His defense, of course, falls on deaf ears in this air of "maternal satisfaction," and Galatea pronounces her Oedipal sentence on Dean: "'The sooner he's dead the better'" (195). On a brief spin through some jazz joints on their last night in the Bay, Dean attempts to counter with his image of the perfect—that is, perfectly docile—wife (203), but the two men leave town with Galatea's curse ringing in their ears (205).

Once again, their journey involves a homosexual encounter contrasted with a married couple, as Dean and Sal find a ride in an "'[e]ffeminate car'" owned by a gay man and occupied by a tourist couple (206). Passing through Denver, Sal and Dean get into their first argument, instigated by Dean's suggestion that Sal is getting old. All Sal's resentments come spilling out, but his reaction triggers only guilt in himself, making him aware "how ugly I was and what filth I was discovering in the depths of my own impure psychologies" (213). In Denver, Sal arranges for them to stay with an Okie family who had been his neighbors only two weeks before. The single mother, Frankie, has the same name as Kerouac's first wife, and one of her daughters, Janet, bears the name given by his second wife to their daughter, who was born while Kerouac was writing Doctor Sax. Dean and Sal now become rivals in this fatherless household. When Frankie refuses to buy a car on Dean's recommendation, he faults her for being just like his father, who, rumor has it, is working for the railroad in New England (215), a job Maggie fantasizes for Jacky Duluoz in *Maggie Cassidy* (75). While staying in Frankie's home, Dean discovers that his family has disinherited him. Reeling from the news, he gets drunk and steals a detective's car. By refusing to be his accomplice, Sal establishes his moral superiority, which he confirms by protecting little Janet from Dean's frenzy. In fact, when they leave, Sal notes, "Little Janet was crying to see us, or me, or whatever it was, go" (223). Here, Kerouac's guilt about leaving his own wife and daughter comes very near the surface of his fiction.

The Oedipal themes recur in their trip east, as they pick up two Irish Catholic boys as riders, then stop at the ranch of Ed Wall, whose wife fixes them all a huge farm meal while she complains of the boredom of her life: Kerouac even inscribes a reference to the scroll manuscript of *On the Road* into their trip across the plains: "The magnificent car made, the wind roar; it made the plains unfold like a roll of paper." At times, Dean slows to search a crowd of bums for his father (232), and approaching Chicago he engages in a race with a hipster traveling with his mother (233). Sal, for his part, recalls Eddie as they cross Iowa (234) and imagines that the residents of Illinois towns think they are gangsters (236). The disguise of his autobiography continues, as Sal and Dean stop in Detroit en route to New York. In life, Jack and Neal stopped there to visit Edie, as Duluoz explains in *Visions of Cody* (373–74), but in *On the Road* they spend the night in an all-night movie house alternately watching a Western and a mystery thriller. Sal's attempt to synthesize the cowboy hero and the sinister paranoia of the thriller results in a kind of nervous breakdown. He concludes, "All my actions since then have been dictated automatically to my subconscious by this horrible osmotic experience" (244). Sal's desire to exonerate himself recalls Oedipus's rejection of his own guilt on the grounds that he was merely acting out the curse laid upon his father. Sal also seems to be speaking for Kerouac when he implies that some deep-seated flaw in his subconscious causes him to repeat himself compulsively. In New York, Sal's aunt officially ends their trip by trying to get rid of Dean as soon as possible, while through Sal's agency Dean himself falls in love with the beautiful Inez and determines to make her his third wife.

The message of the whole trip seems to be that no matter how he strives, the mythic hero is bound to fulfill the destiny decided for him before his birth. Perhaps if Sal could escape from Dean's influence, he could break the pattern that binds him to his brother-figure by its similarity to Dean's compulsion. He would then, it seems, also free himself from Dean's obsession with his father. Free of the negative model, Sal might pursue his own frequently stated desire to find a loving wife. Like many evils, Dean's enthusiasm for sex at all costs is attractive, but his influence on all his "disciples," including Sal, is detrimental, as the wives and girlfriends of these disciples well know. By casting his elegiac romance as an ambivalent relationship of attraction and repulsion between two brother-figures, Kerouac gave himself the opportunity to work out his own ideas and feelings about the influence on his adult life of his infantile rivalry with Gerard. In *On the Road*, the father, who had forsaken his son in *Vanity of Duluoz*, fades into the background. Granted, he returns in the form of various ghosts, but unlike the ghost of Hamlet's father, the revenant of the father in the Duluoz Legend carries no specific message. Rather, he presents himself as an enigma who serves to distract the protagonist from his true mission in life, a mission that he can discover only by acting it out.

The advance on his book provides Sal with the money to fund his last adventure in *On the Road*, and he begins this trip on a positive note by parting ways with Dean, who is now working to support three children. Dean's fantasies with Sal now revolve mostly around a stable future in which they will raise families side by side. Sal's solitary departure signals his hope that he will be able to escape from Dean's orbit to follow his own heart's true desire. As if to certify his hope, on the bus to Denver he meets Henry Glass, a kid fresh out of jail, who reminds him transparently of Dean. Henry is on his way to live with his brother, and though he invites Sal to be his buddy, Sal perceives that unlike Dean, Henry has "no native strange saintliness to save him from the iron fate" (257). Henry's fate disappears from the story along with his character in Denver, but Sal's is sealed when he learns that Dean, who now takes on a Rabelaisian largeness, is pursuing him like the Shrouded Stranger (259). Dean, always the brother, now also becomes the father to Sal, leading Sal towards a fate he still hopes to escape.

This time around, they seem to break the pattern of their previous journeys, heading south to Mexico, where Dean intends to get a divorce from Camille so he can marry Inez. Here, the itinerary is at odds with the purpose, and the reader senses some final rupture between Sal and Dean in the offing. Many of the Denver characters are present, as well as Ed and Galatea Dunkel, giving the scene a repetitive feel, but Dean and Sal take on a new partner to form a traveling trio similar to the ones in *The Town and the City*. Stan Shepherd, however, comes to them locked in his own Oedipal struggle. His trip is being financed by his white-haired mother over the objections of his aged grandfather. Together, the three travelers represent three stages in Oedipus's relationship with his father, "Dean looking for his father, [Sal's] dead, Stan fleeing his old one" (267). As in Sophocles's drama, the stages in Kerouac's novel occur simultaneously as a result of the introspection of the author. Dean also notes the difference in their route as they cross Texas, vertical as opposed to horizontal, like Sal's experience mountain-climbing in California three years earlier (269). Once again, however, the trip is punctuated by Dean's thoughts of his father and Sal's memories of holding hands with Marylou (271) and of living with Terry (272), and crossing the Mexican border, which should bring them into a new order of things, instead signals further repetition when the border guard announces, Gerard-like, "Everything fine" (275, sic).

Sure enough, Sal shortly finds himself in competition with Dean in a whorehouse in the small town of Gregoria, where the very Indians stand for the generational relationship between father and son (281). Ironically, a young married man with a child provides marijuana for the illicit adventure, and even the Americans' mutual desire for a little son like his doesn't prevent them from patronizing the prostitutes (286). All the whores are women of color still in their teens, and only a baby's cry at the close of the orgy reminds Sal that he is not "in a pornographic hasheesh daydream in heaven" (291). Later, back on the road south, Sal experiences a symbolic apparition when a white horse (similar to the ones Jackie Duluoz imagines rising from the foam of the Merrimack River in *Doctor Sax* [8, 73]) passes over Dean's sleeping body without harming him (295–96), and Dean trades his watch to a little Indian girl for a crystal (298), signifying that they have entered timeless "Biblical areas" similar to the one where Jesus lived. Sal senses, "The end of our journey impended" (300) like doom, but Mexico City turns out to be "one vast Bohemian camp," and Sal discovers at the end of the road that "nothing ever ended" (302). When Sal falls ill with dysentery, Dean ruthlessly abandons him, but Sal considers this betrayal forgivingly, perhaps because it finally releases him from the sphere of Dean's influence.

Looked at from the perspective of Kerouac's life, *On the Road* ends ambiguously, when Sal, like the poet Petrarch, finds his Laura, though in a loft in New York City. In reality Sal's meeting with Laura is modeled on Kerouac's meeting with his second wife, Joan Haverty, who was living in a loft formerly occupied by Bill Cannastra, a friend of Jack's who was killed in a subway accident in the fall of 1950, while Jack was in Mexico (another death discussed in the tape section of *Visions of Cody*). Returning to find his friend, Kerouac instead found his friend's former lover and made her his own. Within a month, to his other friends' astonishment, Jack married Joan and moved into Cannastra's loft. The 18,000-word letter Sal mentions was in life the catalyst provided by Neal Cassady that helped galvanize Kerouac's spontaneous prose. The following spring, using his new method, Jack composed the scroll manuscript of the novel. Further, Joan claims in her memoir, "Nobody's Wife," that while Jack was writing "The Mexican Girl" episode, he impregnated her with their daughter (257–58). Joan believed that Jack's passion was inspired by his feeling of superiority over a poor woman of color, a superiority he could not feel over his independent-minded wife.

In the conclusion to the novel, Dean turns up again in New York, as does Remi, the other brother-figure from earlier in the story. When Remi invites Sal and Laura on a double date to a Duke Ellington concert, Dean begs a ride uptown. Remi refuses, and despite their compassion for Sal's forlorn friend, Sal and Laura can do nothing to change his mind. "Old Dean's gone," Sal thinks, though out loud he mouths Gerard's platitude, "'He'll be all right'" (309). Already, early in his relationship with Joan, Kerouac had apparently begun to identify Neal with his father and himself with Gerard, a convoluted way of identifying himself with Leo. In this context the mystery of the haunted and haunting beauty of the last paragraph of the published version of *On the Road* begins to reveal itself.

Off the road, Sal returns to the river, the paternal, seminal source of his own being. He looks west over the Hudson to Iowa, where he had experienced the loss of his own identity. The image of children crying pervades his nostalgia, signifying his own misery as a child, as well as the misery both Neal and Jack have caused their children by abandoning them. He invokes A. A. Milne's character Pooh Bear, which in the 1950s was often used as a term of endearment by young lovers, suggesting that some spirit of childlike innocence or romantic love presides over the order of things. The evening star, however, comes straight out of Whitman's elegy for Abraham Lincoln, "When Lilacs Last in the Dooryard Bloom'd," carrying with it the implication that the story about to be concluded has, in fact, been a dirge of mourning for "the sweetest, wisest soul of all my days and lands" (l. 204), in Whitman's words, the father addressed as brother. This elegiac tone explains the reference to "the final shore" of death (310) and leads to the chilling repetition of the final sentence.

Sal names his friend, then the father Sal and Dean literally failed to find (but who was, instead, found by Dean's third wife and who announced his whereabouts in a letter from Seattle [252]), then Dean again. This repetition is particularly striking in an Oedipal reading because it brings home subconsciously the theme of fate in the succession of generations. The son plays out the course set for him by the father, and in the end, for better or worse, the son becomes the father. As Sal has tried unsuccessfully to escape the pattern set for Dean by Old Dean Moriarty Kerouac tried unsuccessfully to escape the pattern set for him first by Gerard, who won his mother's love by dying, and later by Leo, who cursed his son with the exclusive care of Gabrielle then forsook them both by dying. The harshness of this fate is tempered by Kerouac's love for his family, which gives rise to the Romantic sentimentality of the closing paragraph. The final meeting with the old hobo (306), repeated from *Pic*, helps Sal assuage the guilt for his own attraction to family irresponsibility and provides Kerouac with the religious justification for his compulsive treatment of the Oedipus myth in the Duluoz Legend. Rather than resist the dictates of fate and the Oedipus complex, he will simply transform them into a lament for the human condition. He will, as the prophet advises, "*Go moan for man.*"

Visions of Cody is to *On the Road* what Melville's *Pierre* was to *Moby Dick* (Hunt 5), a brilliant but tortuous overflow from the monumental creative effort of the novel that immediately preceded it. In fact, Jack Duluoz, the narrator of *Visions of Cody*, distinguishes the text from his "story-novels" by calling it a "record" written to appease his "lone soul" (107), although he admitted many years later that everything he had written about Neal had been written "out of love, the kind of love that one can feel only about his brother" (qtd. in Jarvis 132). It is Kerouac's most experimental and— probably not coincidentally—most misogynistic book. Consisting of a hodge-podge of recollections from the same period covered by *On the Road*; a lengthy transcript of a tape-recording made by Cody (Neal Cassady's character), his wife, Duluoz, and two of their friends; an "imitation" of the tape; various reminiscences from Duluoz's life and recreations of his juvenile writing; and a detailed analysis of a movie shoot, *Visions of Cody* makes reference in some way to every novel Kerouac had conceived or written by 1954 except for *Maggie Cassidy*. It even predicts *The Dharma Bums* by introducing the character of Ray Smith, the protagonist of that much later novel (311). *The Town and the City*, which provides a connective thread for the narrative of *On the Road*, figures here, cryptically, as *H from the C* (92— probably short for "Home from the City" an inside joke). Begun in October 1951, just when Kerouac discovered his sketching method of composition (which he says in the novel, however, "is not for my secret thoughts" [981], the vertical complement to his spontaneous prose, *Visions of Cody* allows Kerouac to probe his memory and imagination unfettered by the demands of a linear plot. The result constitutes his frankest analysis of his own interests and motives and his most intuitive evaluation of his Oedipal dilemma. The difficulty of the novel lies partly in its similarity to free association, which puts the reader in the position of a 1950s analyst conducting a talking cure. Kerouac is blowing as deep as he can blow, following the policy of his 1953 manifesto (*GB&O* 72), but the depth and height of his vertical method disconnect the narrative connections, tempting the reader, in Cody's words, to "continue the continuity" (141). It is safe to say that without the other versions of the road story, or at least a thorough knowledge of the facts of Kerouac's life, most readers would find *Visions of Cody* incomprehensible. With the other versions and the biography in mind, however, the novel provides an unparalleled key to the innermost recesses of its author's mind.

In contrast to *On the Road,* the narrator of its sequel, recalling the repetition of the end of the previous novel, explicitly announces that his new journey will be an interior one: "IN THE AUTUMN OF 1951 I began thinking of Cody Pomeray, thinking of Cody Pomeray" (5). Explaining his need for a tape recorder later in the novel, Duluoz hopes that it will enable him to capture "this lifelong monologue which is begun in my mind— lifelong complete contemplation—what else do I *really* know unless I'm depriving myself of kinds of knowledge that would bring out those qualities in me which are most valuable to others ..." (99). The literary forebears that preside over this experiment are the modern French novelist Marcel Proust, whose *Remembrance of Things Past* provides a model for basing the Duluoz Legend on an exploration of childhood memories, and James Joyce, the inventor of stream-of-consciousness narration, which Kerouac uses here to represent the interaction of observation, memory, and imagination he calls his "lifelong monologue" (99). Once Duluoz leaves the physical road to begin his vertical explorations, the dense symbolic episodes of the horizontal narrative give way to discontinuous memories, thoughts, and feelings, isolated traces of his Oedipal concerns, most of which result from his attempt to understand more fully his true relationship with Cody.

In this version of the story, in which memory and daydream supersede action to a large extent, Cody's missing father seems more present than absent, appearing in the first sentence and persisting until the final paragraphs, and Duluoz's connection between his own father and Cody's reaches back into the previous century, when the fathers were themselves children (5). Even in the pursuit of his other interests, like jazz, Duluoz is haunted by his father's last words (23), and the more he thinks of Cody, the more memories of his own father surface (25). Thinking back to 1933, when Cody was only six or seven, Duluoz recalls that his father's buddy, Mike Fortier, had first made him aware, at age eleven, of the differences that separated him from his father, and though this memory is bittersweet (similar in impact to Uncle Mike's prophecy in *Doctor Sax* [118]), it leads him to the possible discovery of an entirely new memory, the revelation of something that he had considered lost forever (26). "Trying desperately to be a great rememberer redeeming life from darkness" (103), Duluoz reconsiders his fate (34), feels that his father has rejected him (36), and recognizes that a dream about a homosexual orgy (also reminiscent of a scene in *Doctor Sax* [68–69]) has something to do with his tendency to connect his boyhood pals with his adult male friends, especially Cody (36). He quotes a long letter from himself to Cody, in which he reveals his "own personal tragedy" and the "tragedy, the loneliness of my mother," his feeling that he will soon die, and his guilt for having "done wrong, to myself the most wrong" (41).

Duluoz reveals in recounting the story of Cody's life that Cody's father had been a close friend and associate of Old Bull Balloon, the old vaudeville character who plays cards with Duluoz's father in *Visions of Gerard* and reappears in *Doctor Sax*. He also informs the reader that Gaga, old Cody's paraplegic roommate (whom Neal Cassady describes at length in *The First Third*), had once tried to molest young Cody. Cody's adolescent regime included sleeping in Old Bull's roll-top desk, and it also turns out that Cody and his father shared the same woman. Indeed, on Halloween Night of 1939, Cody pushed his father off Big Cherry Lucy and took over so much that "they fist fought like rivals" (56). Yet later he pleaded with a Denver judge to have mercy on the old man (80). The result of his early experiences is that Cody, himself grown older, "goes now haunted in the streets of Saturday night in the American city with his eyes torn out like Oedipus who sees all and sees nothing." In this state, despite his efforts, Cody has come to resemble his father, who "had never done anything but stare dumbly in alleys" (83), yet also meandered "in blind chagrin" (84).

Recounting Cody's life leads Duluoz to review his own, beginning with a dream of his early childhood in Centralville in which his father is "ignoring me again as I now ignore my own boyСand have to, as *he* had to" (89, italics in original). This sense that Duluoz is avoiding his own paternal responsibilities is reinforced by a stray image of a woman and her infant in a beat car on the same white hill he has previously associated with his father's rejection of him (36). Here the association suggests that Kerouac was already worried about his second wife's demands for child support, because he thinks of "her, the baby, and jail for me" (88). In the last section of the novel, the narrator goes so far as to ask himself rhetorically, "Do I have a baby daughter somewhere?" He feigns lack of concern by answering, "I have not troubled to find out" (335). Duluoz attributes all his troubles to a curse associated with the discarded galleys of his first published novel (92). He wonders why his father, Emil, was especially cursed and "when will the troubles of this *cursed* family end" (92, italics in original). He begins to conceive of himself almost in Uncle Mike's terms as "Duluoz of the Dolours" (94) as he again associates the failure of his father's business with the beginning of his writing career. The scene of his first story writing on Sarah Avenue in Lowell prompts him to think of an earlier scene on Phebe Avenue, which in turn leads him to ask about the child he was then: "[D]id he come to live just to be buried?" (94). Thinking of his birthday in 1950, he longs for bygone days when "birthdays were birthdays and not anniversaries of guilt and culpritude" (94). Finally, he associates the year of Gerard's death, the same year as Cody's birth, with his father's grave, regretting that his father is no longer alive to feel pride in his son's accomplishments. "It appears," observed biographer Charles Jarvis, "that Jack Kerouac saw the wonder of his apotheosized Gerard through the revelations of Cody, another holy brother" (128).

While there is no exact equivalent in *Visions of Cody* to the woman in the fish-and-chips shop in *On the Road*, Duluoz does recognize the strong presence of his mother in the text. While out walking one Sunday, he sees an old woman who reminds him of her. He fantasizes that the old woman considers him insane for watching her: "'[H]e plays with himself too late,'" she thinks (317). This incident, which links the sketching aspect of Kerouac's composition process with masturbation and its mythical result, madness, further recalls Duluoz's mother's unsuccessful attempts to prevent him from masturbating. "My mother was real rough on me in that respect," he declares, "she wouldn't allow any kind of sex in the house" (317). In *The Compulsion to Confess* Theodor Reik expressed his belief that "the actual gratification of a forbidden impulse can, at the same time, satisfy the need for punishment." The Freudian theorist adds pointedly, "We can observe this in cases of masturbation that unconsciously also have the character of self-castration" (249). In a passage near the very beginning of the novel, Duluoz envisions feeling "castrated with legs-tangled-in-pants position" as he masturbates while sitting on the toilet (8). Near the end of the novel, while he is recounting the last trip east from *On the Road*, Duluoz is reminded of his fear as he hides in a public toilet stall while Cody has gymnastic sex with the man in whose car they are riding (358). In this latter episode, he links masturbation, fear of castration, and homoeroticism. The self-consciousness of these allusions becomes documentary when Cody asks Jack on tape whether he has read the winter 1952 number of the proto-Beat magazine *Neurotica*, which is entirely devoted to discussion of the castration complex (179). In *Rebel Without Applause* Jay Landesman, the founder of *Neurotica*, describes an actual meeting with Kerouac and Cassady in which Jack suggested an idea for a future issue of the magazine (141–42). The specific issue of *Neurotica*, edited by Gershon Legman and referred to in *Visions of Cody*, features an article by the Freudian analyst Otto Fenichel on "Castration Anxiety in Boys," as well as a fragment from Melville's *Pierre* and F. Scott Fitzgerald's story, "The Boy Who Killed His Mother" (*Neurotica:1948–51* [*sic*]).

Duluoz is quite aware that one of the similarities between Cody and himself is their early attachment to their mothers, which makes it difficult for them to sustain a relationship with other women. "[W]omen are impractical for me ...," Duluoz asserts, because "I'm doomed to these universal watchfulnesses" (32). His resignation here recalls his response to Johnnie's annulment of his first marriage in *Vanity of Duluoz*, where he avers that he "was of no more use to her as a husband" (*VD* 208). His fear of castration derives from his sense that he has violated his father's sexual prerogative, and when he discusses Cody's mother, who died when Cody was nine years old, Duluoz perceives that "like me, he sinned against his father" (381).

Interestingly, Duluoz associates his sin with New Haven, where his parents were living when he finally quit football to pursue a literary career, a scene described fully in *Vanity of Duluoz*. Earlier in *Visions of Cody*, the narrator's description of the Duluoz family curse had also led him to think of New Haven, which he says he left "to comply with the evil hidden wishes of this world." Though he prayed to his father to make his mother happy, realizing the futility of that prayer, he vows to leave home "'to save trouble all around.'" In leaving New Haven, Duluoz intuits the connection between his love for his mother, "the great and final protector of my life and soul," and his failed second marriage, when he summarizes his parting words in this way: "'This is my last night in your house, mother, that you so lovingly prepared for me yet how could you foresee or even prevent my evil which precipitated its own evils, and the first evil was not putting her down when I first realized I didn't love or like her at all eight days before our marriage.'" By concluding this address with the ejaculation "O dull clown" (93), Kerouac probably alludes to Hamlet's conversation with the gravedigger, suggesting that the madness supposedly caused by masturbation is of the antic variety, feigned for the sake of outwitting the mother's husband, but nevertheless leading ultimately to tragedy.

The presence of antic madness would also explain another allusion to Shakespeare's Oedipal tragedy in the "Joan Rawshanks in the Fog" section, when Cody mocks "Jack's Dictionary" by proclaiming, "Make way for the King, the Queen has dropped dead, he's come to see Poloniopolos, the Greek tragedian" (323). In the film Kerouac saw being made, *Sudden Fear*, which was released in August 1952, Joan Crawford is a playwright whose life is threatened by an actor she has rejected for a leading role, heightening the connection in the novel between the drama and death. In the consciousness of Kerouac's narrator, as in the self-revelation of Oedipus, all the phases of the tragedy happen at once, so that the son here has usurped his uncle's place in his mother's bed after she is already dead and has belatedly come to seek advice from the pedantic counselor, who instead seals his doom by reinforcing the inevitability of his fate. His initial response to his own doom, like that of Oedipus, is Promethean. Duluoz sounds like Ahab defying the forces of nature in *Moby Dick* when he warns the gods, "[B]e careful of me, I can catch thunderbolts and pull you down and have done it before" (93). Surely this is the hubris of a hero riding for a fall.

No wonder that when Duluoz, recounting his first visit to Denver in 1947, after meeting Cody, sees a successful young business executive—the image his mother tried to create for him when he went off to college—he finds beneath this prosperous disguise "a bored old Tiresias" (293) forecasting Duluoz's demise. To account for his own behavior, Duluoz invents his own version of the rivalry between the younger males in their antagonism for their father that Freud believed motivated our prehuman ancestors, a caveman who "had the right to kill his wife and child and move on to another woman; of course, it also meant moving on to other men" (265). But in his version of Jack's personal myth, Cody identifies the shrouded stranger as "the eternal husband coming back to peek at the tortured lover who stole his wife away" (312), an allusion to Dostoevsky's novella *The Eternal Husband*. Duluoz now realizes that Cody, made attractive to Duluoz by his own Oedipal tendencies, has exacerbated Duluoz's troubles. Alluding to the fact that they have shared the same woman, he damns Cody for being a false friend: "[M]y benefactor whispers his wife to me in the dark" (361). While pretending to be a true brother but insisting that they share the same woman, Cody shows himself to be both an angel and an enemy (298). Just as Oedipus suspects that his brother-in-law, Creon, may be a rival for the throne in Sophocles's play, in *Visions of Cody* Duluoz begins to doubt the beneficence of both Gerard and his surrogate. In assessing his own ambivalence, he even admits that he and Cody might be capable of killing each other (330). Duluoz concludes that, like both Oedipus and himself, Cody is "no struggling babe, he's a raging murderous man" (331).

There is a strange moment in the final section of the novel, the recapitulation of Cody and Jack's 1949 trip from San Francisco to New York City, when Duluoz figures himself as the defendant in a murder trial. Kerouac places this mock trial just after the homosexual sex scene, and the sentence itself has homoerotic overtones. As a mitigating factor in his own defense, the protagonist says, "I, Jack Duluoz, have not been the same since my brother Gerard died ..." (359), but before he can enter his plea, Cody, as judge, informs the jury that Jack is "'an impostor French-Canadian from New England,'" but "'in any case he deserves punishment'" (360). Perhaps Cody's accusation relates to the (presumably fictitious) newspaper story in the "Imitation of the Tape" section, which carries the headline "LOCAL BOY INDICTED FOR FORGERY" and names the perpetrator as "Jack L. Duluoz" (254), implying that the act of writing in English is an act of imposture. In the Oedipus tale, of course, the hero is a criminal impostor, pretending to be his mother's husband instead of her son and forging his father's identity in her bed, but in *Vanity of Duluoz*, the hanging, like the Hanged Man in the Tarot, is a harbinger of change. Duluoz, condemned to death by his brother, expiates his guilt and lives on simply by realizing that "Dead eyes see" (336). He gives Cody a symbolic slap in the face, telling him to "snap out of it" (314). By redressing his grievance against Francis Martin (i.e., Gerard), who had slapped his brother Peter in an invalid's fit of pique (*T&C* 35), Duluoz disengages himself from his identity with his brother and finds new hope for a future free from his Oedipal rivalry with him. By the same token, he assumes responsibility for his own creativity, instead of obsessively attributing it to his brother or his father. In this convoluted fashion, the vertical experiment of *Visions of Cody*, by allowing Kerouac to plumb the depths of his psyche, showed him how he could use the same instrument of composition that had bound him to the ghosts of his past to liberate him from them, at least in theory.

A brief bilingual section near the close of the novel testifies to its author's personal triumph. Like Dante, Duluoz finds himself at midlife in the midst of a dark forest, but unlike his poetic predecessor, he finds his guide unreliable. Rather than rely on a brother who suffers from the same malady as himself, he must commune with the French-speaking part of his mind, even if that seems to be "conning nature." By saying in French what cannot be expressed in English, Duluoz discovers the truth of his own instincts: "Cody is full of shit; let him go; he is your friend, let him dream; he's not your brother, he's not your father ..." (362). The identity between Cody and Gerard or Leo has been broken, and if Jack can recognize the danger in that identity, presumably he can recognize the danger of identifying himself too closely with either his brother or his father. Psychically, he has put himself in a position to will to become his own man. If the force of compulsion proves stronger than that of will, it will not be for lack of self-awareness. Finally, in *Visions of Cody*, victory over self-destructive urges depends on "loving your own life, loving the story of your own life" (307), regardless of whether it has a conventional happy ending. If Kerouac never overcame his Oedipal urges in life, in *Visions of Cody* we see him in the act of transforming them into a new kind of Oedipus tale. Perhaps this kind of inward journey "gets worse and worse and darker all the time till time disappears," but Duluoz urges us with ironic humor to accompany him just the same: "O reader just follow me blindly into the hell and gone!" (96). Or as Duluoz's French-speaking self concludes less romantically, "[D]on't go down the hill of the other side of your life for nothing" (363).

"Adios, King" (398), the final words of *Visions of Cody*, resound as ambiguously in the mind of the Oedipal reader as the "doublewords ringing" in Duluoz's ears at the end of the "Imitation of the Tape" section (274), for he bids farewell to his angel and enemy as though he were Hamlet taking leave of Claudius or Oedipus lamenting the loss of Laius. There is no way of knowing how thoroughly Kerouac hoped to delude himself with his own literary language, but his tendency is to confront his Oedipal dilemma by representing it repeatedly throughout his road narratives with as much variety as the plots and characters will allow. In the allegorical *Pic,* where such opportunities are limited, Kerouac still managed to found the story on an Oedipal act of violence. *On the Road,* by contrast, offers so many Oedipal situations as to suggest, as Sal Paradise perceives, that for Kerouac every human encounter was merely the revisitation of some primal scene. In the context of the Duluoz Legend, the romantic ending of Kerouac's most famous novel seems as pat in its resolution as any of Shakespeare's comedies, and the Oedipal reader cannot quite accept it as successful. In view of what was actually happening in Kerouac's life at the time, Sal's future happiness with Laura, as suggested by the fully edited version, seems like a smoke-screen thrown up temporarily to shield both author and readers from the relentless—and disturbing—effort of self-analysis. Likewise, the end of *Visions of Cody* offers a similar sense of closure, but the discontinuity of its experimental form deconstructs its finality. Rather than being forced to kill his father, like Oedipus, or to avenge his father's murder, like Hamlet, the purpose of Duluoz's journey seems to be to transcend his identity with his brother. But this transcendence does not allow him to avoid the Oedipal fate; rather, it seals his fate. For in transcending his brother's influence, he makes it his own, becoming in the process more like his brother than his brother himself. For if Cody's lack of a mother drove him to recreate her in the image of many wives and lovers, Duluoz's possession of one led him to fulfill the curse more literally.

Kerouac gives us an inkling of his destiny, appropriately, in a dream Duluoz dreams in Mexico, of "a little golden road, a house, a treeshade, the which Shroudy inhabits in the disguise of my mother" (384). Here, the Shrouded Stranger, always variously identified with the ghost of Gerard or Leo—and sometimes even with Neal—reveals itself to Kerouac's subconscious as his mother. In *The Visions of the Great Rememberer,* his annotation of the novel, Allen Ginsberg remarks, "But the shrouded stranger's his Mother, he's smothered by the shroudy stranger's 'dress'!" (37). It is his inevitable relationship with her that he fears will prevent him from attaining the Eternal City, but he finds instead that she will be not only his companion but also his guide to their mutual destination. Perhaps that is why Pic, in the version of his story written at the end of Kerouac's life, so easily attains his goal of combining a mother with a sister, or why the tape section of *Visions of Cody* concludes not with a transcript of the words of the characters, but with the recording of a revival meeting, which ends uncharacteristically and (except to an Oedipal reader) incongruously, with the congregation chanting, "MOTHER! MOTHER!" Like the preacher at that revival, Duluoz tries to give his readers a sense of his own assurance that everything is all right, that evil disposes of itself, that only the original sacrifice of the father repeated by the son, that is, the return to the mother, will heal "the great Natal Sore" (274).

OMAR SWARTZ

The Vision of Social Deviance

Kerouac's "path" is laid out in his fiction, most popularly in *On the Road*, and is represented in three predominant rhetorical visions: the Vision of Social Deviance, the Vision of Sexuality, and Dean as Vision. Each vision serves as a general base supporting the next vision in a pyramid form. The primary vision that grounds the bulk of the narrative has to do with the rejection of popular culture; this I call the Vision of Social Deviance.

On the Road begins with the narrator's immediate rejection of the world that American culture has to offer him. "I first met Dean not long after my wife and I split up" (1957, 5), begins Sal Paradise, a young, noncommitted college student surviving on the G.I. Bill. We meet Sal after he has just gotten over "a serious illness ... that had something to do with the miserably weary split-up and [my] feeling that everything was dead" (1957, 5). We are never told what this illness is, and there is never any further reference to Sal's former wife. The past is clouded in mystery.

Sal reveals that the "split" was "miserably weary." Was this a divorce? A separation? Was this a long marriage that left the pair emotionally distraught? Did Sal leave his wife? Did Sal's wife leave him? We are not given any details. We are not even sure what "miserably weary" means. While the context is not clear, the tone is: Sal feels as if everything is dead. Even so, the careful reader has reasons to interrogate the text further—this is especially

From *The View from* On the Road: *The Rhetorical Vision of Jack Kerouac.* © 1999 by the Board of Trustees, Southern Illinois University.

true for the reader who blurs the distinction between fiction and nonfiction, as well as one who realizes that Kerouac made little effort to hide the fact that his "fiction" was largely autobiographical.

In real life, Kerouac met Neal Cassady in December 1946. Kerouac had married Edie Parker in August 1944 but left her in October (they were divorced later after attempts at reconciliation). Parker was connected to Kerouac's arrest as material witness and accomplice after the fact to Lucien Carr's killing of Dave Kammerer. To raise money for bail, Parker's family lawyer insisted that Kerouac marry Edie (Nicosia 1994, 129). Under these marital conditions, it is difficult to imagine that the split would have been "miserably weary." Thus, Sal's narrative, although not necessarily biographically accurate in terms of Kerouac's life, is textually significant. The book *begins* with the element of death. The larger narrative that follows becomes, by extension, an after-death experience or, more neoreligiously, a rebirth. Thus, from the first lines of the text, Kerouac positions the reader for a major transformation.

Death, disease, and weariness characterize the old world from which Kerouac has moved away. The new world, suggested but not articulated at this point in the text, promises something else. More than a new beginning, the text promises a new life, literally. Even the name that Kerouac chose for his persona is suggestive of this experience of rebirth. "Sal" is etymologically related to Paul (originally named Saul), a chief persecutor of Christ's followers who changed his axiology and his identity and became an important herald of the gospel.[1] "Paradise" is the state or condition of the reborn soul in Christian mythology. Both Sal and Paul experience a spiritual death at the beginning of their narratives, and both are transformed by the coming of a new cultural order. Seen in another way, the social institutions of marriage, formal education, and the military failed to supply Paradise with the energy and self-fulfillment that his soul desired. These three institutions, along with work and traditional religion, are the cornerstones of American culture and are widely rejected in the text.

The book's opening sentence presents two important rhetorical breaks from prior literary tradition and infuses in the reader the volatility of Sal's not-quite-so-unique predicament. First, Sal's declaration of discontent breaks from "literature as entertainment to writing as a necessary mode of expressing a particular vision" (Tytell 1976, 70). In other words, Kerouac's style warns the reader that something different is going to happen in the text; the opening tone is a flag that prepares the reader for a different type of reading experience.[2] The effect of this new style is captivating. Bruce Cook explains what happened to him when he first read *On the Road*:

That started it for me. I soon came to regard the Beats as my generation. I felt the same keen sense of identification with them that thousands of others my age did, and I had the same feeling that I was lucky to be in on the beginning of something big. (1971, 3)

That "something big" was a new life, a life that could only be appreciated once people understood that the old life was "dead," at least symbolically. People may have felt that something was wrong with American culture, as discontent existed prior to its naming in *On the Road*. Yet the situation had not been named, at least for middle-class white America, as Kerouac named it by positioning the life that his book documents against the death and the cultural void present and transcended in the opening paragraph.

Extending from the first, the second rhetorical break is evident in the opening sentiment. After shifting from "literature as entertainment" toward "literature as equipment for living," and after contrasting the death and weariness of the old with the promise of something better in the new vision of the world that Kerouac is offering, Kerouac implicitly does something else: he effectively offers an empathetic lure into the hungry cultural waters of young readers who "felt trapped in the bind of societal or parental expectations, bound by the ethos of personal secrecy and self-confinement" (Tytell 1976, 160). This was an age of loyalty: to parents, to country, to God. Each of these loyalties placed demands on young people and forced them to think and feel in certain ways.

The 1950s were a time of suspicion, as exemplified in loyalty oaths and expectations of obedience (Lamont 1990). As the United States government was preparing its citizens for a stultifying Cold War mentality, anything that was considered different was immediately suspect. This was a time when the government provoked fears of Communism and instigated mass witch hunts that condemned many Americans for their legitimate and constitutionally protected actions on behalf of the American political Left (Klehr and Haynes 1992). This culture of suspicion is exemplified in the 1956 Allied Artists film *Invasion of the Body Snatchers*, based on the book by Jack Finney (1955). While the film is ostensibly about space aliens who take over people's bodies in an attempt to control the world, it is, in effect, an anti-Communist film that helped to cultivate an atmosphere of fear (Johnson 1979).

In the film, the "good" characters (red-blooded Americans) can never tell who is or who is not an alien. The aliens *look* like everyone else, but there is something sinister about them, something cold, calculating, ruthless.

Likewise, "good" people in the real world of Cold War politics can never tell for sure who is or who is not a Communist. The aliens are analogous to the Communists, who are just as sinister, according to the official propaganda of the United States. As De Villo Sloan explains:

> To be recruited into [the aliens'] ranks is to join the legions of the living dead. When Benell [the hero of the narrative] encounters [the aliens] at the end of the narrative, they calmly try to reason with him, describing a utopian vision of the future, if only all humans would join them. At this juncture, the discourse is political. It easily conjures up images of Marxist utopians, possible only if the self is given up to the collective. (1988, 185)

Films such as *Invasion of the Body Snatchers* accentuated a fear of Communism in the American public and, by extension, a fear of any social idea that was "left of center." As Glen M. Johnson explains:

> No one can be trusted: the plot of *The Body Snatchers* develops thorough an accumulation of paranoid denunciations of familiars—niece accuses uncle, wife accuses husband, students accuse teacher, son accuses mother. The political parallel is inescapable. "Remember, always," J. Edgar Hoover wrote in *Masters of Deceit*, "that there are thousands of people in this country now working in secret to make it happen here." (1979, 6)

Thus, Hollywood played (as it continues to play) an important role in providing the U.S. government with ideological weapons to justify the arms expenditures that were necessary for it to run its colonies during the Cold War (as well as its current client-states) and to reify the consciousness of consumerism (Bird 1989; Fyne 1985; Parenti 1992; and Smoodin 1988).

As the above suggests, 1950s America was a culture in which any deviance was considered *moral* deviance and was deemed a threat. This threat was not just political. John Tytell highlights the rhetorical atmosphere embedded deeply in the puritanical roots of this country and the concomitant notion that "one's inner being was really suspect, a source of embarrassment or liability, shame or incrimination" (1976, 160). This suspicion, in many ways, was sexual, but it was more than that; any reduction of 1950s conservatism to sexual repression is an oversimplification. Rather, suspicion was based on an irrational fear that was deliberately and rationally presented by the United States government in order to manipulate the American public (Herman and Chomsky 1988; Chomsky 1989; Carey 1997).

U.S. propaganda constantly maintained that the American way of life was about to end, that it was menaced on multiple fronts, and that plurality itself was its greatest threat.[3] To guard the United States against this danger, the social/cultural realm was closely policed by agents of the status quo.

The agitation of Kerouac's rhetorical fantasy struck against the above sentiments and prevailing consciousness, contributed to the identity of a subculture, and cracked the wall of cold mores that was bound eventually to crumble. *On the Road* is a call for plurality; it rejects the culture of suspicion and control. It is not pro-Communist or pro-Socialist, but it is not anti-Communist or anti-Socialist either. Rather, it is pro-body, pro-desire, pro-experience—similar in many ways to the Left politics found in the writings of such social theorists as Gilles Deleuze and Felix Guattari (for example, 1983).[4] Kerouac sees through the propaganda of anti-Communism and asks difficult questions about what it means to be an "American." The book takes us through all parts and experiences of American society—the dirty, the dark, the alternative rationalities and potentialities, things that were formally alien to Kerouac's middle-class reading public.

Cook, for instance, notes the effect *On the Road* had at the time of its publication: "There was a sort of instantaneous flash of recognition that seemed to send thousands of [youth] out into the streets, proclaiming that Kerouac had written their story" (1971, 7). These were the children of the middle class, and they identified with the book so immensely because it broadened their experiences and suggested something more than the limited and limiting messages that they were receiving from their parents, churches, and government, all of which were busy encouraging them to think in politically safe ways. Similar to Sal, they were struggling with their sense of feeling dead. Ironically, these children felt the *inverse* of what movies such as *Invasion of the Body Snatchers* were trying to establish. It became increasingly clear to those who felt alienated from the traditional notions of American culture that the "real" zombies were not the "indoctrinated" citizens of Communist countries but were the American people themselves. The threat to U.S. freedom was not the Soviet Union or the American Communist party, but rather the state religion of anti-Communism and other social pressures that gave the Church and State a tyrannical power over the lives of many young people. This is not an entirely new observation. In 1944, Albert Camus was able to give public support to the claim that "[a]nticommunism is the beginning of dictatorship" (1991, 59).

To the alienated youth of America, Kerouac provides an alternative. Striking out against the death and deprivation of his era, Kerouac, in the third sentence of the novel, introduces Dean Moriarty as the catalyst of his salvation. From beyond the cultural grave, the persona of the narrator speaks out, guided by the shining light of rebirth. Immediately, the reader senses this shift from death to life as Moriarty appears in the text, evoking Kerouac's vision as well as Sal's spiritual redemption. Sal muses, "With the coming of Dean Moriarty began the part of my life you could call my life on the road" (1957, 5). With Moriarty, the reader is introduced to a critical change in perspective. Sal's narrative is about being on the road. But what is so special about the *road* that it becomes the central motif of the novel? For an overt answer to this question, the reader has to wait, although there are clues early in the novel that suggest the "true" value of Kerouac's road. Simply, "the road is life" (1957, 175), Kerouac explains. In Kerouac's world, the road leads away from his symbolic death in the city—the world of work, marriage, school, and the military. Dean is the prophet of the road because he is able to teach others the true metaphysical significance of the road. Sal comments that "Dean is the perfect guy for the road because he actually was born on the road, when his parents were passing through Salt Lake City in 1926, in a jalopy, on their way to Los Angeles" (1957, 5).

The road takes Kerouac from the spiritual poverty of traditional American life. The road, stretching across the breadth of this nation, becomes the symbol of America's true wealth and potential. Kerouac's road is literal; it is the highway to the West, the old Oregon Trail by which the dispossessed and the hopeless could travel in search of a new life. But the road is much more than that; it is the symbolic expression of all spiritual "roads"—it is the dharma path made manifest in asphalt. Since the road is as much spiritual as it is physical, Kerouac needs a spiritual as well as a physical guide. When Kerouac writes that he is going "on the road," he does not mean that he is driving to St. Louis. Destinations are not important. Rather, the "road" represents an odyssey; it itself is a drama. In other words, the "road" is a wilderness; it is *not* the most direct path between two cities. This is why Dean Moriarty is such an important figure in the text and in Kerouac's world. Dean is not simply the companion figure to Sal in the novel, the "other" to Sal's observations. Dean is the novel. Sal could spend his entire life traveling across the country, but without Dean, that travel could not be a transcendence. Likewise, people traveled before Kerouac wrote *On the Road*, but such travel often became a transcendent experience for those who had read the book.[5]

Dean literally is the spirit of the text, just as Neal Cassady is the spirit of the counterculture. Dean/Neal is also the driver of the cars in which Sal/Kerouac sometimes travels. It is ironic, but it also makes sense when considering the above, that Kerouac never got a driver's license—Kerouac is not the driving force of his oven vision. Kerouac simply amplifies the vision that he finds embodied in Neal. Or perhaps both visions are symbiotic: Kerouac's vision, embodied in Neal, helps define Neal, and Neal, in turn, gives Kerouac a concrete set of values to amplify and celebrate. Either way, in *On the Road*, it is Dean, not Sal, who is the outcast prophet through whom the road becomes meaningful, becomes something more than a path between two cities. Dean's spirit is the backdrop upon which the drama of the road can be witnessed. In short, Dean Moriarty is the incarnate soul of the deity Paradise witnesses while passing through the great Western desert: "As we crossed the Colorado–Utah border I saw God in the sky in the form of huge gold sunburning clouds above the desert that seemed to point a finger at me and say, 'Pass here and go on, you're on the road to heaven'" (1957, 150).

Prior to meeting Moriarty Paradise was drawn to the allure of the road and planned to travel, yet he never actualized those plans due to what we can assume to be the responsibilities of the systemic world: the world of marriage, work, and school. Sal's opening comments emphasize the fundamental antithesis between the vision Paradise is breaking from and the one that he is working toward. The friction that Sal feels as he contemplates moving from one worldview to another is the result of a conflict in values between the two structures. The actual process of Sal's shifting between two worldviews affects his life perspective. We can gain a clearer understanding of the importance of this change in Sal's development by applying John Waite Bowers and Donovan J. Ochs's discussion of lateral and vertical deviance to the text (1971).

For Bowers and Ochs, vertical deviance (or "agitation") involves discontent *within* a value system. An example of this involves workers who strike for higher wages, more time off, better working conditions, and improved health privileges, but who do not fundamentally disagree with the business institution itself or the economic culture of society at large. The questioning, in this instance, is not of the value system behind the economics of the community. The system remains intact; dissenters question effects of those values in their lives but do not attack the values themselves. Such a position is not revolutionary: it is an attempt to get the system to reconcile itself to its own meanings, potentialities, and promises.

The above is the position of "agitation" as it is represented by the official rhetoric of this country. For propagandistic reasons, the government often subsumes social unrest by co-opting it and making it appear as if the system is voluntarily working for dissenters. This sentiment is exemplified in Bill Clinton's first inaugural address when he emphatically states, "There is nothing wrong with America that cannot be cured by what is right with America" (1993, 75). Clinton, as a representative of U.S. liberalism, recognizes that there are problems in America but denies that the problems have systemic roots, thus cutting off the possibility for institutional change. Considering that Clinton is the president, his rhetoric is understandable: he co-opts dissent by recognizing it and diffusing its challenge to fundamental American economic practices. In the typology of political positions, this is a "progressive" position (Rossiter 1962). Yet such progressivism is not confrontational; both parties in the dispute are working from the same fundamental vision. The question becomes, How will their differences be managed? (Cathcart 1978, 237–38). This is a reformist position, characteristic of American liberalism that transcends the peculiarities of the two Clinton administrations.

Sal had been working from a vertical position of discontent prior to meeting Dean. Along with millions of other Americans, Paradise was able to divorce his wife, reject the authority of the armed services, work haphazardly toward a college education, and engage in a succession of part-time and temporary jobs, all without directly questioning the values behind these institutions. In other words, Paradise was unhappy with his life and his world but could not see the cause of his problems as being systemic to the dominant culture that had no place for him. In traditional Marxist terms, people such as Sal are suffering from ideology—a false consciousness that is imposed on them by the hegemonic social order (Eagleton 1991). According to this position, the disenfranchised, the poor, and the masses of the lower working classes and unemployed have every reason to rebel against the social order that impoverishes them. The fact that they do not rebel and instead have their revolutionary consciousness thwarted by television, racism, sexism, and other tantalizing candies dangled in front of them is the result and function of ideology.[6]

Paradise clearly desired to be outside of the institutions that forced their hold on him, clearly struggled for a new life, but in vain. All he could experience, all he could *hope* to experience given the epistemology (or ideology) that he was subject to, led him to a miserable state of weariness and despair. The structural condition of Sal's predicament can be understood better in Roland Barthes's terms:

> For the very end of myths is to immobilize the world: they must suggest and mimic a universal order which has fixated once and for all the hierarchy of possession. Thus, every day and everywhere, man is stopped by myths, referred by them to this motionless prototype which lives in his place, stifles him in the manner of a huge internal parasite and assigns to his activity the narrow limits within which he is allowed to suffer without upsetting the world. (1972, 155)

In short, Sal lacked the direction and insight to be able to break from his past (that is, to "upset the world") and to gain agency and influence over his future. His initial attempts to escape from his old life were ruinous: he was still trapped in the value system that the situations of work and family represent, and this powerless feeling led Paradise to the perception of death and disease in his static existence. Sal had reached a point at which he could go no farther, and his vertical perspective prevented him from actually dropping out and taking to the road, which would have been a transformation into lateral agitation. This sentiment is evident in the line "I'd often dream of going West to see the country, always vaguely planning and never taking off" (1957, 5).

As evidenced above, the first page of the novel is where we find a stunted, disgruntled, and symbolically dead Sal, a man who could not find peace with himself or with the world, a man in need of a cultural space in which to transform (as a caterpillar needs a specific space to transform into a butterfly). With his relationship to Dean, that space opens up, as if Dean's presence has the power to reorder physical as well as conceptual space. Life begins to change for Sal. Sal undergoes a metamorphosis—and it is here that the "text" begins.

Obviously, the first page is the beginning of the book in a chronological sense. More importantly, however, we can say that the book conceptually begins in its first paragraph rather than somewhere deep in its body, as is the case with many novels. In contrast, we can also say that the book does not start in the first sentence, as the first sentence is narrated by a dead man. Another way to get at the same idea is to explain how the book conceptually begins with Sal's metamorphosis—his change from a position of vertical agitation to one of lateral agitation. Bowers and Ochs explain that "[a]gitation based on lateral deviance occurs when the agitators dispute the value system itself" (1971, 7). With that change in Sal, our entire perspective with regard to the text changes.

One of among many passages illustrates the effect that Dean has on Sal:

I had been spending a quiet Christmas in the country, as I realized when we got back into the house and I saw the Christmas tree, the presents, and smelled the roasting turkey and listened to the talk of the relatives, but now the bug was on me again, and the bug's name was Dean Moriarty, and I was off on another spur around the road. (1957, 96)

This new perspective is reinforced throughout the book and questions the value system of American institutions. A passage from *Visions of Cody* clearly illustrates that Kerouac, having made the break in his personal life, is writing from a point of lateral agitation:

> In America, the idea of going to college is just like the idea of prosperity is just around the corner, this is supposed to solve something or everything ... because all you had to do was larn [*sic*] what they taught and then everything else was going to be handled; instead of that, and just like prosperity that was never around the corner but a couple of miles at least (and false prosperity—) going to college by acquainting me with all the mad elements of life, such as the sensibilities, books, arts, histories of madness, and fashions, has not only made it impossible for me to learn simple tricks of how to earn a living but has deprived me of my one-time innocent belief in my own thoughts that used to make me handle my own destiny. (1972, 259)

This is a particularly cogent passage. In it, Kerouac is more than a disgruntled or frustrated student; he is more than a college "dropout." Kerouac does not fail in school; rather, he comes to recognize that school *is part of the problem.* School, like so many other systemic pressures, prevents Kerouac from handling his "own destiny." But the passage is about more than destiny: it is about lying, illusions, false pretense; it is about a game that most people are made to play and a value system based upon a myth. Kerouac reinterprets the dominant myths that guide our middle-class culture and stakes his personal existence in direct opposition to it.

Kerouac's questioning in the above passage is exemplified in the persona of Dean. Dean is not school-educated like Sal, and this is one of his strengths. Unlike Sal, who is "deprived" of his "innocent" thoughts that helped him to handle his own destiny, Dean does nothing else but live out his destiny. Throughout the book, Dean is also portrayed as "innocent"—his crimes and transgressions are always "angelic" because Dean lives in "time," in "destiny," in "truth." Dean is free while the rest of us suffer through formal educations that enslave us to the decrepit morality that Kerouac fears. Dean's education is from the university of life where he "spent a third of his time in the pool hall, a third in jail, and a third in the public library" (1957, 8).

As the mechanism for Sal's transformation, Dean's life becomes an extension, a manifest form of Sal's innate questioning. From the outset of the book, Sal strives for a complete spiritual identification with Dean. However, by the end of the book, when Sal sits on the broken-down pier in New Jersey and muses about Dean's missing father, there is a sense in which Sal has failed to maintain the intensity of that identification. Dean's father remains Dean's father; he does not become "our" father. Sal and Dean are clearly separate, but this does not matter. Identification is never complete as Dean is too intense and too holy for Sal to achieve total consubstantiality with him. The questioning itself ultimately becomes a powerful form of social agitation. As Gregory Stephenson explains, "For Sal, Dean represents a psychological and spiritual reorientation, a new pattern of conduct, a new system of values, including spontaneity, sensuality, energy, intuition, and instinct" (1990, 156).

Bowers and Ochs discuss social agitation as occurring "when a group has a grievance or grievances" and no alleviation is built into the existing social structure (1971, 7). These theorists define agitation as the state in which "people outside the normal decision making establishment ... advocate a significant social change and ... encounter a degree of resistance within the establishment" (4). By this definition, Sal's opening lines and Kerouac's distinct tone in *On the Road* qualify as instances of agitation. But why, for what reason, and for and against whom?

On one level Kerouac, through Paradise, is striving to create for himself a situation of freedom and experience by rejecting as insufficient the value base offered to him by his culture. The values of this culture and its moral deficiencies are mocked by Sal and Dean when they arrive in Washington during President Truman's second inauguration. They encounter, on Pennsylvania Avenue, "Great displays of war might ... B-29's, PT boats, artillery, all kinds of war material that looked murderous in the snowy grass; the last thing was a regular small ordinary lifeboat that looked pitiful and foolish." Dean's reply to all this is, "What are these people up to? Harry's sleeping somewhere in this town.... Good old Harry.... Man from Missouri, as I am.... That must be his own boat" (1957, 112). However, their discontent with the dominant values of this society soon changes from naive mockery to a more soul-grating realization of what the values of their rejected culture have held for the peoples of the Earth. Here Paradise describes a meeting with some Indians of the Sierra Madre:

> [The Indians] watched Dean, serious and insane at his raving wheel, with eyes of hawks. All had their hands outstretched. They had come down from the back of mountains and higher places to hold forth their hands for something they thought civilization could offer, and they never dreamed the sadness and the poor broken delusion of it. They didn't know that a bomb had come that could crack all our bridges and roads and reduce them to jumbles, and we could be as poor as they someday, and stretching out our hands in the same, same way. (1957, 24)

The inability of materialism to provide for the spiritual/cultural needs of Americans becomes obvious when Kerouac writes of the above scene in *Visions of Cody*: "All the Indians along the road want something from us. We wouldn't be on the road if we had it" (1972, 380).

Kerouac's discontent with American capitalism and its destructive qualities is more bluntly communicated by Bull, another character in *On the Road*, modeled after William S. Burroughs. Bull exclaims, "The bastards right now are only interested in seeing if they can blow up the world" (1957, 128). Bull continues his condemnation of the establishment's consciousness:

> "These bastards have invented plastics by which they could make houses that last forever. And tires. Americans are killing themselves by the millions every year with defective rubber tires that get hot on the road and blow up. They could make tires that never blow up. Same with tooth powder. There's a certain gum they've invented and they won't show it to anybody that if you chew it as a kid you'll never get a cavity for the rest of your born days. Same with clothes. They can make clothes that last forever. They prefer making cheap goods so's everybody have to go on working and punching timeclocks and organizing themselves in sullen unions and floundering around while the big grab goes on to Washington and Moscow." (1957, 124)

The deficiency of American values and the type of world that these values have created are also judged by Sal as they appear personified in the guise of the police. Throughout the novel, Sal and Dean repeatedly encounter cops who harass them, jail them, trail them in the cities, and take their money.[7] In the middle of the book, Paradise finally condemns, in a way that is highly prophetic of the 1960s, this manifestation of the old values:

> The American police are involved in psychological warfare against those Americans who don't frighten them with imposing papers and threats. It's a Victorian police force; it peers out of musty windows and wants to inquire about everything, and can make crimes if the crimes don't exist to its satisfaction. (1957, 113)

Kerouac later contrasts this image of American police with what he found in Mexico: "Such lovely policemen God hath never wrought in America. No suspicions, no fuss, no bother: he was the guardian of the sleeping town, period" (1957, 242).

What is important in the above discussion is the attitude of social deviance that accentuates the romanticized reality that Kerouac was striving to create; it is the sense of freedom through questioning that Kerouac represents. In the 1950s, most middle-class Americans, whose only negative experience with the police would be traffic violations, would not think of criticizing them. During this time, the police were, as they have usually been, staunch supporters of middle-class privilege and racist ideology (Walker 1980). In contrast, Kerouac's attitude demarcated a demystification of an important American institution, thus contributing to a growing social rift between the police and the white, privileged American public.

Kerouac's perspective polarizes two worldviews and vitalizes an opposition to the psychological and potentially physical oppression of the corporate state. Tytell explains the effect that Kerouac had:

> For many, [On the Road] was the book that most motivated dissatisfaction with the atmosphere of unquestioning acceptance that stifled the fifties; ... its audience grows and young people gravitate to a force in it that seems to propel by the material itself, almost as if its author did not exist as an outside agency of creation. (1976, 157)

Tytell uses the word "gravitate" to suggest the magnetic quality found in On the Road. In an effort to rephrase what Tytell terms as gravitation, I substitute the phrase "chaining-out process." Tytell is merely writing in nonrhetorical terms what Bormann explains as the influence of "dramatizations" in creating spheres of attraction, understanding, and influence:

> The dramatizations which catch on and chain out in small groups are worked into public speeches and into the mass media and, in turn, spread across larger publics, serve to sustain the members' sense of community, to impel them strongly to action ... and to provide them with a social reality filled with heroes, villains, emotions, and attitudes. (1972, 398)

Dramatizations are, in a sense, self-contained gravitational systems, marked by spheres of influence. People become attracted to dramas and enter orbits around particular visions. In this case, the Vision of Social Deviance is a call to action, a questioning of motivation, and a suggestion for a new social reality with a reordering of priorities. People who read Kerouac's book and enter the orbit of its drama are logologically encouraged to see social deviance as a political and social option. As discussed by Burke, logology is the study of "words about words" (1970, 1). Specifically, logology refers to the relationships *among* words, what words imply for each other in terms of an incipient action (see Bridges 1996). In short, readers who are affected by Kerouac's book learn a vocabulary and an attitude to help them to focus their discontent and to gain the support of others who feel the same way. Readers of the novel are taught that their alienation has roots in a problematic and systemic world and that, in their alienation, they have ideological peers.

NOTES

1. More obviously, "Sal" is Latin for "salt" (as in "salt of the earth") and Salvadore, Sal's proper name, is Italian for "savior."

2. Specifically, Kerouac's style is an example of "foregrounding." For a discussion of foregrounding, see Leech and Short (1981, 28).

3. This argumentative tactic is exemplified in the discourse of J. Edgar Hoover. See Swartz (1996c) for a specific study.

4. While this claim has theoretical and intuitive integrity, it is true that Kerouac personally expressed contrary behaviors at times.

5. Primeau (1996) places Kerouac's novel in the history of road narratives and argues that *On the Road* defines the genre in the United States.

6. The complexities of "ideology," as a concept, is the subject of much critical theory. For a selective overview of critical theory, see Bronner and Kellner (1989).

7. See Walker (1980) for a discussion of police corruption in U.S. history.

BEN GIAMO

WHAT *IT* IS?

Kerouac wrote to his "Dear Ma" back in Ozone Park, Long Island, during the first leg of his journey across America in July 1947: "I've been eating apple pie & ice cream all over Iowa & Nebraska, where the food is so good. Will be in Colorado tonight—and I'll write you a letter from Denver. Everything fine, money holding out." He signed the note "Love, Jacky xxx" and included a postscript: "You ought to see the *Cowboys* out here."[1]

So did you ever read a book billed as the classic novel of the Beat Generation, in which the narrator and one of two protagonists in the novel makes his way cross-country eating apple pie and ice cream at every roadside diner simply because it's "nutritious and ... delicious"? You won't find much rebellion in that homey Norman Rockwellian act. Yet it is part of being on the road, as integral to it as taking a spoonful of the "greatest laugh in the world" by an old-time Nebraska farmer and holding it to one's ear. Or hitching a ride on the back of a flatbed truck with an odd assembly of drifters linked by the crapshoot of time and motion and direction and by the hypnotic white lines of the highway's unwinding immensity. "This is a narrative of life among the wild bohemians of what Kerouac was the first to call 'the beat generation,'" Malcolm Cowley wrote in his acceptance report for *On the Road* to Viking Press in April 1957.[2] The report then goes on to highlight the juicy details that turn the story into a litany of mad adventures

From *Kerouac, the Word and the Way: Prose Artist as Spiritual Quester.* © 2000 by the Board of Trustees, Southern Illinois University.

and kicks—the crazy antics of protracted juvenile delinquents "always on wheels." It would have been better to write merely what Sal Paradise states in the midst of his third trip back and forth across the continent—"the road is life."

What then is life? Life is suffering, the precepts of both Buddhist and Christian teaching. But in Kerouac's second novel, written in April 1951 and published in September 1957, the sorrows of young John do not stand alone; rather, for Jack, the road of life entails certain sadness paired with exuberant joy. The up and down scale of the novel is so exact that it brings Frank Sinatra's famous lyric to mind: "riding high in April, shot down in May"— "That's Life." And so it is, a most honest record of experience, especially from a writer "interested in life, any kind of life, all of it!" The oscillation between ecstasy and suffering—elation and dejection—appears to be the maxim of the novel. It simply goes with the territory, as if a physical law of motion—"our one and noble function of the time." This oscillation, in which characters and events both expand and contract, results in an uncanny state of equilibrium whereby the states of creation and annihilation balance out. Thus, for every IT one takes a HIT, and so on. Such a condition, especially when accelerated and telescoped as it is in the novel, generates rich insights into self and other, society in general, the stuff of human nature, and nature itself—its movement from high to low energy states and back again.

The proposition that the road is life, and life itself the equilibrist, demands a writing style that can respond to the movement between opposite emotive forces. In part, this is one reason why Kerouac turns away from the profound and ponderous lyricism of *The Town and the City*, that "Wolfean romantic posh," as Carlo Marx (Ginsberg) puts it from his Denver doldrums dungeon in *On the Road*, and toward a much more factualist narrative style. The style, though conventional and more objectively oriented, does contain a syncopated positive charge in order to heat up the novelistic system and capture that oscillation between the swells of excitement and the drain of despair. The proposition also leads Kerouac away from a strictly Christian form of ecstatic mystical union and towards an embrace of the aesthetic and hedonistic factors in the nature of existence, and their consequences. Though both Dean Moriarty and Sal Paradise refute the Nietzschean notion that God is dead—"God exists without qualms"—and although the pursuit of IT finally devolves to the biblical magic of Mexico, the frantic dynamism and will to power embodied in Dean Moriarty kick up the spectral dust of Nietzsche's ghost and conceal those highest values, anchored in the eternal and/or the enlightened one. These qualities do not necessarily make for an amoral novel. Rather, the altered morality expressed in *Road* descends, in part, from D. H. Lawrence's attribution of Whitman's achievement: "He was the first to smash the old moral conception, that the soul of man is something 'superior' and 'above' the flesh.... Whitman was the first heroic seer to seize the soul by the scruff of her neck and plant her down among the potsherds."[3] Such a passional soul, which finds its true home along the open road, naturally embeds the spiritual quest in the phenomenal world of sensation and, at times, in sensory indulgence.

In the Buddhist sense, however, to be unenlightened is to be simply ignorant. According to D. T. Suzuki, "so long as passions ... were not subdued, and the mind still remained enshrouded in ignorance, no Buddhists could ever dream of obtaining a Moksha (deliverance) which is Nirvana, and this deliverance from Ignorance and passions was the work of Enlightenment."[4] Therefore, as viewed from his Buddhist phase of the mid-1950s, Kerouac's designation of On the Road as "'Pre-enlightenment' work" reveals the clarity with which he distinguished the spiritual dimensions and stages of his literary work. During this middle period, Kerouac often associated this Buddhist emphasis on deliverance with the Christian notion of self-denial and detachment from the spurious pleasures of the world so as to rest peacefully in the arms of God and/or heavenly Buddha. This direct relation led at times to Kerouac's superimposed perspective on Buddhism and Catholicism.

But for now, grinding through the gears of Kerouac's early phase, it is to that world of sensation we must return. The surface of Road is buzzing with frenetic activity, for the road provides the necessary link and lifeline to the busy, restless, energetic multiplicities of the too-worn yet still-possible world. As Dean Moriarty puts it, "'Yes! You and I, Sal, we'd dig the whole world with a car like this because, man, the road must eventually lead to the whole world'" (230). It is all there for the taking, providing one has the wheels, the jack, and the knack: old highways, cars, hotels and flophouses, lunchcarts and diners, smokestacks, railyards, red-brick and gray-stone cityscapes, neon-glazed streets, insane bars and jazz clubs, cantinas and whorehouses. All stretched out *ad infinitum* along the road-world of the earth-bound eternal now, all madly and strangely and variously peopled with hepcats and musicians, Susquehanna ghosts, the phantom of Dean's lost father—bum, women, and the fellahin. However it is laid out, whether short or long, straight or curved, the road is the perfect vehicle for expressing all the "pure products of America go[ne] crazy," to borrow an apt poetic line from William Carlos Williams.

Think of Dean Moriarty, the hero of Road, lost western frontiersman turned urban cowboy-brakeman always on the make—a wild roaming being in perpetual motion. Gone, though not gone beyond. The character of Dean Moriarty (based on Neal Cassady) is the very personification of restlessness, "a wild yea-saying overburst of American joy" (10). Sal Paradise (alias Duluoz) catches the itch from him, going on the cross-country road by his own adventurous self and with his bosom buddy on several occasions—bosom because in Dean, with "suffering bony face," Sal sees his "long-lost brother" and lost bliss of boyhood among the rough trade of Paterson (another stand-in for Lowell). But whether or not Sal actually finds his "brother" and recovers that lost bliss is another question altogether. In the meantime, in between time, and all along the way, Sal "knew there'd be girls, visions, everything; somewhere along the line the pearl would be handed to me" (11).

Along the road; however, it seems as though the pearl of wisdom Sal desires has been exchanged for the ball bearings of cumbustive metallic flight in the form of a 1949 Hudson sedan. Paradise soon sees that Moriarty's soul is "wrapped up in a fast car, a coast to reach, and a woman at the end of the road" (230). As always, Sal goes along for the ride. On the one hand, Dean represents the perfervid Beat Generation chase for IT, which may be defined as the "ragged and ecstatic joy of pure being" (195). As a form of ecstasy, the search for IT spins on the wheels of free, spontaneous, fleeting, hedonistic existence blurring the lines of our mortality. On the other hand, the tumult of Moriarty's life conveys the "sorrowful sweats" that result from crisscrossing the continent, driven by the mad rush of blind passion and momentary whim of desire so that, by the end of the novel, Dean has collected three wives, divorced two of them, spurted four kids, and forsaken the East Coast to live once again with his second wife on the West Coast. On his first solo trip cross-country, Sal makes Denver and gets his initial glimpse into the organized chaos of Dean's life from their mutual friend Carlo Marx. Sal asks Marx, "'What's the schedule?'"

> "The schedule is this: I came off work a half-hour ago. In that time Dean is balling Marylou at the hotel and gives me time to change and dress. At one sharp he rushes from Marylou to Camille—of course neither one of them knows what's going on—and bangs her once, giving me time to arrive at one-thirty. Then he comes out with me—first he has to beg with Camille, who's already started hating me—and we come here [Marx's apartment] to talk till six in the morning. We usually spend more time than that, but it's getting awfully complicated and he's pressed for time. Then at six he goes back to Marylou—and he's going to spend all day tomorrow running around to get the necessary papers for their divorce." (42–43)

Both the road and Dean Moriarty are treated ambiguously by Kerouac. Together they form the hard surface and romanticized subject for celebration as well as for registering sorrow—especially the sadness bound up with suffering and the feeling of an impending mortality. For the vehicle for joyous adventurous kicks is also the agency for one's passing through, and the very nature of passing through accentuates the fact that "time's running, running," as Dean puts it on one occasion. Despite the frantic pace, despite the speeding rush onward, Dean is still contained by chronological time; "'cause now is the time and *we all know time!*'" he shouts (114). But does he know or betray time? For to know time is to understand that it is impossible to beat time—the "death-delivering ravages of time."[5] "Where go? what do? what for?—sleep" (167). The road may be preferable to the inn, as Cervantes wrote, but movement for the sake of movement on modern mid-twentieth-century American highways and byways is a sure path to pain—no pearl.

Even during Sal's first solo cross-country venture, where Dean is encountered only briefly in Denver, the force and counterforce of time tinged with desire are deeply felt. The false start from Bear Mountain is the first minor indication. Sal had wanted to follow the red line of Route 6 on the map because it spanned the continent, from Cape Cod to Los Angeles. But getting a ride proved impossible, and then the rains came to drench his idealism. He ends up hitching back to New York City and taking a bus to Chicago and picking up Route 6 in Illinois, a much more practical maneuver. By the end of chapter 9, while Sal is still in Denver, the oscillation between exuberant joy and certain sadness is already established. During a ribald night after the opera—which enlarges Sal's gloom—in the high altitude of Central City, he begins to reflect on the spectacle of man in nature:

> I wondered what the Spirit of the Mountain was thinking, and looked up and saw jackpines in the moon.... In the whole eastern dark wall of the Divide this night there was silence and the whisper of the wind, except in the ravine where we roared; and on the other side of the Divide was the great Western Slope, and the big plateau that went to Steamboat Springs, and dropped, and led you to the western Colorado desert and the Utah desert; all in darkness now as we fumed and screamed in our mountain nook, mad drunken Americans in the mighty land. We were on the roof of America and all we could do was yell, I guess—across the night, eastward over the Plains, where somewhere an old man with white hair was probably walking toward us with the Word, and would arrive any minute and make us silent. (55)

The old prophet appears several times throughout the novel, as if reminding readers to dig like miners for the meaning in experience, to ascertain the wisdom—if any—behind sheer sensual transient desire. This figure, so well positioned by Kerouac to question, at times ironically, the whole purpose of blurring thoughtless movement, first appears while Sal travels from Cheyenne to Denver: "I pictured myself in a Denver bar that night, with all the gang, and in their eyes I would be strange and ragged and like the Prophet who has walked across the land to bring the dark Word, and the only Word I had was 'Wow!'" (37). This is nothing but the hissing surface of the road shaped into three letters—the sound is all exclamation and no depth. Kerouac matches this amusing visceral high of experience with the sad stale low of the morning after in Central City: "Everything seemed to be collapsing." The following night, after the sigh of impatient sex, Sal and a girlfriend gaze up at the ceiling and wonder "what God had wrought when He made life so sad" (56–57). The only response is a reflexive one—move on to San Francisco.

Sal's itch to get on to the next destination and sign on board a ship to parts unknown numbs into a rather comical episode of entrapment in the land of everyday bourgeois domesticity. Not only does Sal live amid the incessant squabbles of his friend Remi Boncoeur (Henri Cru) and his cantankerous girlfriend Lee Ann in Mill City, California, but he signs on to work with Remi as a security guard in the barracks that temporarily quarters overseas construction workers. So thus far he has spent only about two weeks on the road before he is landlocked for a good two and a half months as he watches crew after crew ship out: "I was sworn in by the local police chief, given a badge, a club, and now I was a special policeman" (63). Sal is a somewhat inept and mildly subversive Chaplinesque cop as he makes his rounds, getting drunk with the dormers and accidently raising the American flag upside down on one occasion. But he hangs in there, sending most of his paycheck back home to his aunt and learning the difference between thieves and conformists, which isn't great, until the whole tedious affair overwhelms him. During a big night out with Lee Ann, Remi, and his stepparents, Sal lets loose: "I forgave everybody, I gave up, I got drunk.... Everything was falling apart. My stay in San Francisco was coming to an end. Remi would never talk to me again.... It would take years for him to get over it. How disastrous all this was compared to what I'd written him from Paterson, planning my red line Route 6 across America. Here I was at the end of America no more land—and now there was nowhere to go but back" (77–78).

On the return, however, Sal finds someone and someplace to go before heading back—an amorous interlude with Terry, his Mexican girl whom he meets on a bus to LA. After a skittish start, the romance blossoms and Sal finds love in the midst of Mexican and Okie migrant farm worker communities. The combination of romance, ethnicity, and field-hand labor (at this time Sal alternately fashions himself an "old Negro cotton-picker" and a Mexican) unleashes his deep *sympatico* with the oppressed who live out the script of a premodern fellahin folk culture rooted to the land: "I looked up at the dark sky and prayed to God for a better break in life and a better chance to do something for the little people I loved. Nobody was paying any attention to me up there. I should have known better. It was Terry who brought my soul back" (96–97).

The expansive interlude proves tender and compassionate and also doomed to failure. Although vague plans are made to continue the affair in New York City, Sal and Terry both know deep down that this will never happen. "Everything was collapsing.... I told Terry I was leaving. She had been thinking about it all night and was resigned to it. Emotionlessly she kissed me in the vineyard and walked off down the row. We turned at a dozen paces, for love is a duel, and looked at each other for the last time" (99–101).

Tired, haggard, and weary, Sal begins to know the ravages of time by the end of his first trip across the country and back. As if to exaggerate his condition, Sal comes across the Ghost of the Susquehanna outside of Harrisburg, Pennsylvania—a misdirected "walking hobo of some kind who covered the entire Eastern Wilderness on foot.... poor forlorn man, poor lost sometimeboy, now broken ghost of the penniless wilds." Thrown out of a railroad station in Harrisburg at dawn, where he was sleeping on a bench, Sal Paradise begins to contemplate the cruel injustice of it all: "Isn't it true that you start your life a sweet child believing in everything under your father's roof? Then comes the day of the Laodiceans, when you know you are wretched and miserable and poor and blind and naked, and with the visage of a gruesome grieving ghost you go shuddering through nightmare life" (104–5). This feeling of disillusionment "Gad, I was sick and tired of life"— is deepened even further by the time Sal returns to the swirl of Times Square with eight thousand miles under his belt. He takes in the futility of the "mad dream—grabbing, taking, giving, sighing, dying, just so they could be buried in those awful cemetery cities beyond Long Island City" (106). To make matters worse, the trip that launches Paradise on the road ends with a missed connection with Dean in New York City—Sal's "long-lost brother" lost again.

Thus awakened to the interplay of fervent dreams, suffering life, and drifting souls, Sal goes home to figure out what was lost and what was gained from the adventure. One thing, however, is for certain: he now knows time— both its shifting ravages and its threads of continuity—for while he was gone his aunt "worked on a great rag rug woven of all the clothes in [Sal's] family for years, which was now finished and spread on [his] bedroom floor, as complex and as rich as the passage of time itself" (107). In this rough design, a certain equilibrium is stitched throughout the whole pattern: as time beats Sal down it also restores him.

Throughout the remainder of the novel, however, after the beginning of the second trip—this time with Dean more than a year later—there is no more mention of Sal's family (reduced to one brother, Rocco, and his Southern relatives), save for his lone aunt whom he lives with when off the road. What happened to the big joyous family togetherness of *The Town and the City*? Increasingly, the beats—the "sordid hipsters of America that [Sal] was slowly joining" (Dean/Cassady, Carlo/Ginsberg, Bull Lee/Burroughs, Remi/Cru, and so on)—command more and more of Paradise's attention and energy as the family recedes into near oblivion. In fact, all of the key members of "the gang" appear to be orphanlike: Sal lives with his aunt; Dean's mother died when he was a boy and his father—the "tinsmith" wino, who raised his son on the Denver skid row—is now a gone hobo; Carlo, who resides in his grotesque cave, the perfect placement for his subterranean designs, never mentions family; and Remi, a real orphan, was brought up by stepparents and, therefore, is "out to get back everything he'd lost; there was no end to his loss" (70). Such loss and alienation are the driving forces behind "all this franticness and jumping around" that the beats insist upon, revved up in their search for freedom of spontaneous action, liberation of spirit, self-willed individualism, and brotherhood. Therefore, as abundant American progress shifts into overdrive during the unprecedented military-industrial state of the 1950s, the conformist ideal of social stability gets exchanged for the careening, full-throttled seizure of mobility.

The second trip, which brings Dean and Sal into their first real encounter, sees them shuttling back and forth between Testament, Virginia, and New York City to move some furniture for Sal's aunt. (Dean arrives out of the blue and so Sal's aunt finds something useful for him to do.) The shuttle service is really a warm-up for a longer cross-country trip to San Francisco by way of Texas and the Southwestern route. Now, even before embarking on the long road trip, Sal wonders briefly whether it's better to race or rest his soul. Should he move or stay put? Which one is more beneficial to his well-being? Should they plan on finding a real destination somewhere—"go someplace, find something?" Or should they be magicians of the short stay, barely leaving their meaningless breath behind as they streak through the American night to the next place beyond the bend?

The answer: "The only thing to do was to go" (119). But not without some reservations, or at least a nagging absence of something vaguely felt left undone, incomplete, unattended. "Just about that time," Sal admits, "a strange thing began to haunt me. It was this: I had forgotten something. There was a decision that I was about to make before Dean showed up, and now it was driven clear out of my mind." The haunting decision had something to do with Sal's dream about the Shrouded Arabian Traveler chasing him across the desert, and who finally overtook Paradise just before he could reach the Protective City. In a moment of narrative calm and reflection, Sal considers the collective import of the dream:

> Naturally, now that I look back on it, this is only death: death will overtake us before heaven. The one thing that we yearn for in our living days, that makes us sigh and groan and undergo sweet nauseas of all kinds, is the remembrance of some lost bliss that was probably experienced in the womb and can only be reproduced (though we hate to admit it) in death. But who wants to die? In the rush of events I kept thinking about this in the back of my mind. I told it to Dean and he instantly recognized it as the mere simple longing for pure death; and because we're all of us never in life again, he, rightly, would have nothing to do with it, and I agreed with him then. (124)

The dream and its interpretation are soon left in the cloud kicked up by the red dust of the Hudson—"the too-huge world vaulting us, and it's good-by" (156). Ah, the protective device of escapism on the run. But at least for the duration of a rest stop, Sal managed to grip something fundamental about the *alpha* and *omega* of human existence—its mixture of bliss and mortality, joy and sorrow, and the beauty inherent in the appreciation of it all. Although Dean and Sal turn their backs on the spiritual significance of the dream, their minds "enshrouded in ignorance," Kerouac does not, for he lets the reader know that Sal Paradise "agreed with [Dean] *then*," as if to suggest that in time a different viewpoint might take hold, a perspective that would confront the realities of impermanence: the pain of birth, old age, sickness, and death.

But, for now, "we lean forward to the next crazy venture beneath the skies" (156). And merrily they go along, blurring time, which ends like the long stretch of the road itself, in death. The only reprieve from the terminus of chronological time is a high-octane mixture of speed and desire embodied in IT. IT, a transcendent state of pure excitement, stops the felt experience of linear time screeching in its tracks. It is first evoked by Dean when in the company of Rollo Greb, whose sense of excitement with life "blew out of his eyes in stabs of fiendish light." Dean tries to explain this strange suspension of being and time to Sal in a rush of hipster bopisms: "'That's what I was trying to tell you—that's what I want to be. I want to be like him. He's never hung-up, he goes every direction, he lets it all out, he knows time, he has nothing to do but rock back and forth. Man, he's the end! You see, if you go like him all the time you'll finally get it.'" Sal seems perplexed: "'Get what?'" Dean exclaims: "'IT! IT! I'll tell you—now no time, we have no time now ...'" (127). Dean's utterance is really a double entendre, for he means not only later we'll discuss this matter, but also this is IT—"now no time, we have no time," or, in other words, we've beat the shroudy specter of time, and somehow sprung ourselves from the prison house of calendar and clock into an eternal now. The rush of IT blossoms at Birdland, where Dean and Sal immediately go after leaving Greb to hear George Shearing, a renowned jazz pianist, elevated by Dean to the stature of God. "And Shearing began to rock; a smile broke over his ecstatic face; he began to rock in the piano seat, back and forth, slowly at first, then the beat went up, and he began rocking fast, his left foot jumped up with every beat, his neck began to rock crookedly, he brought his face down to the keys, he pushed his hair back, his combed hair dissolved, he began to sweat" (128). Shearing, like Greb, rocks back and forth, not to a metronome, not to keep the cool beat of time's deterministic tick-tockery, but to escape it altogether. This is the intimate body language of IT—a hotly affirmative Dionysian gesture to "spastic ecstasy." Although "Dean was popeyed with awe," Sal registers skepticism, as if to take the rhythm of back and forth to another existential level—hot and cool, fast and slow, high and low, ecstatic and flat, IT and NOT. "This madness would lead nowhere. I didn't know what was happening to me, and I suddenly realized it was only the tea that we were smoking" (128–29). Though initially dismissive about IT, Sal continues to rock along for the ride through "old tumbledown holy America from mouth to mouth and tip to tip."

For the most part, the road keeps Paradise in the groove of time, but Sal does manage to slip away once in the story and experience that which had been scattered by the sparks of hedonistic activity, that which had been buried under the heap of unsubdued passion. This amounts to a countervailing sense of IT, and perhaps a glimpse into a spiritual form of ecstasy that will take root after the road trails off. After an amusing visit with Bull Lee, his wife Jane, and Carlo Marx in Texas, the ragged crew finally make San Francisco, where Dean abandons both Sal and Marylou, his first wife, in order to make amends with Camille, his second wife. "Where is Dean and why isn't he concerned about our welfare? I lost faith in him that year" (171). Sal, without food, money, or friends, growing delirious with hunger, picking up butts from the street near the Tenderloin, having the "beatest time of [his] life," is suddenly delivered from despair and the devastating jazz of time. Walking about, he seems to hear another note in the air—the long hollow breath of a bamboo flute signifying nothing.

IT begins to happen during an imaginary encounter with a proprietress of a fish-and-chips shop on Market Street, whom Sal takes to be his "strange Dickensian mother" from two centuries ago in England. He becomes unstuck in time, "now only in another life and in another body," unsure if he is in Frisco or N'Orleans or da city city city. In a projection of remorse, the mother lashes out at him and the son suffers the good Christian opprobrium for his inclination toward unbridled pleasure, the lush life of drunkenness and routs. "'O son! did you not ever go on your knees and pray for deliverance for all your sins and scoundrel's acts? Lost boy! Depart!'" And so he does, taking a leave of absence from the conditioned nature of things—from time itself

> And for just a moment I had reached the point of ecstasy that I always wanted to reach, which was the complete step across chronological time into timeless shadows, and wonderment in the bleakness of the mortal realm, and the sensation of death kicking at my heels to move on, with a phantom dogging its own heels, and myself hurrying to a plank where all the angels dove off and flew into the holy void of uncreated emptiness, the potent and inconceivable radiance shining in bright Mind Essence, innumerable lotus-lands falling open in the magic mothswarm of heaven.... I realized that I had died and been reborn numberless times but just didn't remember.... I felt sweet, swinging bliss.... I thought I was going to die the very next moment. (172–73)

This "step across chronological time," a wondrous adjustment to the fated dream of the Shrouded Traveler, is another form of ecstasy, an enlightened sense of IT, one that, though not a controlling principle in the novel, works momentarily to suggest what is missing from the first definition, that is, the "ragged and ecstatic joy of pure being." For Sal's shimmering glimpse of IT in the "timeless shadows" limns a form of Buddhist ecstasy (mixed with Catholic notions of angels and heaven) associated with liberation *from* being and not the more conventional liberation *of* being inherent in the original sense of IT. Such a liberation, in the former sense, is clearly present in Sal's vision, for he reaches the plank of the Protective City of his Shrouded Traveler dream, which is located much further east of the Arabian desert—the Far East. Springing from the plank of previous conceptions and cultural restraints, Sal dives deeply into the "holy void of uncreated emptiness." The Buddhist terms, concepts, and images that flash through the passage deliver Sal into a briefly felt state of nirvana or the All-At-One-Ment, as the Buddha puts it in the *Diamond Sutra*, and what F. S. C. Northrop refers to as the undifferentiated, all-embracing, indeterminate aesthetic continuum. Other arbitrary conceptions for this state of nonbeing include emptiness—void—ultimate escape; by any other name, it would feel like "sweet, swinging bliss."

In an instant, having tasted the fruits of nirvana, Sal is back in the realm of samsara—the born, created, shaped, differentiated. The normal gray quotidian is made fragrant by the fact that he is on the street starving. At this point, the narrator makes an interesting confession about the vision: "I was too young to know what had happened." It is a revealing remark that highlights the aesthetic distance between Kerouac and the character of Sal Paradise, while also taking the reader beyond the limits of this *Road* so as to suggest a sense of maturity and insight that have come in time/out of time. One assumes that such an admission, and the meaning that it packs, is the result of leading the examined life and the discovery of Buddhist teaching. In fact, given the pattern, tone, and dominant impulse of the novel, it seems as if the visionary passage is less a foreshadowing of Kerouac's keen interest in Buddhism and more of a retrofit once his self-study was underway in 1954, almost three years since he completed the *Road* manuscript, which was not published until 1957, thus allowing much time to play with various insertions and perform related editorial tasks.[6]

Be that as it may, snared by samsara, the youth resumes his lush course of desire through the here and now dreamworld of sensory delights. "In the window I smelled all the food of San Francisco"—bluefish, lobster, steamed clams, beef *au jus*, roast chicken, hamburger and coffee, chili beans, chow mein, pasta, soft-shelled crabs, ribs. How could this young man's dream of San Francisco be improved? Simply "add fog, hunger-making raw fog, and the throb of neons in the soft night, the clack of high-heeled beauties, white doves in a—hinese grocery window" (173–74). Clearly, Sal is back on track with the design of the novel, the thrust of the *Road*, especially after Dean arrives to rescue him from the plank of idle visions in strange shadows of butt-crusted San Francisco street emptiness. Then, as the second tour ends, the by-now predictable state of collapse ensues—back and forth, back and forth: "What I accomplished by coming to Frisco I don't know. Camille wanted me to leave; Dean didn't care one way or the other.... At dawn I got my New York bus and said good-by to Dean and Marylou. They wanted some of my sandwiches. I told them no. It was a sullen moment. We were all thinking we'd never see one another again and we didn't care" (177–78).

But only several months later, in the spring of 1949, Sal initiates the third trip—from New York City to San Francisco via Denver. In Denver, the rhythm of the road kicks in, and by now the reader understands the beginning point of the quest: movement from a state of rest to the early stirrings of desire. Walking around the African American quarters of Denver at "lilac evening," Sal feels uneasy in the lowlands of his soul. He realizes that he is simply a "'white man' disillusioned." Romanticizing the life of the "Negro" and Mexicans, Sal complains about the emptiness he feels at the very core of his existence, "feeling that the best the white world had offered was not enough ecstasy for me, not enough life, joy, kicks, darkness, music, not enough night.... It was the Denver Night; all I did was die" (180–81).

Sal's keen awareness of the nothingness within creates an insatiable hunger for life, an intense attachment to the "mad dream" envisioned from Times Square. When he hooks up with Dean in San Francisco, Sal's restless longing to affirm something passionate in every breath he takes is manifolded by Dean's "pious frenzy." Together, Sal and Dean find each other and see through each other; they meet again not only as companions of the road but as true friends in search of experience and meaning and togetherness. The sense of care that the two friends display, and the clarity of IT that occurs, gives the third trip a degree of tenderness and a growing depth of insight displayed by the narrator. Such development and maturation that Sal undergoes proves that Kerouac is no fool, no happy delinquent who, like a latter-day version of Peter Pan in zoot suit and chains, will never grow up. No, Kerouac is quite deliberate about IT all.

Shortly after Sal finds Dean in San Francisco, they both get thrown out of the house by Camille, quite deservedly I might add. Drawn and disoriented but still suffused with pointless excitement, Dean stumbles and circles around in a wild spin of pure blank random intensity. "Poor, poor Dean—the devil himself had never fallen further; in idiocy, with infected thumb, surrounded by the battered suitcases of his motherless feverish life across America and back numberless times, an undone bird" (188–89). In a pure moment of compassion and concern, Sal offers to pay his way to New York and then Italy—somehow he'll find the money. Dean, at first incredulous, giving Sal a look like the blinking sight of someone suddenly released from a dark closet, slowly adjusts himself to the fact that Sal is serious:

> Resolutely and firmly I repeated what I said.... I looked at him; my eyes were watering with embarrassment and tears. Still he stared at me. Now his eyes were blank and looking through me. It was probably the pivotal point of our friendship when he realized I had actually spent some hours thinking about him and his troubles, and he was trying to place that in his tremendously

involved and, tormented mental categories. Something clicked in both of us....

"Well," said Dean in a very shy and sweet voice, "shall we go."

"Yes," I said, "let's go to Italy." (189–90)

Before they head out for the long impossible voyage, Sal defends Dean—"the HOLY GOOF"—to one of Camille's friends who has called him on the carpet. To Sal, Dean, in the face of this moral battering, appeared simply "Beat—the root, the soul of Beatific." " 'Very well, then,' I said, 'but ... he's got the secret that we're all busting to find and it's splitting his head wide open and if he goes mad don't worry, it won't be your fault but the fault of God' " (195). The secret Sal alludes to is the one bound up with further swayings into the ecstatic rhythm of IT. As with most things in life, first comes the direct unmediated experience and only later the reflection and explanation. So, once again, the novel turns to the sight and sound of jazz music (led by a tenor sax man) to pick up the tempo and transport the audience into an exaltation of mind and feelings:

The behatted tenor man was blowing at the peak of a wonderfully satisfactory free idea, a rising and falling riff that went from "EE-yah!" to a crazier "EE-de-lee-yah!" and blasted along to the rolling crash of butt-scarred drums hammered by a big brutal Negro with a bullneck who didn't give a damn about anything but punishing his busted tubs, crash, rattle-ti-boom, crash. Uproars of music and the tenor man *had it* and everybody knew he had it. Dean was clutching his head in the crowd, and it was a mad crowd. They were all urging that tenor man to hold it and keep it with cries and wild eyes, and he was raising himself from a crouch and going down again with his horn, looping it up in a clear cry above the furor....

Everybody was rocking and roaring. (196–97)

The tenor man continues blowing and blasting and breathing be-bop to his heart's content until the senses are aptly deranged and Dean and the crowd curiously stand apart from themselves, outside of time, which is the posture of ecstasy. "Dean was in a trance. The tenor man's eyes were fixed straight on him; he had a madman who not only understood but cared and wanted to understand more and much more than there was." Then a strange thing happens: the tenor man slows IT down with a song from "this sad brown world"—"Close Your Eyes." The juxtaposition of ecstasy and sorrow confirms Kerouac's belief in paired emotive forces: the swoon of rapturous delight and frenzy will soon give way to the placid tenderness of weary reflection, "because here we were dealing with the pit and prunejuice of poor beat life itself in the god-awful streets of man." This is what it must mean to know time truly, over and over again. Later, when Dean and Sal meet the tenor man after his gig ends, Dean, still lit up, tells the musician that he's looking for a ball. The tenor man tells it to him straight: "'Yah, what good's a ball, life's too sad to be ballin all the time.... Shhee-it!'" (198–99). In cooling down the orgiastic high of the human system, the tenor man hits those necessary flat notes that make life (and time) known in both its moments of emotional ferment and calm comprehension. In the meantime, Sal and Dean go back in the club for more. And so it goes.

On their way from San Francisco to Denver in a travel-bureau car, Dean and Sal, rocking the boat in the back seat, begin to draw from their own perceptions and recollections in order to enact the direct experience of IT. First, however, Sal wants to know what IT means, and Dean refers back to the previous night:

> "Now, man, that alto man last night had IT—he held it once he found it.... Up to him to put down what's on everybody's mind. He starts the first chorus, then lines up his ideas.... and then he rises to his fate and has to blow equal to it. All of a sudden somewhere in the middle of the chorus *he gets it*—everybody looks up and knows; they listen; he picks it up and carries. Time stops. He's filling empty space with the substance of our lives.... He has to blow across bridges and come and do it with such infinite feeling soul-exploratory for the tune of the moment that everybody knows it's not the tune that counts but IT—" (206)

The model seems clear enough: to know time is to escape its structure through improvisation, then the secret note is hit and the moment enlivened. But one begins from within the structure, some patterned chorus or thought that will, when deeply felt, sidestep itself and generate spontaneity. The moment then transports one out of the Periodicity of time and into the fullness of being or pure spatial excitement. One only has to think of Coltrane's method and sound. There you have it, and—once you do—IT carries you away.

Once Dean and Sal begin their incessant yakking in the back seat, that which is normally concealed suddenly reveals itself, without plan or preparation. The thread of one recollection cross-stitches to another and "'NOW, I have IT'" Dean exclaims, and proceeds to another patchwork in the story of his life—something that must be told, must be heard, some bright burning illumination that will make all the difference. "We were hot; we were going east; we were excited.... 'Yes! Yes! Yes!' breathed Dean ecstatically.... We had completely forgotten the people up front.... The car was swaying as Dean and I both swayed to the rhythm and the IT of our final excited joy in talking and living to the blank tranced end of all innumerable riotous angelic particulars that had been lurking in our soul all our lives" (207–8).

This is what it means, then, to experience IT and to know TIME—not only entering a momentary state of pure possibility, but, curiously, realizing the psychic equivalency of Einstein's inverse relationship between velocity and time (as stated in his special theory of relativity). Phenomenologically, the difference this makes to Sal and Dean is that space and time are released from their fixed trajectory of rational sequential stages. Likewise, the meaning of their high-tingled experience of being-in-time is perceived as not set in any absolute sense. Hence, for the moment, they are liberated, that is, they do not live in a state of consciousness in time, which is tantamount to betraying time, but rather bend time to consciousness. As Genevieve Lloyd explains: "The idea that consciousness is in time is the idea of self as determined. The idea that time is in consciousness is the idea of self as determining."[7] This relationship between IT and NOT helps to explain the oscillation from ecstatic joy to certain sadness that Kerouac projects into the novel. Dean perfectly expresses the notion of consciousness in time by making reference to the passengers up front: "'They have worries, they're counting the miles, they're thinking about where to sleep tonight, how much money for gas, the weather, how they'll get there—and all the time they'll get there anyway, you see. But they need to worry and betray time'" (208).

Once in Denver, while waiting to pick up another travel-bureau car to Chicago, Dean accelerates the momentum of IT into an energized state so charged that he seems to be a free electron, spinning out of control. He can only collide and bounce, stealing one car after another for random joy rides, but his fierce activity betrays the happiness: "All the bitterness and madness of his entire Denver life was blasting out of his system like daggers. His face was red and sweaty and mean." Sal stays free of the attraction and tries to put some ironic distance between himself and the "unbearable confusion" in the Denver night. In doing so, he draws a caricature of IT in a hillbilly road-house: "Everything was collapsing, and to make things inconceivably more frantic there was an ecstatic spastic fellow in the bar who threw his arms around Dean and moaned in his face, and Dean went mad again with sweats and insanity" (220–21). The irony is pointed and shows Kerouac's ability to stand apart from IT, in fact, to call IT into question, not only by veering toward the complementary pole of collapse, but by portraying how it can all go berserk. Extending this critical distance, as if to suggest a different vehicle for getting ecstasy—other than sheer speed raised to the nth power, Kerouac plants another Buddhist image while Sal tries to sleep: "At night in this part of the West the stars ... are as big as roman candles and as lonely as the Prince of the Dharma who's lost his ancestral grove and journeys across the spaces between points in the handle of the Big Dipper, trying to find it again. So they slowly wheeled the night" (222). The view, which is so skyward, so altogether beyond, and such an overlooked complement to the oft quoted "mad ones" that "burn, burn, burn like fabulous yellow roman candles," temporarily takes Sal out of the dualistic oscillation and projects him onto a higher plane.

The road reclaims Sal in the morning and before long he is back into the grand rhythm of life. In the middle of the trip from Denver to Chicago, however, he feels the horrific hiss of the "senseless nightmare road," and hunkers down on the floor of the back seat to deliver his consciousness to time. No doubt, it's time to pay the piper for knowing IT. "Now I could feel the road some twenty inches beneath me, unfurling and flying and hissing at incredible speeds across the groaning continent with that mad Ahab [Dean] at the wheel. When I closed my eyes all I could see was the road unwinding into me. When I opened them I saw flashing shadows of trees vibrating on the floor of the car. There was no escaping it. I resigned myself to all" (234). Sal does not resist the rule of the road, for it has been laid down well in advance, and so gives himself up to the inevitable rushing rhythm of this human condition: knowing time and betraying time.

Once they make Detroit, the deterministic grip of consciousness in time is reinforced by the images of popular culture. Sleeping all night in a ramshackle movie-house, where the double feature plays and replays until dawn, Sal and Dean are entirely stuffed in their waking and sleeping hours with B movies, namely the "Gray Myth of the West"—"Singing Cowboy Eddie Dean"—and the "dark Myth of the East" set in Istanbul with George Raft and Peter Lorre. Sal comically comments on the awful effect of subjecting himself to the flicks: "All my actions since then have been dictated automatically to my subconscious by this horrible osmotic experience." In fact, at dawn Sal is almost swept up with the rubbish by the ushers—just another speck in the "come and gone" of the night: "Had they taken me with it, Dean would never had seen me again. He would have had to roam the entire United States and look in every garbage pail from coast to coast before he found me embryonically convoluted among the rubbishes of my life, his life, and the life of everybody concerned and not concerned" (244). This generalization extends the experience of entrapment, and its correlate of spiritual pollution, to all, for are we not all betrayed by time and its mindless reels of hegemonic culture remotely controlling us from afar?

This sense of consciousness in time, which subverts the ecstatic liberation of IT, is further heightened by virtue of repetition. As trip four winds down, along the way from Detroit to New York City, Sal starts to recognize the landscape. He'd been there before: "I realized I was beginning to cross and recross towns in America as though I were a traveling salesman—raggedy travelings, bad stock, rotten beans in the bottom of my bag of tricks, nobody buying.... The trip was over." Five days after they land in New York, at a party, Dean falls in lust with Inez; "he was kneeling on the floor with his chin on her belly and telling her and promising her everything and sweating." Not long after, Dean and Camille are discussing divorce on the telephone while she has his second baby, and a few months later Inez gets pregnant. What of Dean? Oh, he "was all troubles and ecstasy and speed as ever. So we didn't go to Italy" (245–47). Ah, rubbish—betrayed again! That's life.

Sufficiently rested and buoyant once again, Sal moves on during the following spring (1950) by himself to launch the final trip of the novel. The destination is Denver, but life has more surprises under its sleeve for Sal. By this time, Sal's uneasy feeling and deterministic dreamscape of an ultimate mortal reality rises to the surface again. This time the Shrouded Traveler combines with a vision of Dean storming toward Denver (unannounced and uninvited) to pick up Sal and a buddy and head down to Mexico—"the magic land at the end of the road," and the final place to attain IT in the novel. The vision describes a menacing image of Dean which is a view mostly submerged in the novel—subordinate to the hero's glamorization. Nonetheless, its force is great as it erupts into narrative consciousness. Even early on in the novel Sal sees the darker aspects of his friend and alter ego: "And Dean, ragged and dirty, prowling by himself in his preoccupied frenzy" (58). By the end of the novel, the sight has developed into a complete vision of Dean:

> a burning shuddering frightful Angel, palpitating toward me across the road, approaching like a cloud, with enormous speed, pursuing me like the Shrouded Traveler on the plain, bearing down on me. I saw his huge face over the plains with the mad, bony purpose and the gleaming eyes; I saw his wings; I saw his old jalopy chariot with thousands of sparking flames shooting out from it; I saw the path it burned over the road; it even made its own road and went over the corn, through cities, destroying bridges, drying rivers. It came like wrath to the West. (259)

The Shrouded Traveler, who reaps all consciousness and all time down the road—however they are equated, thickens with meaning and flares with intensity as Dean merges with this pursuer, making the figure notorious as well as perilous. Such a merger greets Sal with "bony purpose and gleaming eyes." Angel of death—like a clip of Groucho Marx hunched over, low to the earth, long strides, wings tucked, leering and muttering under cigar-breath while fluttering by uttering "hello I must be going." Time's despite. Is there no escape? Must there be no exit? Is that *it*?

Now it seems that only the route south of the border can restore sensations, intoxicate the emotions, and intensify the spirit of fellowship with humankind. Dropping down to Mexico is magical because it not only promises the new and unknown, but guarantees flight from the confines and "broken delusion" of corporate America and its aggressive technoid (and Cold War) civilization. Mexico's attraction for both Sal and Dean is that the road running through it unwinds time from present to past (the transition from advanced modern industrial state to a premodern folk society). They find in this devolution a chance to transcend both geographical and conceptual boundaries associated with the constraints of chronological time—its tireless goose steps toward the future and its progressive form of historic development that always insists—onward! Sal compares the road south of the border to

> driving across the world and into the places where we would finally learn ourselves among the Fellahin Indians of the world, the essential strain of the basic primitive, wailing humanity that stretches in a belt around the equatorial belly of the world.... These people were unmistakably Indians and were not at all like the Pedros and Panchos of silly civilized American lore—they had high cheekbones, and slanted eyes, and soft ways; they were not fools, they were not clowns; they were great, grave Indians and they were the source of mankind and the fathers of it. The waves are Chinese, but the earth is an Indian thing. As essential as rocks in the desert are they in the desert of "history." And they knew this when we passed, ostensibly self-important money-bag Americans on a lark in their land; they knew who was the father and who was the son of antique life on earth, and made no comment. (280–81)

These noble thoughts aside, the magic of Mexico is first experienced sensually in a whorehouse before the spiritual discovery of the land and its people fully emerges. Sal and Dean cannot escape that traditional masculine dualism of the virgin and the whore, and enter the latter before adoring the former. There does not seem to be any concrete mean in any part of the

Americas for this duo. Listening to mambo amplified over loud speakers in the brothel, it seems to Sal that "the whole world was turned on.... It was like a long, spectral Arabian dream in the afternoon in another life—Ali Baba and the alleys and the courtesans" (289). After their mighty lust is quenched, they move on toward Mexico City, turning away from the pull of their loins and toward the push of more lofty images. On the way, they encounter some Mexican girls selling rock crystals: "Their great brown, innocent eyes looked into ours with such soulful intensity that not one of us had the slightest sexual thought about them..... 'Look at those eyes!' breathed Dean. They were like the eyes of the Virgin Mother when she was a child. We saw in them the tender and forgiving gaze of Jesus.... Their mouths rounded like the mouths of chorister children." The road finally spreads out into a holy vista—"the golden world that Jesus came from .... these vast and Biblical areas of the world." And in the midst of the sacred ancient site sits the profane City—"one vast Bohemian camp.... This was the great and final wild uninhibited Fellahin-childlike city that we knew we would find at the end of the road" (298–302).

But Sal speaks too soon, for the real end of the road typically results in disaster—this time terrible feverish sickness—which takes away all of his appetite for IT. To make matters worse in this foretaste of helpless mortality, Dean checks out of the picture and abandons Sal in Mexico City to go about his mad business of divorces, marriages, remarriages, and flings into the neon recesses of America, "dreaming in the immensity of it." Sal, recovered and heading back to New York City, at last crosses the prophet's path just over the Laredo border. It is the prophet's fourth and final appearance in the novel, the last chance to convey the word, and he does: "'Go moan for man'" (306). This strange but persistent figure thus gives Sal (and Kerouac) a way out of the endless oscillations between intense pleasure and devastating sorrow. It is no less than an admission that all life is suffering; this is where the road begins and ends, and the various detours around such a condition and first principle can only result in a peace that is hollow and restless. The mission of the writer is therefore discerned.

Kerouac jams the brakes on the novel in part five—a mere five pages— and skids to a stop. Actually, throughout the novel the road has been thinning out: part four (recounting the trip to Mexico) is only about half as long as the first trip of part one, which is the longest account; parts two and three, almost identical in length, each comprise two-thirds of the first part. Back in New York, Sal closes the novel with a farewell to Dean, who pops back up in his life once again. In perhaps much-too-facile a manner, Sal finds that concrete mean and falls in love with the woman of his dreams. So he seems to be settling down both to his life's work and to his heart's content. On the other hand, Dean, still traveling back and forth across the continent, a clanging caboose rattling through dawn and dusk, seems to have rocked himself off the proverbial rocker—derailed. He appears utterly senseless when Sal finds him unexpectedly with his girlfriend at their New York pad: "He hopped and laughed, he stuttered and fluttered his hands and said, 'Ah—ah—you must listen to hear.' We listened, all ears. But he forgot what he wanted to say. 'Really listen—ahem. Look, dear Sal—sweet Laura—I've come—I'm gone—but wait—ah yes.... Can't talk no more—do you understand that it is—or might be—But listen!'" (306–7).

Several days later, Sal says good-bye to Dean as he departs for the West Coast, "bent to it again." There is an unmistakable sadness in the air and this sets up the final paragraph of the novel—a sort of paean to the American dream and the passage of time, and to our home in the universe where we live it out, ending in a lone reflection on the ever transient nature of being-in-the-world. This closing reads like a final blessing, in which the author tucks in the story, characters, and reader, too, bidding all a fare-thee-well. One can tell that this is offered by someone who has finally reached a very deserved and knowing state of rest:

> So in America when the sun goes down and I sit on the old broken-down river pier watching the long, long skies over New Jersey and sense all that raw land that rolls in one unbelievable huge bulge over the West Coast, and all that road going, all the people dreaming in the immensity of it, and in Iowa I know by now the children must be crying in the land where they let the children cry, and tonight the stars'll be out, and don't you know that God is Pooh Bear? the evening star must be drooping and shedding her sparkler dims on the prairie, which is just before the coming of complete night that blesses the earth, darkens all rivers, cups the peaks and folds the final shore in, and nobody, nobody knows what's going to happen to anybody besides the forlorn rags of growing old, I think of Dean Moriarty, I even think of Old Dean Moriarty the father we never found, I think of Dean Moriarty. (309–10)

This elegiac note, which unites the panorama of space with the curvature of time, makes good on the prophet's message, for Kerouac, through Sal, expresses his mantric moan for humankind. The passage, both sad and joyful, as mixed as existence itself, achieves an equilibrium of sensibility, and thus provides solace and sustenance. Moreover, it works to disengage Sal and the reader from action in order to reflect and consider, to take in the immensity of it all: self, others, nation, world and universe. What remains to think on? Where is the meaning here—both hidden and overt? Now what? What of IT? In such a mood and in light of the legend's spiritual quest, one wonders about the pearl. Is it just now being handed to Sal and, in turn, to us?

The stillness and evocation of the passage—the sense of love, adoration, and wonder about the ultimate nature of existence—delivers the story from confusion and desire, from rocking back and forth and going up and down in ecstasy and sorrow. It also seems to invite calmness, self-possession, and contemplation. (Kerouac would later write in his biography of the Buddha, "Composure is the trap for getting ecstasy" ["Wake Up," episode two, 13].)[8] Dean may be hustling about at that very moment, but Sal sits on an old river pier, located squarely within linear time but still open to possibility, watching, summing up one phase of his life and opening the door to another. In doing so, he does not try to cross-step chronological time; a pier is not a plank. There is no springing into "the holy void of uncreated emptiness"—not yet. For the time being, Kerouac acknowledges our mortality—"the forlorn rags of growing old," but he also grants immeasurable freedom to us in the meantime, as if to ask each and every person somewhere along that road: What will happen? for "nobody, nobody knows." Taken in conjunction, this amounts to Kerouac's generous nod and wink to both states of existence: consciousness in time (self as determined) and time in consciousness (self as determining).

Without diminishing the joyful spontaneity of IT, the hedonistic lifestyle celebrated in *On the Road*, the novel also calls IT into question in the interstices of restless busy action and through the forms of unconscious dreamscapes and transcendent visions. Somewhere in the midst of all this earthbound clutter an image emerges, momentarily flickering, of a finger pointed at the moon. That is all. But it is enough to challenge hedonism, not on the basis of morality, but simply in terms of the nature of things as they are. Northrop elaborates on the limitations inherent in treating IT as the ultimate mode of being in the world: "Hedonism as a complete philosophy of life is inadequate—not because it is naughty or because sensed things are not real, but merely because determinate things are transitory; and a philosophy which treats determinate pleasures as if they were a basis for living under all circumstances treats pleasure as an immortal law rather than the actual transitory thing which it is."[9] Therefore, the spiritual challenge facing Kerouac, or anyone on such a search for the divine or ultimate truth, is to reject what the senses perceive as the ontological be all and end all of this life. What the senses perceive is not unreal. It's just that, in the scheme of things, the frenzy of the phenomenal world must give way to an acceptance of the noumenal as the form of ultimate reality. How then to secure peace of mind and spiritual contentment? What are the conditions necessary for insights into the cross or the diamond of enlightenment? How shall one think of this fleeting world? Wherein lies the path (or device) to get beyond the *phenomenal* tricks of time:

> A star at dawn, a bubble in a stream;
> A flash of lightning in a summer cloud,
> A flickering lamp, a phantom, and a dream.[10]

NOTES

1. Kerouac's correspondence with his mother (24 July 1947), Berg Collection, New York Public Library.

2. Cowley's acceptance report to Viking Press, dated 8 April 1957, is contained within the Cowley-Kerouac File, the Malcolm Cowley papers, Newberry Library, Chicago, Illinois. On the inside of one manila folder in the file, in Cowley's own hand, is written "Kerouac looked like Gregory Peck."

In the first draft of the report, Cowley hedged on the merit of the novel: "It isn't a great or even a likable book, but it is real, honest, fascinating, everything for kicks, the voice of a new generation." In the final version, the negative judgment is deleted so that the sentence simply reads: "It is real, honest, fascinating," etc. In the final report Cowley also added the praise for Kerouac's style: "The writing at its best is deeply felt, poetic, and extremely moving."

In retrospect, this acceptance report stands as the first official attempt to codify Kerouac as the King of the Beats and to characterize the Beat Generation as wild and reckless; Cowley amplifies the novel's nervous energy and devotion to sensory indulgence, but nowhere does he mention the attempt to affirm anything spiritual in the process. For example: "The characters are always on wheels. They buy cars and wreck them, steal cars and leave them standing in fields, undertake to drive cars from one city to another, sharing the gas; then for variety they go hitch-hiking or sometimes ride a bus. In cities they go on wild parties or sit in joints listening to hot trumpets. They seem a little like machines themselves, machines gone haywire, always wound to the last pitch...."

3. Lawrence, pp. 255–56. In one of his many sketch notebooks (no. 9), Kerouac copied a long quote from Lawrence's *Studies in Classic American Literature* prior to composing *On the Road*. The quote is from the essay on Whitman and shows his impact on Kerouac, especially with respect to the importance of sympathy, which was Kerouac's definition of "beat" given on *The Steve Allen Show* in 1958 (i.e., "sympathetic"), followed by a reference to Whitman's *Specimen Days*. In addition, the quote reaffirms Whitman's democratic and transient location of the soul as well as his identification with the oppressed. What follows are excerpts from Lawrence's quote:

> Stay in the dark limbs of negroes. Stay in the body of the prostitute. Stay in the sick flesh of the syphilitic. Stay in the marsh where the calamus grows. Stay there, soul, where you belong.
>
> The Open Road. The great home of the Soul is the open road. Not heaven, not paradise. Not "above." Not even "within." The soul is neither, "above" nor "within." It is a wayfarer down the open road....
>
> Having no direction, even. Only the soul remaining true to herself in her going.

Meeting all the other wayfarers along the road. And how? How meet them, and how pass? With sympathy, says Whitman. Sympathy.... Feeling with. Feel with them as they feel with themselves. Catching the vibration of their soul and flesh as we pass.

It is a new great doctrine. A doctrine of life. A new great morality. A morality of actually living, not of salvation.... The soul living her life along the incarnate mystery of the open road.

See Kerouac's holograph sketch notebooks ("SK means SKETCHINGS"), Berg Collection, New York Public Library.

4. Suzuki, *Essays in Zen Buddhism*, p. 63.

5. Northrop, p. 354. In distinguishing between transitory and nontransitory factors in the nature of existence, Northrop argues the following: "The Buddhist merely reminds one of the ... immediately apprehended fact that the self and all things are not merely the many distinguishable and different transitory differentiations, but also the all-embracing, indeterminate aesthetic continuum of which the transitory factors are the temporary differentiations. This ... indeterminate aesthetic manifold, since it contains the temporal, arrow-like sequence of transitory differentiations within itself, instead of being itself within this arrow-like passage of time, is timeless and hence immortal; or put more exactly, it is outside the death-delivering 'ravages' of time and hence escapes its consequences. It embraces time as one of its determinate differentiations, instead of time embracing it."

6. Only several months before writing the roll manuscript of *On the Road*, Kerouac conveyed his "Strange Dickensian Vision on Market Street ... in San Francisco in the month of February 1949" to Neal Cassady. In a letter dated 8 January 1951, Kerouac gives Cassady a detailed account of the "little fish-n'-chips joint" and the proprietress he takes to be his English mother in a former lifetime. Although this reads like a first draft of the novel in part two, section 10, there is no mention at all of a Buddhist sense of ecstasy. All of the terms, images, and references in the letter to Cassady are limited to the "Strange Dickensian Vision." Furthermore, the reincarnation that is felt in Kerouac's account is simply not extended to a Buddhist vision of innumerable reincarnations. In the letter, he never takes that "complete step across chronological time into timeless shadows" as he does in the published version of *On the Road*. This suggests that the Buddhist sense of IT was added to this section and passage of the novel sometime after the roll manuscript was written. An inspection of the roll manuscript and various states of the manuscript thereafter (right up to publication) would be necessary to verify such a claim. In closing his letter to Cassady, Kerouac clarifies matters in his own way concerning the fate of the vision—its "glimpse of possible reincarnation" and "presence of God": "It's all in the air and is still there for me to grasp another day, and I hope to, I want to, I know I will" (*SL*, 275–81).

7. Lloyd, *Being in Time*, p. 84.

8. The eight episodes of the biography, which appeared in *Tricycle: A Buddhist Review*, were also given the heading—"Shakyamuni Buddha: A Life Retold." The biography ran consecutively from summer 1993 to spring 1995. Kerouac relied heavily upon Asvaghosha's *Buddha-Charita* and Narasu's *Life of the Historic Buddha* to complete the biography. His other important sources included the following: the *Surangama Sutra*, the *Lankavatara Scripture*, the *Dhammapada*, the *Anguttara Nikaya*, the *Itivuttaka*, the *Digha Nikaya*, the *Majjhima Nikaya*, the *Theragatha*, the *Vinaya Pitaka*, the *Prajna-Paramita-Hridaya Sutra*, the *Samyutta Nikaya*, along with the *Tao-te-Ching*, the *Life of Milarepa*, and the *Mahayana Samgraha*.

9. Northrop, p. 339.

10. Quoted from *The Diamond Sutra and the Sutra of Hui Neng*, p. 74.

MARK RICHARDSON

Peasant Dreams: Reading On the Road

Will we stroll dreaming of the lost America of love past blue automobiles in driveways, home to our silent cottage?

Ah, dear father, graybeard, lonely old courage-teacher, what America did you have when Charon quit poling his ferry and you got out on a smoking bank and stood watching the boat disappear on the black waters of Lethe?
                                    —Allen Ginsberg, "A Supermarket in California"

No revelation ever made Jack a whit less selfish.
                                    —Gerald Nicosia, *Memory Babe*

"We can learn something about the naive artist," Nietzsche writes in *The Birth of Tragedy*, "through the analogy of dream. We can imagine the dreamer as he calls out to himself, still caught in the illusion of his dream and without disturbing it, 'This is a dream, and I want to go on dreaming,' and we can infer, on the one hand, that he takes deep delight in the contemplation of his dream, and, on the other, that he must have forgotten the day, with its horrible importunity, so to enjoy his dream" (32). Its Dionysian ecstasies notwithstanding, Jack Kerouac's *On the Road* belongs to the tradition of Apollonian art that Nietzsche conceives of here: an art of

From *Texas Studies in Literature and Language* 43, no. 2. © 2001 by the University of Texas Press.

willful illusion sustained against the encroachments (as Nietzsche later puts it) of "a whole world of torment" (33). Kerouac's is the work of forgetting, though the residues of memory, the shafts of daylight that trouble this dreamer's sleep, are precisely what intrigue me.

I am interested in whether or not *On the Road* finally believes, and in what sense believes, in the mythology of America on which it depends. At times Kerouac seems directly to question the faith his narrator Sal Paradise has in all Dean Moriarty comes to represent: a peculiarly intense and charismatic masculinity, a vital relation to the body, cultural and spiritual authenticity, the promise of America itself. *On the Road* achieves, at times, a certain distance from its own enabling myths, quite as if it were holding them up for scrutiny even as it plays them out. This has the effect of putting us and the novel itself in a strangely abstract relation to its ideological basis, which is why the problem of faith is crucial. *On the Road* constantly tests the limits of its own creed but refuses, often poignantly, to abandon it. Kerouac's road novel outruns its own horizon and at the same time always fails to achieve escape velocity. Its dawning, at times anxious, awareness of this fact makes *On the Road* an Emersonian fiction, an affiliation that provides a clue about the origins of another characteristic of the book: its exuberant, frustrated optimism. *On the Road* is a book that simply refuses to be jaded, no matter how canny, ironic, and self-aware it becomes.

I

On the Road involves a familiar American idea about belief: the *act* of believing in Dean actually brings Dean about—makes him, renews him, creates him. We do not believe in Dean; we *believe Dean in*, to adapt a phrase Robert Frost once used about God and the future. Dean Moriarty cannot exist apart from our fictions of him, which is why even Neal Cassady, upon whom the character is based, is not essentially real. He had a legendary kind of existence as the "cocksman and Adonis of Denver," as Allen Ginsberg put it. Kerouac, Ginsberg, and Cassady himself were always inventing and reinventing "Neal Cassady," who, as Ginsberg writes in the dedication to *Howl and Other Poems*, had published several books in heaven. Neal is simply too fine a creation for this world; his genius can never be adequately embodied. And the same goes for America, with which Dean Moriarty is mythically identified. (When Carlo Marx addresses America in the person of Dean, he only makes explicit what Kerouac always implies: "Whither goest thou, America, in thy shiny car in the night?")

On the Road tells a Young Goodman Brown sort of story. We look out on America and see double: promise and piety on the one hand, wickedness and fraud on the other. Dean Moriarty, in all his dubiety, simply is America: "tumbledown holy America," Sal equivocally says, catching the seediness and the grace. On the whole, his fidelity, his affection for Dean, makes *On the Road* an optimistic work in the tradition of Whitman. It says "yes" to America in the way Mark Twain's "road" novel, *Huckleberry Finn*, says "no"—and this despite the fact that *On the Road* invokes dystopian possibilities. Kerouac's is another in a long line of American fictions (and nonfictions) in which utopian and dystopian modes weirdly cooperate. The dubiety of *On the Road* is easy enough to see: it records a long, post-adolescent drunken odyssey that *also* purports to be a spiritual journey of personal and national dimensions. Those with no faith—for example, the copywriters who marketed early paperback editions of the book as a salacious, lurid tale—see only the orgy and the drunkenness, only the kicks. The faithful see something else altogether: Dean Moriarty, new American Saint, as Sal Paradise puts it (34). Of course, nothing can fulfill the promise of Dean Moriarty. Sal's faith at times seems a deliberately naive refusal to face the truth. His gee-whiz doggedness, taken to an extreme level of piety, defines a childlike character, a Forrest Gump, whose vast appeal for American audiences is not hard to explain. He flatters our fidelity and optimism. In *On the Road* as in *Forrest Gump* we are invited to admire a faithful, forward-looking hero and discouraged ever from regarding his faith and goodwill as mere gullibility, which we could never respect. *On the Road* is tragically optimistic—a fine figure for the 1950s, a haunted, hopeful, doomed decade.

Kerouac's novel emerged as a new sense of American national identity was consolidating itself: both internally with respect to the possible full Americanness of Black men and women and externally with respect to its conflict with the USSR. Kerouac went west in 1947, and *On the Road* appeared in 1957: the novel imaginatively spans the first decade of the American National Security State and of the Civil Rights struggle. The Internal Security Act became law in 1950, to be followed in 1954 by the Communist Control Act. 1954 also brought the decision in *Brown v. Board of Education*. In 1949 eleven American Communist leaders were convicted under the Smith Act of 1940. Ethel and Julius Rosenberg were executed in 1953. During the same period, many states considered, and some passed, laws requiring oaths of loyalty for state employees. The U.S. detonated the first hydrogen bomb at Eniwetok Atoll in November 1952. Between 1950 and 1953 defense spending quadrupled as the peacetime economy was partly militarized. By the end of 1950, U.S. soldiers were fighting the Chinese in Korea. In 1955 Emmett Till was murdered in Mississippi, and Rosa Parks arrested in Montgomery, Alabama.

On the Road almost never refers directly to these events, but they are, in a nebulous sort of way, everywhere felt. Dean and Sal pass through Washington on the day of Truman's inauguration in 1949: "Great displays of war might," Sal says, "were lined up along Pennsylvania Avenue as we rolled by in our battered boat. There were B-29s, PT boats, artillery, all kinds of war material that looked murderous in the snowy grass" (112). The next two paragraphs tell how the Virginia police harassed Dean just for the hell of it. Sal points the moral: "The American police are involved in psychological warfare against those Americans who don't frighten them with imposing papers and threats. It's a Victorian police force; it peers out of musty windows and wants to inquire about everything, and can make crimes if the crimes don't exist to its satisfaction" (113). In a more paranoid vein, Old Bull Lee— the character based on William S. Burroughs—rants about predatory "bureaucracies" and what he calls "the big grab" going on "in, Washington and Moscow" (123–24). *On the Road* plainly belongs to the era of containment: containment of the USSR without, containment of un-American elements within. All the essential Cold War questions trouble Kerouac's novel: What is America? Who are Americans? Are we the chosen or the damned? Kerouac need hardly address these questions directly, because the structure of feeling of *On the Road* is itself tempered by the Cold War, with its restless anxiety, its troubled optimism, its delirium and depression. Kerouac has Sal say, at a crucial moment late in the novel, when Sal and Dean are in Mexico:

> Strange crossroad towns on top of the world rolled by, with shawled Indians watching us from under hatbrims and *rebozos*.... They had come down from the black mountains and higher places to hold forth their hands for something they thought civilization could offer, and they never dreamed the sadness and the poor broken delusion of it. They didn't know that a bomb had come that could crack all our bridges and roads and reduce them to jumbles, and we would be as poor as they someday, and stretching out our hands in the same, same way. Our broken Ford, old thirties upgoing America Ford, rattled through them and vanished in the dust. (246)

Sal's peculiar optimism—his *"upgoing* America"—always has a haggard air of defeat about it.

"Everything was dead," Sal tells us in the first paragraph of the novel. What follows is a story of rebirth—an Emersonian story of the agitation always to redraw the outer boundaries of the soul's horizon. To Sal, Dean appears as "a western kinsman of the sun" (11). Sal speaks of "the coming of

Dean" as if it were an advent, saying: "I could hear a new call and see a new horizon, and believe in it at my young age" (11). Dean is a Christ-like, vernal figure, and *On the Road* is a gospel of his life and works.

But after sounding an overture to Dean, *On the Road* presents him to us in equivocal terms. His talk is a kind of hipster-intellectual-comical patois. (Here is how he asks his girlfriend to fix breakfast and clean up their apartment: "In other words we've got to get on the ball, darling, what I'm saying, otherwise it'll be fluctuating and lack true knowledge or crystallization of our plans" [6].) His relations with women are abusive and obtuse enough to occasion wonder. We cannot discredit the judgment of Sal's aunt that Dean is a "madman." And there is no lack of suggestion that Dean is an evangelical fraud. Sal Paradise admits it at the outset: "[Dean] was simply a youth tremendously excited with life, and though he was a con-man, he was only conning because he wanted so much to live and to get involved with people who would otherwise pay no attention to him. He was conning me and I knew it (for room and board and 'how-to-write,' etc.), and he knew I knew (this has been the basis of our relationship), but I didn't care and we got along fine" (8). This perfectly expresses the complexity of the novel: its ambivalence about Dean and its happy, good-humored candor about its own mythology.[1]

It would be hardhearted of us to debunk Sal's faith. Such is the conciliatory position *On the Road* forces us into if we are at all susceptible. Maybe everyone else but Sal is a Philistine, we say without being able to decide; maybe to lack faith is actually worse than to invest it in a fraud or fiction. All truly valuable things, this novel suggests, come about only through the creative and possibly deceitful agency of belief—through yea-saying, not through skepticism and denial. There are those in *On the Road* who lack faith, but they are always made to seem petty. Sal says early in the novel: "All my other friends [besides Dean] were 'intellectuals'—Chad the Nietzschean anthropologist, Carlo Marx and his nutty surrealist low voiced serious staring talk, Old Bull Lee and his critical anti-everything drawl." He adds by way of summary that these men "were in the negative, nightmare position of putting society down" (10–11). All of our sympathies lie instead with Dean, whose "criminality," as Sal says, was "a wild yea-saying overburst of American joy" (11). In this book it is *un-American* not to believe. And belief in Dean becomes belief in the possibility of the mythic "lost America of love" with which he is always identified.

America, Kerouac seems to say, has always been a beautiful fiction believing itself into existence as it unfolds west. Sal gets ready for his first trip west by reading books about "the pioneers." He gives himself over fully to what he calls "hearthside" ideas about America (12–13). Once on the road he subsists on apple pie and ice cream: "That's practically all I ate all the way across the country, I knew it was nutritious and it was delicious, of course" (15). Such is the patriotism of *On the Road*, which was a pretty good advertisement for America. Kerouac's novel chooses the West, as the saying used to go, and how different a document it is in this respect from *Howl and Other Poems* (1957), with its tormented, cagey animosities.

In any case, Carlo Marx and Dean, we read in chapter one, "rushed down the street together, digging everything in the early way they had, which later became so much sadder and perceptive and blank" (9). Kerouac is saying that to see "perceptively" is to be "sad" and "blank." He leaves us to infer that to be "digging everything," to live in faith and goodwill, is also to labor under a fortunate illusion—under the dominating power of belief; to be digging everything is somehow willingly to be subject to a con, willingly to turn away from the "whole world of torment" that "naive artists" like Kerouac can't bear to contemplate. The association of disillusion with perception, and of illusion with belief, has great consequence in a novel that in certain respects cannot imperil its belief in its most central and enabling American cultural illusions—illusions that have, it happens, chiefly to do with race. On the other side of the color line lies the world of "horrible importunity" that *On the Road* will not allow itself to register. That is the subject of the balance of my essay.[2]

II

To be "beat" is to be among what Sal Paradise calls "the Fellahin peoples of the world." This explains Sal's feeling of solidarity—even of identity—with his Mexican-American lover Terry in Part One of the novel. "Fellahin," as Kerouac uses the word, can refer either generally to peasants, or more specifically to peasants (and other persons) of color. (The word is of Arabic origin.)[3] In the passages describing Sal's life with Terry, Kerouac essentially crosses the color line, as by an act of sophisticated minstrelsy: he puts on a mask of color.[4] But minstrelsy is only one generic category in play here. The second is pastoral, and the most remarkable thing about this interlude is the idyllic cast Kerouac gives to the lives of the Mexican and African American migrant farm laborers.

> We bent down and began picking cotton. It was beautiful. Across the field were the tents, and beyond them the sere brown cottonfields that stretched out of sight to the brown arroyo foothills and then the snow-capped Sierras in the blue morning air. This was so much better than washing dishes on South Main

Street [in Los Angeles]. But I knew nothing about picking cotton. I spent too much time disengaging the white ball from its crackly bed; the others did it in one flick. Moreover, my fingertips began to bleed; I needed gloves, or more experience. There was an old Negro couple in the field with us. They picked cotton with the same God-blessed patience their grandfathers had practiced in antebellum Alabama; they moved right along their rows, bent and blue, and their bags increased. My back began to ache. But it was beautiful kneeling and hiding in that earth. If I felt like resting I did, with my face on the pillow of brown moist earth. Birds sang an accompaniment. I thought I had found my life's work. (81)

Sal's pastoral eye is hardly the eye of a migrant worker, whose felt relation to the cotton field is probably more economic in character than literary and romantic. His phrases are deeply evocative; they carry him away. "Kneeling" catches the piety of the scene, as Sal describes it; "hiding," the sense that he has managed among these simple folk something like an escape. The "pillow" of earth on which Sal lays his head alerts us to the fact that his ruminations are oddly like a dream—a "peasant" dream, we might say. Sal is composing a "plantation tale": "antebellum Alabama" is as keenly felt here as post–World War Two California. All of this encourages Sal, more and more sanguine by the hour, to believe he has found his "life's work" picking cotton. He says: "I was a man of the earth, precisely as I had dreamed I would be" (82).[5]

The latter remark opens up a crucial chain of associations affiliating "earthiness" with "the Fellahin" and with "the primitive." To become a man of the earth is to take on color—to shed the over-civil skin of White cultivation in order to bring to life the essential man (and masculinity) that lie beneath. By this logic, to put on the mask of the Fellahin people of the world is really to take off the mask of the White bourgeois. Movement across lines of color and class leads Sal Paradise to conclude that the primitive and the (to him) Other are actually what is *essentially* human: it was with him all along, though Whiteness had alienated him from it. *On the Road* is a fantasy of the sort Emerson entertains in "Self-Reliance":

What a contrast between the well-clad, reading, writing, thinking American, with a watch, a pencil, and a bill of exchange in his pocket, and the naked New Zealander, whose property is a club, a spear, a mat, and an undivided twentieth of a shed to sleep under! But compare the health of the two men, and you shall see that the white man has lost his aboriginal strength. If the traveller tell us truly, strike the savage with a broad axe, and in a day or two the flesh shall unite and heal as if you struck the blow into soft pitch, and the same blow shall the send the white to his grave. (279)

The "aboriginal" self is in essence "Black" and "savage"; it is suckled with the she-wolf's teat. Kerouac's idea in *On the Road* is more temperately expressed, certainly more sentimental, than Emerson's is in "Self-Reliance." But for both men Whiteness is a condition of decadence-an unsoundness of mind and body.

As Sal and Dean move deeper into Mexico, Sal tells us that it was not like driving across Carolina, or Texas, or Arizona, or Illinois; but like driving across the world and into the places where we would finally learn ourselves among the Fellahin Indians of the world, the essential strain of the basic primitive, wailing humanity that stretches in a belt around the equatorial belly of the world" (229). Primitivism, color, the earth, authenticity, and sexual vigor (as we move below the "belt"): the constellation is familiar in American writing. Reading *On the Road* I think of such passages as the following from Jean Toomer's *Cane*, where Toomer conveys his character Dan Moore's impressions of a Black woman seated near him in a theater: "A soil-soaked fragrance comes from her. Through the cement floor her strong roots sink down. They spread under the asphalt streets.... Her strong roots sink down and spread under the river and shoot in bloodlines that waver south. Her roots shoot down" (65). The idea in *Cane* is the same one we encounter in *On the Road*, as in much of Beat writing, which in this case Toomer anticipates. A certain problem of social and psychological alienation is set forth in these works, a problem associated with a specifically White middle-class culture; and the therapy proposed in each book is a kind of psychosexual pastoral, a return to the earth, to the soil, to sexual vitality, and to color. *On the Road* and *Cane* look among the Fellahin for what can "stir the root life of a withered people" (59), to borrow Toomer's words.

In the long passage quoted above, Sal Paradise says he had always "dreamed" of becoming "a man of the earth." The remark is more revealing than he probably intends because the episode describing his life with Terry in California surely follows the logic of his dreams about what the lives of hard laborers are really like. In this way, ideology gives us a dream of the world rather than a "direct" or unmediated experience of it. Dreams are fictions rooted in the world beyond the dream, with all its "horrible importunities," and they are somehow designed (so to speak) to accommodate us both to that world and to those importunities; in turn, fictions are finally also "cons"—which, I will argue, brings us full circle back to the question of literary belief and credulity that *On the Road* implicitly raises.[6]

When, in the sequence with Terry, Sal reports that he "sighs like an old Negro cotton-picker" (82), one is entitled to wonder just how an old Negro cotton-picker sighs. What is the "method," as the actors say, for Sal's little piece of stage business? The question is to the point because this is precisely the sort of role-playing (or displacement) that *On the Road* exists to make possible—but also to hold up for scrutiny. Sal loses himself in Blackness, shedding the "white ambitions" (148) that had saddled him through life until now. But notice that Sal's way of dreaming about Mexican-American and Black laborers is an eminently White way of dreaming about them. To put the matter most uncharitably to him and to Kerouac: White Americans reduce Mexican-American and Black farm workers to poverty only to flatter them with suggestions that their lives are idyllic and charmed, free of White worry, White responsibility White inhibitions—in a word, with suggestions that they are "natural." This calls to mind the patronizing reflection Charles Chesnutt has his White narrator John deliver in *The Conjure Woman* (1899). John is speaking of Uncle Julius, a former slave who serves as his coachman: "He was a marvelous hand in the management of horses and dogs, and manifested a greater familiarity with them than mere use would seem to account for, though it was doubtless due to the simplicity of a life that had kept him close to nature" (55). Uncle Julius might well smile ironically at these remarks—or bitterly, depending on how tolerant he felt disposed to be—because they present Julius's life as a slave in extraordinarily romantic terms: as a "simple" life lived "close to nature" in an almost genetic sympathy with the animals. John offers us a dream about slavery, not an account of it. This way of thinking about hard labor informs Sal Paradise's idealizing response to a later generation of agricultural workers. A deep continuity connects Chesnutt's John to Kerouac's Sal—two White Northerners at liberty (and at play) among the Fellahin peoples of the world. Of course, Chesnutt qualifies John's way of thinking about Uncle Julius with irony. No equivalent irony is at work in *On the Road*: Sal pretty clearly speaks for his author in episodes like the one being discussed. These episodes mark a weird Beat revival of the plantation tale of the post-Reconstruction era. Sal's remarks about the California cotton field transport him to that other place and time, misty with elegiac grace: "There was an old Negro couple in the field with us. They picked cotton with the same God-blessed patience their grandfathers had practiced in antebellum Alabama."

White Americans have often described themselves as repressed even as they oppress others. There is a kind of mythic truth in this Hegelian idea that the master enslaves himself. But the politics of it are dubious. This is the dreamwork of a cruel social order because it presents a way of thinking that erases oppressive conditions—a naive way of thinking that strategically forgets the "horrible importunities" of life on the other side of the line. Such a dream of the world makes it impossible to see what is really happening: entrapment becomes freedom, and poverty an idyll chiefly to be envied. As Kerouac's reader identifies with Sal, he or she occupies a particular structure of feeling. To occupy it is to enter into a specific set of relations to the world presented in *On the Road*. It doesn't matter that this is an imaginary world: every world that we can be aware of is an "imagined" one in some sense. Kerouac encountered real men and women in the cotton fields of California, but he took them up into a dream of what he might be as Sal Paradise, and of what possible America he and they might inhabit together. Our relation to "real" men and women can be as imaginary as our relation to Sal Paradise and Dean Moriarty, characters who themselves stand in an "imaginary" relation to "real" men—Jack Kerouac and Neal Cassady. (In early drafts of the novel Kerouac had used his friends' names. His publisher required that he change their names and obtain releases for the use of their stories.)

The peculiar generic status of *On the Road* is pertinent here: as nonfiction fiction it subtly but clearly registers the slippage between the real and the imagined, between waking and dreaming life. *On the Road* equivocally offers itself as a document of America, but it is really a fiction of it. In the California interlude the relation into which we are invited to enter with "old Negro cotton pickers" and with Terry and her son is a relation of idealizing envy.[7] Kerouac does not ask us to pity them, to champion them, or anything else. He asks instead that we wistfully love them best (and need them most) just as they are. Implicit in this relation is a specific practice: this imaginary relation to real laborers is probably as necessary to the maintenance of the agricultural system that employs them at three dollars a day as are any governmental or police agencies.[8] Gary Snyder's remarks about his friend Kerouac in *A Place in Space* are therefore terribly misleading. "There is [in Kerouac] no self-pity or accusation or politics," Snyder writes, "simply human beings and facts" (10). He goes on to suggest, a little incredibly, that Kerouac had "abandoned all classes" in his own mind and life.

A Marxist would sum it up like this: There is nothing much in *On the Road* to disrupt the reproduction of existing relations of production and much that actually helps to reproduce those relations. But we can turn to Ralph Ellison for language more specific to American contexts. He writes, speaking generally of the "black mask" of minstrelsy: "Its function was to veil the humanity of Negroes thus reduced to a sign, and to repress the white audience's awareness of its moral identification with its own acts and with the human ambiguities pushed behind the mask" (*Shadow and Act*, 49). This "repression of [its] white audience's awareness" makes *On the Road* a conservative novel. Sal Paradise never really sees the poverty in the California work camps, though he lives in and around them for several weeks. This blindness is what enables him to reflect with such amused charm at what he considers the quaint *mañana* culture of the Mexican-American workers: "It was always *mañana*. For the next week that was all I *heard*— mañana, a lovely word and one that probably means heaven" (79). As he sees them, these workers are carefree, happy, true-hearted, and ecstatic (to use terms Sal elsewhere favors). Everything can wait until tomorrow. *On the Road* gives us no way to comprehend or anticipate the struggles that would culminate in the 1967 strike organized in California by Cesar Chavez and the United Farmworkers. These struggles are simply unthinkable within the terms established in Kerouac's novel.

In the episode about Terry we are indirectly made aware of the struggles she undergoes, even if they aren't described as she might describe them: hard labor from dawn to dusk for three dollars a day and no security. *On the Road* achieves at least this much distance from its ideological basis. It almost wakes up from its "peasant dreams," as Kerouac sometimes comes close to exhibiting the novel's ideological grounds (so to speak) rather than simply articulating them. These moments are like crises of faith. But even so, such details about the hard lives of migrant farm workers as we do become aware of in reading this part of *On the Road* never color the episode as a whole, or very much perturb its air of beatific complaisance: its sleep may be disturbed but it is never interrupted. Sal's sojourn on the plantation is underwritten by his aunt back in New Jersey. He has a sponsor. We smile at the irony, and wonder if Kerouac intends the irony at Sal's expense, when Sal says: "I was through with my chores in the cottonfield. I could feel the pull of my own life calling me back. I shot my aunt a penny postcard across the land and asked for another fifty" (83). Feeling the pull of her own life calling her back is a luxury that Terry simply never has. But then again she really is Mexican, whereas the dreamer Sal is, as he himself puts it, only Mexican "in a way"—that is to say, only figuratively (82). That makes all the difference. There are Mexicans "in a way" (Sal) and then there are Mexicans (Terry); there is freedom (what Sal has), and then what might be termed freedom "in a way" (what Terry has). In this case, similitude is not identity, though *On the Road* seems at times to mistake the point. In fact, the novel may be said to exist in order to make precisely this sort of mistake.[9]

III

The passage idealizing migrant farm labor, and others like it, involve a certain blindness on Kerouac's part. It isn't, I think, merely a matter of blindness on Sal's part, though I see how that argument might be made. There are facts about the struggles of the Fellahin that for ideological reasons *On the Road* cannot allow itself to see. This is what keeps Kerouac's book well within the assumptions of American liberalism, as Norman Mailer, a more radical thinker than Kerouac, describes them in "The White Negro," his controversial essay about the culture of the hipster. "What the liberal cannot bear to admit [about America]," Mailer writes, "is the hatred beneath the skin of a society so unjust that the amount of collective violence buried in the people is perhaps incapable of being contained, and therefore if one wants a better world one does well to hold one's breath, for a worse world is bound to come first" (321). This is what *On the Road* cannot bear to admit. This is the nightmare, the "horrible importunity," that Kerouac's Apollonian dreamwork has supplanted.

At times, Kerouac's turning away from this grim possibility is keenly felt by the reader, quite as if it were willful, or a little dishonest. It is hard to tell exactly how we are to take a reference to "the happy, true-hearted Negroes of America." Is it an example of Sal's naiveté or of Kerouac's? The easy way in which Kerouac's narrator takes liberties with the truth in telling this story about America is perhaps an artistic fraud. There is a cheat in this "nonfiction fiction." Kerouac's vision is probably affected by the color-blindness that Richard Wright ingeniously (so to speak) characterized in *Native Son* as *Daltonism*. The word, a medical term, refers to an organic color-blindness, and Wright borrows it in naming the philanthropic family that hires Bigger Thomas in the novel's first section, and whose daughter, Mary Dalton, Bigger kills. Whether we are meant to feel the hollowness of Sal's remark about happy, true-hearted Negroes is not entirely clear. But one can conclude that Kerouac and Sal never met Bigger Thomas, or had somehow refused to recognize him even when they did meet him, whether in Wright's novel or in America itself. The refusal evolves out of diffidence, shame, fear, perhaps out of hypocrisy. It is a mode of what the existentialists call bad faith.[10]

The failure to recognize Bigger Thomas—his invisibility to White men and women—forms the main theme of *Native Son*, which is an incisive critique of the literary tradition to which Mark Twain's Jim and Kerouac's strategically misrecognized "happy negroes" alike belong. Kerouac and Sal are essentially like Wright's Jan Erlone, the young White Communist who awkwardly tries to befriend Bigger Thomas in the first part of the novel. Jan and Mary Dalton—surely acting in bad faith—ask Bigger to take them to a place where real people eat, by which they mean colored people; they speak liberally of how emotional Black folk are; somewhat absurdly, they even invite Bigger to join them in singing "Swing Low, Sweet Chariot" as he drives them around Chicago's Loop (78, 88). Only after Bigger has killed Mary, only after he has tried to implicate Jan in the killing, only after he has killed a second time, is Jan able really to see the man he had so condescendingly idealized: "Bigger, I've never done anything against you and your people in my life," Jan says when he first visits Bigger in prison. "But I'm a white man and it would be asking too much to ask you not to hate me, when every white man you see hates you. I—I know my ... my face looks like theirs to you, even though I don't feel like they do. But I didn't know we were so far apart until that night ... I can understand now why you pulled that gun on me" (331).

Sal Paradise never meets this understanding. He never comprehends the hatred of which both Norman Mailer and Wright speak, as is clear from his astonishing remarks at the beginning of part three of *On the Road*: "At lilac evening I walked with every muscle aching among the lights of 27th and Welton in the Denver colored section, wishing I were a Negro, feeling that the best the white world had offered was not enough ecstasy for me, not enough life, joy, kicks, darkness, music, not enough night" (148). Well, neither has Jan Erlone ever had "enough night": enough night is exactly what Bigger Thomas gives him. *Native Son* is a nightmare about America in comparison to which *On the Road* is but a daydreamⅭinnocent, naive, merely charming. Afraid of the darkness by which it is also seduced, *On the Road* reads as if written under the palliating glow of an ideological night-light. In *On the Road* the promise of the "better world" to which Mailer refers in "The White Negro" is essentially willed into existence as a kind of mirage on the horizon by the sheer force of Sal's and Dean's (and Kerouac's) beatific faith. And that "joyous" and "wild" America, where Black and White live together "voluntarily" (as Sal memorably puts it early in the book), is even within the terms of this fiction and faith nothing other than a utopia or "supreme fiction." *On the Road* is nostalgic for a place that never was, which accounts for its distinctive and very American mood of elegiac optimism: a mixture of regret for what is missing, and fond anticipation of what, according to our covenant with the gods, is supposed to lie ahead. Kerouac's utopia is as fragile, hermetic, and unreal as the hours Huck Finn spends alone on the river with Jim. That utopia, like those hours on the raft, is perhaps what we remember best about the book. But it is hardly what the book documents.

On the Road, then, is touched by shamed nostalgia: shame because we are reading a White writer condemn Whiteness, nostalgia because the mood is so thoroughly unprogressive. *On the Road* invites us to suppose that in America Blacks have actually been somehow "freer" than Whites. It accommodates us to their suffering by imbuing it with the prestige of martyrdom, as if suffering were a kind of gift. In *Existential Errands*, Mailer wickedly suggests that Blacks are "sufficiently fortunate to be alienated from the benefits of American civilization" (270). Without Mailer's irony, and without his intention to outrage, *On the Road* makes the same claim. Something sentimental in this false consciousness oddly lends *On the Road* its pathos. All this admiration and wonder, all this talk about freedom, all this regret about the repression the White man visits on himself: these things work, abashed, in the shadow of real oppression in an America which, to borrow W. E. B. DuBois's words, more or less remained "an armed camp for intimidating black folk" (65).

In *Nobody Knows My Name*, James Baldwin says what must be said of Sal's wish to exchange worlds with the "happy Negroes of America": "[It is] absolute nonsense, and offensive nonsense at that: I would hate to be in Kerouac's shoes if he should ever be mad enough to read this aloud from the stage of Harlem's Apollo Theater. And yet there is real pain in it, and real loss, however thin" (231). Had Kerouac read this passage of Sal's in Harlem he might have known what Jan Erlone felt the night Bigger Thomas pulled a gun on him. But Kerouac's pain is real enough, "however thin," as Baldwin concedes, and it is affecting. There is remarkable sincerity in this novel, though it doesn't reveal exactly what Kerouac thought it revealed. We pity him, as Baldwin does, for reasons he wouldn't accept. For here it all is at last: Sal, animated by unspeakable desire, in a dreary funk about his White inhibitions, slumming around in Denver's "colored section." It is a perfect model for what Kerouac does in *On the Road*. That he may be aware of this— he places his alter ego Sal in exactly the same position—lends the book its air of shame. Kerouac's heroism is the odd heroism of a con-artist trying to believe, against mounting evidence to the contrary, that his own patter might just all be true. Still half-asleep in his peasant dream, he tries to ignore the sound of the alarm clock with which Wright famously opens *Native Son*; it never penetrates his oblivion. Call Black Americans free in the mid-1950s, as Sal does, and you have, to borrow Ralph Ellison's indispensable trope, simply rendered them invisible. At times, it is hard not to think that *On the Road*, so well fitted to this end, is somehow "intended" to accomplish it ("intended" not by Kerouac but by the culture of which he is a part).

Given the ideological drift of the novel, Kerouac's later turn toward the right in politics is perhaps less puzzling, and his hostility to the Black radicals of the 1960s less surprising. (He could deal with Uncle Tom, not with Nat Turner.) Anyone who has read the biographical literature on Kerouac knows the racist diatribes he was sometimes given to uttering toward the end of his life. (These were partly associated, it must be said, with the mental and physical deterioration that followed years of alcoholism.) Barry Miles recounts the most infamous such episode in *Jack Kerouac: King of the Beats*: "In the summer of 1962, [Kerouac] got his fourteen-year-old nephew Paul to help him build a cross from two-inch-by-four-inch wooden posts which he then covered with cloth. They drove to a wall which roughly divided the Black neighbourhood from the White section of Orlando [where Kerouac was then staying]. There Jack soaked the cloth in kerosene, stood the cross on the wall, and set fire to it. As his homemade fiery cross burnt, Jack danced up and down, yelling racist obscenities" (278).[11] The dreamy plantation-tale ethos of *On the Road* should never be confused with more viciously forthright, not to mention delirious, manifestations of American racism. But among the novel's troubling lessons for contemporary readers is how continuous—and how coherent—the culture of "racism" actually is, across a spectrum running from embarrassing, to bad, to abominable. At the end of the day, Jack Kerouac's consciousness—his way of being aware of the social world he inhabited—was thoroughly American, *delirium tremens* and all. We simply have to own it: he registers our national failures like a mirror. That he should register our national promise, too, is a thoroughly American paradox, as we shall see.[12]

IV

Driving through southwestern Louisiana, Sal Paradise relates the following exchange between himself and Dean Moriarty: "'Man do you imagine what it would be like if we found a jazzjoint in these swamps, with great big black fellas moanin' guitar blues and drinking snakejuice and makin' signs at us?' 'Yes!' There were mysteries around here" (131). This is the sort of parable Sal and Dean tell themselves once they get to Mexico. Their primitive ideal stands in antithesis to Whiteness, which is, dialectically, as much the subject here as Blackness. Elsewhere Sal speaks of the "essential strain of the basic primitive, wailing humanity" that stretches around the equator among the "Fellahin" peoples of the world (229). This strain, the strain of African American music in the novel generally, is what Sal and Dean listen to jazz in order to hear. They have lived, it seems, in exile from themselves. In an odd revision of antebellum "colonization" schemes, it is White men who require "repatriation" to Africa; and, somewhat selfishly, they require it for the health of their own bodies more than for the health of the body politic. Whiteness, here, is a condition of alienation: from the body, from sexuality, from the primitive alter-ego. *On the Road* takes for granted that we are a nation under the domination of what, in his own analysis of the constitution of Whiteness, Wallace Stevens called "High-Toned Old Christian Women." The association will not seem absurd if we take another look at Stevens's famous poem.

> Poetry is the supreme fiction, madame.
> Take the moral law and make a nave of it
> And from the nave build haunted heaven. Thus,
> The conscience is converted into palms,
> Like windy citherns hankering for hymns.
> We agree in principle. That's clear. But take
> The opposing law and make a peristyle,
> And from the peristyle project a masque
> Beyond the planets. Thus, our bawdiness,
> Unpurged by epitaph, indulged at last,
> Is equally converted into palms,
> Squiggling like saxophones. And palm for palm,
> Madame, we are where we began. Allow,
> Therefore, that in the planetary scene
> Your disaffected flagellants, well-stuffed,
> Smacking their muzzy bellies in parade,
> Proud of such novelties of the sublime,
> Such tink and tank and tunk-a-tunk-tunk,
> May, merely may, madame, whip from themselves
> A jovial hullabaloo among the spheres.
> This will make widows wince. But fictive things
> Wink as they will. Wink most when widows wince.

"A High-Toned Old Christian Woman" concerns a specifically WASP-ish mode of being White.[13] While it is necessary to Stevens's purposes that this Christian be a woman, the poem comes fully alive only as we realize what those squiggling saxophones bring into it. Stevens's imaginative excursion into a 1920s jazz-joint is an excursion across the color line, though this is only implied: it is a sophisticated act of literary minstrelsy. Whiteness, as it attaches to High-Toned Christian Women, is felt chiefly as a constriction of the sensual. That is the meaning of those "flagellations." Whiteness is ascetic, and the masculine voice that roundly teases the old woman promises a release from a civilizing regime that is completely recognizable. Stevens's speaker essentially follows Huck Finn, though he marches to the beat of his own drummer. Having already been subject to the regime of the Widow Douglas and Miss Watson, Huck lights out for the territory when Sally

Phelps, another Old Christian Woman, threatens to civilize him. But Huck's flight from femininity is also a flight from Whiteness, and not simply from the horrifying "fish-belly" Whiteness of his brutish father Pap. Huck's only real happiness in the novel—though he doesn't entirely assimilate this fact—is the time he spends with Jim on the margins of the river, and on the margins of "civilization" itself. The same may be said of Kerouac and Sal in *On the Road*, where "Whiteness" names a suit of clothes too good to be comfortable.

The release Huck feels is Platonic (Leslie Fielder notwithstanding); in *On the Road*, release from White civility is specifically felt as an awakening of sexual vitality. At one point in the novel Galatea Dunkel and her high-toned "sewing circle" attempt to chasten Dean Moriarty. "You have absolutely no regard for anybody but yourself and your damned kicks," Galatea says. "All you think about is what's hanging between your legs and how much money or fun you can get out of people and then you just throw them aside" (160). The cultural distance between this White, feminine reproach and the scene of jazz-joint ecstasy that follows it in the novel is the same distance that separates Stevens's High-Toned Old Christian Woman from those "disaffected" flagellants, "smacking their muzzy bellies in parade." Apparently, the answer to high-toned White women is jazz. Stevens speaks of "squiggling" saxophones. The figure refers at once to the shape, the sound, and the effect of the saxophones: their squiggling sounds make his speaker squiggle in Dionysian dance. The introduction of these saxophones into the poem accomplishes a double reorientation. With a single gesture Stevens's speaker moves toward Blackness and toward masculinity: unleashing his sexual vitality, he repudiates White feminine prudery. This repudiation is felt even in the language of the poem's final lines, just as we feel the rhythms of the tenor-man's ecstasy enter Kerouac's "be-bop" prose as he describes the scene in a San Francisco jazz-joint called Jamson's Nook.[14] Stevens's intense consonance and onomatopoeia register his Dionysian indulgence of a verbal "bawdiness," "unpurged by epitaph," that makes a fine response to the old widow's ascetic flagellants: he coaxes a happy, scat-singing sort of poetry out of the bodies of the words themselves.

To become hip to jazz for these White writers is to enter into a new relation to the body and to sexuality. This makes it possible for Norman Mailer to write, referring to the supposed etymology of the term, that jazz is orgasm; in a word, this is what Stevens also maintains. He brings into his poem all of these associations with the merest allusion to those "squiggling saxophones": such is the economy of the language of race in American writing. *On the Road* unfolds these same associations into a restless journey away from Whiteness into the "Fellahin" darkness of the alter-ego. And we might put it still another way, this time moving from Kerouac back to Stevens: "A High-Toned Old Christian Woman" is exactly the sort of reverie into which Sal Paradise falls in Denver, when, at "lilac evening," he wishes he were "a Negro, feeling that the best the white world had offered was not enough ecstasy for me, not enough life, joy, kicks, darkness, music, not enough night." Still, the better to understand Sal's malaise (and Stevens's) it is good to turn again to James Baldwin.

V

In *The Fire Next Time*, Baldwin suggests that "the price of the liberation of the White people is the liberation of the Blacks—the total liberation, in the cities, in the towns, before the law, and in the mind" (97). The idea is that "inter-cultural" oppression and "intra-psychic" repression are complementary disorders. In "The White Negro," Mailer, like his friend Baldwin, sets about to dismantle these twin structures of racist and psychic repressions—White over Black, conscious over unconscious. He does so in a dual maneuver: he asserts the primacy of the historically or morally subordinate terms and then abolishes subordination altogether. And "The White Negro" helps us see how the racial politics of *On the Road* are perhaps more progressive than at first they seem. "The nihilism of Hip," Mailer writes, "proposes as its final tendency that every social restraint and category be removed, and the affirmation implicit in the proposal is that man would then prove to be more creative than murderous and so would not destroy himself" (319). The revolution Mailer describes would take aim against all prohibitions having to do with sex and race. And his remarks suggest that the blackface tradition of the "white negro" is by no means without insubordinate implications. Mailer's essay brings to a fiercer, much more troubling pitch the argument with White Christianity that Stevens has in "A High-Toned Old Christian Woman" (which remains the utterance of an aesthete, not a rebel). What follows The Revolution is total affirmation of Life, to use Mailer's Lawrentian term for it: "disaffected flagellants," smacking their muzzy bellies in parade.

Mailer believed (maybe only provocatively) that a sexual revolution would reverse the savage turn the West took in the first five decades of this century. For him, psychic repression, racist repression, and military-industrial rapacity, were three aspects of the same pathology: they all added up to The Bomb. This argument remains radical today and explains why, in the fifth section of "The White Negro," Mailer writes that the emergence of Blacks into full participation in American life would revolutionize the country: this emergence, were it genuinely to occur, would mark the abolition of the range of repressions that has constituted the very psyches of Americans, determining what it means to be both "White" and "Black." An integrated America will necessarily be a different America because what it means to be "American" has until now involved a complementary blend of social oppression and psychic repression. This is what Baldwin has in mind when he writes, in *No Name in the Street*: "In the generality, as social and moral and political and sexual entities, white Americans are probably the sickest and most dangerous people, of any color, to be found in the world today" (55).

Baldwin makes it impossible for us to read books like *On the Road* naively. But he also helps us read them with sympathy. He writes in *The Fire Next Time*: "The white man's unadmitted—and apparently, to him, unspeakable—private fears and longings are projected onto the Negro. The only way he can be released from the Negro's tyrannical power over him is to consent, in effect, to become black himself, to become a part of that suffering and dancing country that he now watches wistfully from the heights of his lonely power and, armed with spiritual traveler's checks, visits surreptitiously after dark" (96). "Spiritual traveler's checks" are what Sal Paradise withdraws from the jazz-joints he patronizes after dark. His need for them betrays his poverty, which is also the poverty of the nation. So, psychological integration follows upon, and can only follow upon, racial integration: this hope, which Kerouac shares with Baldwin, is perhaps what most marks *On the Road* as belonging to the era of the Civil Rights struggle. The real heart of the novel comes in an early passage about Mill City, the Northern California village where Sal Paradise's friend Remi Boncoeur lives: "It was, so they say, the only community in America where whites and Negroes lived together voluntarily; and that was so, and so wild and joyous a place I've never seen since" (51). Sal's wild, joyous America is exactly that: a utopia—what we've never seen since. In *Nobody Knows My Name*, Baldwin rightly suggests that, in *On the Road*, Kerouac is "ruminating" on "the loss of the garden of Eden" (230). Eden is where we are headed, though we sometimes mistake it for where we have always already been. Only a possibility and a promise, America has existed nowhere within our geographical or chronological horizons. But in their fictions, as opposed to their frauds, Americans have at times powerfully believed that possibility into existence. This is the abiding faith of *On the Road*—faith in the redemptive fiction of Dean Moriarty, a beat-beatific "white negro," a man psychically and socially integrated, whole and healed. To read *On the Road*, for the White reader it anticipates and requires, is therefore to dwell in possibility, "at sunset" in paradise America, as Kerouac's resonantly named narrator says. This Eden exists nowhere and when we get there we'll find Dean Moriarty publishing his books "in heaven"—which brings us to the conclusion, or western-most horizon, of the novel itself.

The last paragraph in *On the Road* is peculiarly evocative. The road (we know) opens up in spring and always calls us West. But here, Sal Paradise speaks from the winter of his discontent as he charts the Eastern streets of New York City thinking again of Dean.

> So in America when the sun goes down and I sit on the old broken-down river pier watching the long, long skies over New Jersey and sense all that raw land that rolls in one unbelievable huge bulge over to the West Coast, and all that road going, all the people dreaming in the immensity of it, and in Iowa I know by now the children must be crying in the land where they let children cry, and tonight the stars'll be out, and don't you know that God is Pooh Bear? the evening star must be drooping and shedding her sparkler dims on the prairie, which is just before the coming of complete night that blesses the earth, darkens all rivers, cups the peaks and folds the final shore in, and nobody, nobody knows what's going to happen to anybody besides the forlorn rags of growing old, I think of Dean Moriarty, I even think of Old Dean Moriarty the father we never found, I think of Dean Moriarty. (253–54)

The verbs applied to the coming of night ("blesses," "cups," "folds," etc.) suggest a tender, maternal act. It is an act in keeping with the idea, gently impressed on us by the language, that the narrator—and Dean Moriarty, and even Old Dean Moriarty—has in some sense become a child again, and that, like the fabled children of Iowa, he knows that God is Pooh Bear beneath the prairie's sparkler stars. The literary mode, here as elsewhere in the novel, is part lullaby, part national anthem, and part elegy—a patriotic lullaby-elegy. Sal is the father-child America, singing itself to sleep in its own life, as Wallace Stevens once put it. (Truly American parents like Kerouac and Stevens themselves believe the bedtime stories they tell the children.) The mythic, sad optimism of *On the Road* is inseparable from sentiments like these. We are made to feel at times that the book is willfully naive, as when Sal, at the road's end, adopts his Huck-like persona in a gesture that essentially limits the point of view of the narrative as a whole: we sense at last in its closing strains that the novel is told to us as by a faithful child. (From here it is but a short step down to *Forrest Gump*. And we ask: What is it about White American male writers and childhood? Why the appeal of naive heroes, from Huck to Sal to Forrest himself? From what knowledge do these authors wish to protect themselves?) And it is not only the absent father we feel the need of in this last paragraph—Old Dean Moriarty—but the lost mother and brother as well, as the final phrases of the novel plainly show that Sal's imaginative sympathy with Dean is now complete: he speaks the veritable language of the orphan, with specifically American inflections of longing and dislocation. And the wholesome American dream that the father-child Sal has, with its prairies, stars, sparklers, and nighttime Iowa blessings, is just the impossible dream of *On the Road*: its wild utopia, the joyous America that exists nowhere beyond the border of this fiction, but where Dean and Huck and Jim, where White and Black alike, at last find their happy, true-hearted, ecstatic place together in this world. *On the Road* sings its White readers to sleep dreaming of this world elsewhere: the place where America has the only reality it has in fact ever had. We have always dwelt merely in possibility, as migrant farm laborers in California, though not in *On the Road*, know full well. *On the Road* is therefore a novel steeped in forgetfulness, an Apollonian dream willfully set against a whole world of torment. It tells us a bedtime story about the power of our supreme national fiction to inspire belief, the better to bring into view its never-realized but always possible object, just over the western horizon. We simply have to keep telling ourselves that America can exist, as Baldwin knew when he wrote *The Fire Next Time*: "We, the black and the white, deeply need each other here if we are really to become a nation—if we are really, that is, to achieve our identity, our maturity, as men and women" (97).

NOTES

1. I acknowledge here a general debt to Gary Lindberg's *The Confidence Man in American Literature*, which taught me much. Lindberg's discussion of Neal Cassady and *On the Road* may be found on pages 259–70 of the book. My arguments ultimately diverge from Lindberg's in that they highlight in any reading of Kerouac the great American congame of "race." Which, of course, is only to say: I am instructed by the original of Lindberg's title—Melville's *The Confidence Man*. I have in mind particularly the section of that labyrinthine fiction describing the confidence man in what appears to be his first incarnation: in blackface.

2. In what follows, my general outlook is informed by several books. First among them is George Frederickson's excellent *The Black Image in the White Mind: the Debate on Afro-American Character and Destiny, 1817–1914*. The period during which Kerouac wrote and published *On the Road* falls outside Frederickson's area of immediate concern; but his arguments are more far-ranging and more suggestive than the modestly descriptive title of his book suggests. In connection with *On the Road*, see especially these two chapters: "Uncle Tom and the Anglo-Saxons: Romantic Racialism in the North" (97–129) and "The New South and the New Paternalism, 1877–1890" (198–227). I would also cite Thomas F. Gossett's influential study *Race: the History of An Idea in America*, recently reissued in a new edition. Eric Lott's fascinating *Love and Theft: Blackface Minstrelsy and the American Working Class* encouraged me to consider the relation *On the Road* has to the tradition of

minstrelsy. Toni Morrison's productive essay *Playing in the Dark* also further clarified for me the meaning of "color" in American writing.

3. As others have pointed out, Kerouac borrowed the term "Fellahin" from Spengler's *The Decline of the West*. See Robert Holton for a helpful discussion of Kerouac's investment in Spengler (270–72, 277).

4. Robert Holton has also pointed out the affiliation to black-face minstrelsy (269).

5. My thinking about the social function of the plantation-tale is conditioned by two works in particular: Richard Brodhead's introductory essay to the edition of Chesnutt's *Conjure Woman* published by Duke University Press (1–21) and C. Van Woodward's *Origins of the New South*, especially the chapter on "The Divided Mind of the New South" (142–74).

6. In speaking of ideology, and of the work it does, I have in mind arguments variously advanced by several writers: Louis Althusser in "Ideology and Ideological State Apparatuses," an essay collected in his *Lenin and Philosophy* (127–86); Raymond Williams, throughout *Marxism and Literature* but especially in the sequence of chapters titled "Literature," "Ideology," "Base and Superstructure," and "Determination" (45–89); and Kenneth Burke in *Attitudes toward History* (passim) and *A Rhetoric of Motives* (90–110). Most productive for me has been Althusser's suggestion that "ideology represents the imaginary relationship of individuals to their real conditions of existence" (162).

7. Robert Holton finds in Kerouac's cotton-field fantasy a "depthless" "nostalgia" characteristic of post-modernity (276–77). The suggestion is intriguing. (It derives, in part, from Frederic Jameson's arguments in *Postmodernism; or, the Cultural Logic of Late Capitalism*.) But though I am generally in sympathy with Holton's illuminating essay, I cannot agree that Kerouac's curious "nostalgia" is peculiarly postmodern, or distinctly associated (*pace* Jameson) with "*late* capitalism." It is of course a nice problem. But I would say that Kerouac's brand of fellahin nostalgia has been doing its ideological work at least since the 1840s; as the passage quoted above from "Self-Reliance" is intended to suggest. I am persuaded—by George Fredrickson and other historians—that Kerouac's thinking about the "fellahin" is, in its essentials, quite in harmony with ideologies supporting White hegemony in the antebellum period. True, Kerouac revised—even reversed—certain values which formerly attached to "Whiteness" and "Blackness." But Whiteness and Blackness are for him constituted pretty much as they were for Americans of Emerson's and Hawthorne's day: color is all about the life of the body, of the senses; Whiteness, all about the life of the mind. And bear in mind what James Baldwin will not let us forget about "color" in American history: the sheer *persistence* of its basic ideological contours. This persistence, among other things, discourages me from thinking of Kerouac's experience of race as "postmodern," or even as very novel at all. Such changes as he does ring on the old White tunes chiefly illustrate, to my mind, the resourcefulness of White hegemony, which can comfortably contain even the King of the Beats.

8. That literary culture—even an apparently oppositional wing of it—can serve this end leads Louis Althusser to range it among what he calls "*ideological* state apparatuses," in contradistinction to such manifest "state apparatuses" as the courts, the legislative assemblies, the army, and the police. In Althusser's scheme, "ideological state apparatuses" help reproduce the "*relations* of production," as distinct from the "*means* of production" (128–34; 142–57). This is not to suggest, I need hardly add, that Kerouac himself intends any such repressive destiny for his novel. Robert Holton hits more or less the right note (though he is a bit more generous to Kerouac's writing than I would be): "One might question whether Kerouac's work does not ultimately do far more to confuse the issues than to clarify, more to augment than to destabilize the reified racial and gender categories of social identity. Still, to dismiss Kerouac entirely would be as simplistic as to elevate him to the level of a cult hero, which many hagiographic Kerouac studies continue to do" (270).

9. I thank Tony Hilfer for directing my attention to Tomas Rivera's novel of life among Chicano migrant laborers, *y no se lo trago la tierra* (1971). It is instructive reading for anyone interested in Kerouac's treatment of Mexican-American farmworkers in *On the Road*. Rolando Hinojosa's English "rendition" of the novel appeared in 1987 under the title *This Migrant Earth*; that is the text I have read.

10. To some extent, I am following a line of argument sketched out by Robert Holton: "[Kerouac's] suggestion [in speaking of "happy Negroes"] seems to be that African Americans are insulated from disappointment because they are lacking in aspiration, a notion that can be sustained only at a considerable distance from the actually existing African American community. Nor could these fantasies of the placid fellahin survive exposure to the African American literary culture of the time which included Richard Wright, Ann Petry, Chester Himes, and Ralph Ellison, writers whose articulations of disappointment and frustration are, to put it mildly, unmistakable" (269–70). Among my aims in the present essay is to bring *On the Road* decisively into contact with that literary culture.

11. The source for the story about the cross-burning is Paul Blake, the nephew who was involved. Gerald Nicosia interviewed him while working on *Memory Babe* in 1978 (739). In writing up the episode, Nicosia offers it as evidence that the "endless cognac and Irish whiskey [had driven Kerouac] out of his mind at last" (634). It is not hard to accept this humane suggestion.

12. For a very different assessment of Kerouac in this regard, see Omar Swartz's recent study *The View From On the Road: The Rhetorical Vision of Jack Kerouac*. After quoting Kerouac on "the happy, true-hearted, ecstatic Negroes of America," Swartz remarks: "This passage is obviously problematic in its representation of the African American, whom Kerouac portrays paternalistically, as he does *all* minorities; yet, he never does so maliciously, and this is the most extreme example of it in *On the Road*. His condescending tone must be discounted in light of Kerouac's larger poetic framework. Kerouac typically poeticized the world, and this is particularly evident in his books of reminiscence" (87; emphasis in the original). The fact that Kerouac treats "*all* minorities" this way is, to my mind, probably beside the point: the minorities in question are, as White America sees them, uniformly people of color—whether African American, American Indian, Hispanic, or "fellahin"; and *that* is the rub. Moreover, the point is not to choose between a "malicious" or "racist" Kerouac, and a Kerouac in whom "paternalistic" attitudes must finally be "discounted." The point is to trace out the continuities linking "paternalistic" attitudes to those larger patterns of White hegemony which contain Kerouac, as they contain so many of us; and which contain as well so much of our literature, *even when that literature is in certain respects radically countercultural*. I would add in passing that the strongest literary work done in America is often precisely the work which makes us feel the confining limits of its own ideological horizons; *Huckleberry Finn* is a case in point. So it seems of limited use to say, with Swartz, that "Kerouac is not a racist but a romantic" (86). My way out of the dilemma is rather to suggest that, at its best, *On the Road* makes a claim on behalf of literary writing generally: to wit, that great writing often exists in an abstract—in a withdrawn or estranged—relation to the ideological medium in which it is suspended (so to speak). Literary works may not transcend that medium; but, like Mark Antony and the dolphins to which Shakespeare compares him, they can show their backs above it. For this reason, even Louis Althusser allows "authentic" artworks a certain autonomous energy (221–27). They do not merely inculcate in us a particular way of seeing the world; they also make apparent the limits of what they find it possible to think, to feel, and to say. Really strong writing can say the truth—as Emerson puts it—even though it "try," at times, "to say the reverse" (881). Surely that is something to care about as a literary critic, and something to criticize as a literary curate. *On the Road* may bind us

to the American past, with its sad contingencies. But it can also make us "citizens, by anticipation, in the world we crave," to borrow a phrase from Santayana (vi). Mill City always exists somewhere in *On the Road*, as I have suggested: "It was, so they say, the only community in America where Whites and Negroes lived together voluntarily; and that was so, and so wild and joyous a place I've never seen since" (51).

13. I refer readers to Rachel Blau DuPlessis's essay on Stevens and Vachel Lindsay, "'Hoo, Hoo Hoo': Some Episodes in the Construction of Modern Whiteness." DuPlessis does not discuss "A High-Toned Old Christian Woman" in detail, nor is she chiefly concerned with jazz (she is writing instead about the language of "hoo-doo" and "voo-doo" in popular culture). But her essay has much to offer anyone interested in Whiteness and Blackness as these things were understood by Americans in the first half of the twentieth century.

14. Kerouac often spoke of his effort to adapt improvisational "be-bop" techniques to the writing of "spontaneous prose"; the result, ideally, is something called "bop prosody." Most interpreters have taken him at his word. But Douglas Malcolm has lately demonstrated—persuasively, to my mind—that the matter bears looking at again. "While jazz does play a significant role in [*On the Road*]," Malcolm writes, "its impact lies in the music's ideological, behavioral, and semiotic implications—in particular their roots in African American culture—rather than in the direct application of its formal rules" (85). In short, the analogy between jazz improvisation and "spontaneous prose"—an analogy enforced by any number of passages in the novel—has led many readers into mistaking the real significance of jazz in the book, which has to do with race, not technique. As Malcolm puts it: "However much he identifies with African Americans, Kerouac is more interested in the ideology of their 'cultural dowry' [to borrow a phrase from Ned Polsky] than he is in the circumstances that produced it. Indeed, his primitivist view of black culture, one that shapes his use of jazz in *On the Road*, often misrepresents, exaggerates, and suppresses important elements of the music and the culture in which it originated" (94). My purpose in the present essay has been to illuminate some possible social functions of these misrepresentations, exaggerations, and suppressions—these distortions in Kerouac's "dreamwork." Jazz works in his novel (I would suggest) just as it does so much more elliptically in Stevens's "A High Toned Old Christian Woman."

WORKS CITED

Althusser, Louis. *Lenin and Philosophy*. New York: Monthly Review Press, 1971.

Baldwin, James. *The Fire Next Time*. New York: Vintage, 1993.

———. *Nobody Knows My Name*. New York: Vintage, 1993.

Burke, Kenneth. *Attitudes Toward History*. Third edition. Berkeley: University of California Press, 1984.

———. *A Rhetoric of Motives*. Berkeley: University of California Press, 1969.

Chesnutt, Charles. *The Conjure Woman*. Ed. Richard Brodhead. Durham: Duke University Press, 1994.

DuBois, W. E. B. *The Souls of Black Folk*. New York: Dover Books, 1995.

DuPlessis, Rachel Blau. "'Hoo, Hoo, Hoo': Some Episodes in the Construction of Modern Whiteness." *American Literature* 67.4 (December 1995): 667–700.

Ellison, Ralph. *Invisible Man*. New York: Vintage, 1995.

———. *Shadow and Act*. New York: Quality Paperback Club, 1994.

Emerson, Ralph Waldo. *Essays and Poems*. Edited by Joel Porte, Harold Bloom, and Paul Kane. New York: Library of America, 1996.

Frederickson, George. *The Black Image in the White Mind: the Debate on Afro-American Character and Destiny, 1817–1914*. Second edition. Hanover, New Hampshire: Wesleyan University Press, 1987.

Ginsberg, Allen. *Howl and Other Poems*. San Francisco: City Lights, 1957.

Gossett, Thomas F. *Race: the History of An Idea in America*. Second edition. New York: Oxford University Press, 1997.

Hinojosa, Rolando. *This Migrant Earth*. [A rendition in English of Tomas Rivera's novel, *y no se lo trago la tierra*.] Houston: Arte Publico Press, 1987.

Holton, Robert. "Kerouac among the Fellahin: *On the Road* to the Postmodern." *Modern Fiction Studies* 41.2 (Summer 1995): 265–83.

Jameson, Fredric. *Postmodernism; or, the Cultural Logic of Late Capitalism*. Durham: Duke University Press, 1991.

Kerouac, Jack. *On the Road*. New York: Signet, 1982.

Lindberg, Gary. *The Confidence Man in American Literature*. New York: Oxford University Press, 1982.

Lott, Eric. *Love and Theft: Blackface Minstrelsy and the American Working Class*. New York: Oxford University Press, 1995.

Mailer, Norman. *Existential Errands*. New York: Signet, 1973.

———. "The White Negro." In *Advertisements for Myself*. New York: Signet, 1959.

Malcolm, Douglas. "'Jazz America': Jazz and African American Culture in Jack Kerouac's *On the Road*." *Contemporary Literature* 40.1 (Spring 1999): 85–110.

Miles, Barry. *Jack Kerouac: King of the Beats*. New York: Henry Holt, 1998.

Morrison, Toni. *Playing in the Dark: Whiteness and the Literary Imagination*. New York: Vintage Books, 1993.

Nicosia, Gerald. *Memory Babe: a Critical Biography of Jack Kerouac*. Berkeley: University of California Press, 1994.

Nietzsche, Friedrich. *The Birth of Tragedy and The Genealogy of Morals*. Trans. Francis Golffing. New York: Anchor Books, 1956.

Santayana, George. *Interpretations of Poetry and Religion*. New York: Harper Torchbooks, 1957.

Snyder, Gary. *A Place in Space*. Washington, D.C.: Counterpoint, 1995.

Stevens, Wallace. *Collected Poems of Wallace Stevens*. New York: Alfred Knopf, 1954.

Swartz, Omar. *The View From On the Road: the Rhetorical Vision of Jack Kerouac*. Carbondale: Southern Illinois University Press, 1999.

Toomer, Jean. *Cane*. New York: W. W. Norton, 1988.

Williams, Raymond. *Marxism and Literature*. New York: Oxford University Press, 1977.

Woodward, C. Van. *Origins of the New South: 1877–1913*. Baton Rouge: Louisiana State University Press, 1971.

Wright, Richard. *Native Son*. Ed. Arnold Rampersad. New York, Library of America, 1991.

Chronology

1922	Born Jean Louis Lebris de Kerouac on March 12 in Lowell, Massachetts to Leo Alcide Kerouac and Gabrielle Ange Levesque Kerouac, both of whom were French Canadians with family roots in Quebec.
1926	Death of Gerard, Jack's brother.
1939	Graduates from Lowell High School, where he participated in football and track.
1940	After a postgraduate year of high school at Horace Mann, begins undergraduate career at Columbia University with an athletic scholarship.
1941	Drops out of Columbia and works at odd jobs.
1942	Returns to Columbia, but quits the football team when his coach benches him during the first game of the season.
1943	Joins the navy, but is discharged months later on psychiatric grounds.
1944	Meets Allen Ginsberg and William Burroughs. Marries Edie Parker, but separates shortly after and has the marriage annulled the following year.
1946	Father Leo dies. Meets Neal Cassady.
1950	Publishes *The Town and the City*, a novel, in February. Marries Joan Haverty, only to leave her the following year.
1951	Finishes *On the Road*.

1952	Takes a job as a brakeman on the Southern Pacific Railway.
1955	Sued by Joan Haverty Kerouac for child support. Viking Press accepts *On the Road* for publication.
1956	Spends the summer as a fire-watcher in the Cascade Mountains in Washington.
1957	Travels to Tangiers to visit Burroughs. *On the Road* is published in September.
1958	*The Subterraneans* and *The Dharma Bums* are published.
1959	Publishes *Doctor Sax*, *Maggie Cassidy*, and *Mexico City Blues*.
1961	Publishes *Book of Dreams*.
1962	Publishes *Big Sur*.
1963	Publishes *Visions of Gerard*.
1965	Publishes *Desolation Angels*. Researches his family history in France.
1966	Publishes *Satori in Paris*. Marries Stella Sampas, with whom he settles in Lowell, Massachusetts.
1968	Publishes *Vanity of Duluoz*. Neal Cassady dies in Mexico.
1969	Dies October 21 in St. Petersberg, Florida of abdominal hemorrhaging.
1970	*Pic* is published.
1972	*Visions of Cody* is published.

Contributors

HAROLD BLOOM is Sterling Professor of the Humanities at Yale University and Henry W. and Albert A. Berg Professor of English at the New York University Graduate School. He is the author of over 20 books, including *Shelley's Mythmaking* (1959), *The Visionary Company* (1961), *Blake's Apocalypse* (1963), *Yeats* (1970), *A Map of Misreading* (1975), *Kabbalah and Criticism* (1975), *Agon: Toward a Theory of Revisionism* (1982), *The American Religion* (1992), *The Western Canon* (1994), and *Omens of Millennium: The Gnosis of Angels, Dreams, and Resurrection* (1996). *The Anxiety of Influence* (1973) sets forth Professor Bloom's provocative theory of the literary relationships between the great writers and their predecessors. His most recent books include *Shakespeare: The Invention of the Human* (1998), a 1998 National Book Award finalist, *How to Read and Why* (2000), *Genius: A Mosaic of One Hundred Exemplary Creative Minds* (2002), and *Hamlet: Poem Unlimited* (2003). In 1999, Professor Bloom received the prestigious American Academy of Arts and Letters Gold Medal for Criticism, and in 2002 he received the Catalonia International Prize.

CAROLE GOTTLIEB VOPAT specializes in women's and minority literatures and is Professor of English at the University of Wisconsin, Parkside.

GEORGE DARDESS has taught English at Tufts University and is the author of several studies of Kerouac and other Beat authors.

TIM HUNT teaches in the Department of English at Washington State University, specializing in American Literature and Creative Writing. In addition to *Kerouac's Crooked Road*, he has published an edition of Robinson Jeffers' collected poetry.

ROBERT HOLTON is Professor of English at Okanagan University College. He is the author of *Jarring Witnesses: Modern Fiction and the Representation of History*.

DOUGLAS MALCOLM has published essays on Jack Kerouac and Michael Ondaatje, and has written widely on the relationship between jazz and literature.

ALEX ALBRIGHT is Associate Professor of English at East Carolina University. His essays have appeared in *Southern Quarterly*, *North Carolina Humanities*, and *American Film*.

JAMES T. JONES teaches English at Southwest Missouri State University. His books include *Wayward Skeptic: the Theories of R. P. Blackmur* and *A Map of* Mexico City Blues: *Jack Kerouac as Poet*.

OMAR SWARTZ teaches at the University of Colorado at Denver. His publications include *Persuasion and Social Activity* and *Socialism and Communication: Reflections on Language and Left Politics*.

BEN GIAMO is Associate Professor of American Studies at the University of Notre Dame. He is the author of *The Homeless of* Ironweed: *Blossoms on the Crag* and *On the Bowery: Confronting Homelessness in American Society*.

MARK RICHARDSON is Associate Professor of English at Western Michigan University. He has written *The Ordeal of Robert Frost* and has co-edited with Richard Poirier the Library of America edition of Robert Frost's poems, prose, and plays.

Bibliography

Albright, Alex. "Ammons, Kerouac, and Their New Romantic Scrolls." *Complexities of Motion: New Essays on A. R. Ammons's Long Poems.* Ed. Steven P. Schneider. Teaneck, NJ: Fairleigh Dickinson University Press, 1999.

Askew, Melvin W. "Quests, Cars, and Kerouac." *University of Kansas City Review* 28 (Spring 1962).

Berrigan, Ted, et al. "The Art of Fiction XLI: Jack Kerouac." *Paris Review* 11 (Summer 1968).

Butler, Frank A. "On the Beat Nature of the Beat," *American Scholar* 30 (Winter 1960–61).

Cassady, Neal, and Allen Ginsberg. *As Ever: The Collected Correspondence of Allen Ginsberg and Neal Cassady.* Berkeley: Creative Arts Book Co., 1977.

Challis, Chris. *Quest for Kerouac.* London: Faber and Faber, 1984.

Charters, Ann. *Kerouac: A Biography.* San Francisco: Straight Arrow, 1973.

———. "Introduction." *On the Road.* New York: Penguin, 1991.

Clark, Tom. *Jack Kerouac.* New York: Harcourt Brace, 1984.

Cook, Bruce. *The Beat Generation.* New York: Scribner, 1973.

Dardess, George. "The Delicate Dynamics of Friendship: A Reconsideration of Kerouac's *On the Road.*" *American Literature* 46 (May 1974).

Davidson, Michael. *The San Francisco Renaissance: Poetics and Community at Mid-Century.* New York: Cambridge University Press, 1989.

Donaldson, Scott, ed. *On the Road: Text and Criticism*. New York: Viking, 1979.

Feied, Frederick. *No Pie in the Sky: The Hobo as American Cultural Hero in the Works of Jack London, John Dos Passos, and Jack Kerouac*. New York: Citadel, 1964.

Foster, Edward Halsey. *Understanding the Beats*. Columbia, SC: University of South Carolina Press, 1992.

French, Warren. *Jack Kerouac: Novelist of the Beat Generation*. Boston: Twayne, 1986.

Giamo, Ben. *Kerouac, the Word and the Way: Prose Artist as Spiritual Quester*. Carbondale, IL:Southern Illinois University Press, 2000.

Gifford, Barry, and Lawrence Lee. *Jack's Book: An Oral Biography of Jack Kerouac*. New York: St. Martin, 1978.

Hassan, Ihab. *Radical Innocence: Studies in the Contemporary Novel*. Princeton: Princeton University Press, 1961.

Hipkiss, Robert A. *Jack Kerouac: Prophet of a New Romanticism*. Lawrence, KS: The Regents Press of Kansas, 1976.

Holmes, John Clellon. "The Is the Beat Generation." *New York Times Magazine* (16 November 1952).

Holton, Robert. "Kerouac among the Fellahin: *On the Road* to the Postmodern." *Modern FictionStudies* 41, no. 2 (Summer 1995).

Hunt, Tim. *Kerouac's Crooked Road: Development of a Fiction*. Hamden, CT: Archon, 1981.

Jackson, Carl T. "The Counterculture Looks East: Beat Writers and Asian Religion." *American Studies* 29 (1988): 51–70.

Jarvis, Charels E. *Visions of Kerouac*. Lowell, MA: Ithaca, 1974.

Johnson, Joyce. *Minor Characters* Boston: Houghton Mifflin, 1983.

Knight, Arthur, and Kit Knight. *Kerouac and the Beats*. New York: Paragon House, 1988.

Leer, Norman. "Three American Novels and Contemporary Society." *Wisconsin Studies in Contemporary Literature* 3 (Fall 1962): 67–86.

Malcolm, Douglas. "'Jazz America': Jazz and African American Culture in Jack Kerouac's *On the Road*." *Contemporary Literature* 40, no. 1 (Spring 1999): 85–110.

Milewski, Robert J. *Jack Kerouac: An Annotated Bibliography of Secondary Sources*. Metuchen: Scarecrow, 1981.

Millstein, Gilbert. Review of *On the Road*. *New York Times* (5 September 1957).

Montgomery, John. *Kerouac at the "Wild Boar" and Other Skirmishes*. San Anselmo, CA: Fels, 1986.

Nicosia, Gerald. *Memory Babe: A Critical Biography of Jack Kerouac*. Berkeley: University of California Press, 1994.

Parker, Brad. *Kerouac: An Introduction*. Lowell, MA: Lowell Corp. for Humanity, 1989.

Parkinson, Thomas, ed. *A Casebook on the Beat*. New York: Crowell, 1961.

Podhoretz, Norman. "The Know-Nothing Bohemians." *Partisan Review* 25 (1958).

Primeau, Ron. *Romance of the Road: The Literature of the American Highway*. Bowling Green, OH: Bowling Green State University Press, 1996.

Richardson, Mark. "Peasant Dreams: Reading *On the Road*." *Texas Studies in Literature and Language* 43, no. 2 (Summer 2001).

Scott, James F. "Beat Literature and the American Teen Cult." *American Quarterly* 14 (Summer 1962).

Sorrell, Richard. "The Catholicism of Jack Kerouac." *Studies in Religion* 11 (1982).

Stephenson, Gregory. *The Daybreak Boys: Essays on the Literature of the Beat Generation*. Carbondale, IL: Southern Illinois University Press, 1990.

Tonkinson, Carole, ed. *Big Sky Mind: Buddhism and the Beat Generation*. New York: Riverhead, 1995.

Turner, Steve. *Angel Headed Hipster: A Life of Jack Kerouac*. New York: Viking, 1996.

Tytell, John. *Naked Angels: The Lives and Literature of the Beat Generation*. New York: McGraw-Hill, 1976.

Vopat, Carole Gottlieb. "Jack Kerouac's *On the Road*: A Re-evaluation." *Midwest Quarterly* 14 (Summer 1973): 385–407.

Walsh, Joy. *Jack Kerouac: Statement in Brown*. New York: Textile Bridge, 1984.

Watson, Steven. *The Birth of the Beat Generation: Visionaries, Rebels, and Hipsters, 1944–1960*. New York: Pantheon, 1995.

Watts, Allen. "Beat Zen, Square Zen, and Zen." *Chicago Review* 12 (1958): 3–11.

Weinrich, Regina. *The Spontaneous Poetics of Jack Kerouac: A Study of the Fiction*. Carbondale, IL: Southern Illinois University Press, 1987.

Woods, Crawford. "Reconsideration: Jack Kerouac." *New Republic* (2 December 1972): 26–30.

Acknowledgments

"Jack Kerouac's *On the Road*: A Re-evaluation," by Carole Gottlieb Vopat. From *The Midwest Quarterly* 14, no. 4 (July 1973): 385–407. © 1973 by *The Midwest Quarterly*, Kansas State College of Pittsburg. Reprinted by permission.

"The Delicate Dynamics of Friendship: A Reconsideration of Kerouac's *On the Road*," by George Dardess. From *American Literature* 46, no. 2 (May 1974): 200–206. © 1974 by Duke University Press. All rights reserved. Used by permission of the publisher.

"An American Education," by Tim Hunt. From *Kerouac's Crooked Road: Development of a Fiction*. © 1981 by Tim Hunt. Reprinted by permission.

Holton, Robert. "Kerouac Among the Fellahin: *On the Road* to the Postmodern." From *Modern Fiction Studies* 41, no. 2 (Summer 1995): 265–283. © 1995 by the Purdue Research Foundation. Reprinted by permission of the Johns Hopkins University Press.

"'Jazz America': Jazz and African American Culture in Jack Kerouac's *On the Road*," by Douglas Malcolm. From *Contemporary Literature* 40, no. 1 (Spring 1999): 85–110. © 1999. Reprinted by permission of the University of Wisconsin Press.

"Ammons, Kerouac, and Their New Romantic Scrolls," by Alex Albright. From *Complexities of Motion: New Essays on A. R. Ammons's Long Poems*, ed. Steven P. Schneider. © 1999 by Associated University Presses, Inc. Reprinted by permission.

"The Place Where Three Roads Meet: *Pic, On the Road,* and *Visions of Cody,*" by James T. Jones. From *Jack Kerouac's Duluoz Legend: the Mythic Form of an Autobiographical Fiction.* © 1999 by the Board of Trustees, Southern Illinois University, reprinted by permission of the publisher.

"The Vision of Social Deviance," by Omar Swartz. From *The View from On the Road: The Rhetorical Vision of Jack Kerouac.* © 1999 by the Board of Trustees, Southern Illinois University, reprinted by permission of the publisher.

"What IT Is?" by Ben Giamo. From *Kerouac, the Word and the Way: Prose Artist as Spiritual Quester.* © 2000 by the Board of Trustees, Southern Illinois University, reprinted by permission of the publisher.

"Peasant Dreams: Reading *On the Road,*" by Mark Richardson. From *Texas Studies in Literature and Language* 43, no. 2 (Summer 2001): 218–242. © 2001 by the University of Texas Press. Reprinted by permission.

Index